RAHEL LEVIN VARNHAGEN

Rahel Levin Varnhagen

The Life and Work of a German Jewish Intellectual

Heidi Thomann Tewarson

University of Nebraska Press
Lincoln & London

Acknowledgments for the
use of previously published
material appear on page ix
© 1998 by the University of
Nebraska Press. All rights
reserved. Manufactured in
the United States of America.
⊗ The paper in this book
meets the minimum requirements of American National
Standard for Information
Sciences—Permanence of
Paper for Printed Library
Materials, ANSI Z39.48-1984.
Library of Congress
Cataloging in Publication
Data. Tewarson, Heidi
Thomann. [Rahel Levin
Varnhagen. English] Rahel
Levin Varnhagen : the life and
work of a German Jewish
intellectual / Heidi Thomann
Tewarson. p. cm.—(Texts
and contexts) Includes biblio-
graphical references and index.
ISBN 0-8032-4435-5 (cloth :
alk. paper) ISBN 0-8032-9436-
0 (pbk: alk. paper)
1. Varnhagen, Rahel, 1771–1833
—Biography. 2. Authors,
German—18th century—
Biography. I. Varnhagen,
Rahel, 1771–1833. II. Title.
III. Series. PT2546.V22T4813
1998 838'.609 – dc21
[B] 98–12271 CIP

To my daughters, Anita and Monique

CONTENTS

ILLUSTRATIONS

ACKNOWLEDGMENTS

I would like to acknowledge and thank Rabbi Shimon Brand (Oberlin College) and Jeffrey L. Sammons (Leavensworth Professor of German, Yale University) for their helpful suggestions and comments on various aspects of the manuscript. Sections of chapters 2 and 4 appeared in my essay "German-Jewish Identity in the Correspondence between Rahel Levin Varnhagen and Her Brother, Ludwig Robert: Hopes and Realities of Emancipation 1780–1830," *Leo Baeck Institute Yearbook* (1994). I would also like to express my special appreciation to my editor, Dr. Douglas Clayton, for his prompt and judicious advice and steady support. His knowledge of German and German literature and publishing were as helpful as they are rare in today's American publishing world. I am also grateful to Dr. Sarah Disbrow for her care in editing the manuscript.

My very special thanks go to Jack Glazier, whose loving support, intellectual companionship, and practical editorial help have benefited this project in so many ways.

NOTE ON THE TRANSLATIONS

The translations of the primary texts from German, and in a few instances from French, are mine unless otherwise indicated. I have made every effort to keep the translations as close to the original as possible. This meant keeping, wherever possible, Rahel's complex sentences, her punctuation or lack of it, and her idiosyncratic use of colons, with which she conveyed the progressive development or logic of a thought or argument. I have made changes only when the meaning would have been unclear. The reader must bear in mind that Rahel's expression, just like her thoughts, is very much a result of her unique situation as a newly acculturated Jewish woman.

The writing of Pauline Wiesel, Rahel's most important and unconventional friend, is even more difficult to render. Her disregard for the rules of grammar, spelling, and punctuation and her unique way of combining several languages cannot be conveyed in English. Only her tendency to capitalize words or syllables she would have stressed in speech can be to some extent communicated.

Whenever a word or expression could not be rendered adequately in English, either because there is no precise English equivalent or because of Rahel's linguistic peculiarities or love of neologisms, the German word or word sequence follows in parenthesis.

If a German work has appeared in an English translation, I have included the English title (in italics or quotation marks) whenever possible; otherwise, I have provided an English translation of the German title.

[T]here are few things on earth more attractive than the idea of the unspeakable liberty which is allowed the unredeemed. When, beneath the black mask, a human being begins to make himself felt one cannot escape a certain awful wonder as to what kind of human being it is. What one's imagination makes of other people is dictated, of course, by the laws of one's own personality and it is one of the ironies of black-white relations that, by means of what the white man imagines the black man to be, the black man is enabled to know who the white man is.

James Baldwin, *Notes of a Native Son*

RAHEL LEVIN VARNHAGEN

INTRODUCTION

Rahel Levin Varnhagen was a famous and controversial woman in Berlin during the waning years of the eighteenth century and the first third of the nineteenth. She presided over two literary salons, of which the first one especially was renowned for attracting Germany's cultural and, to a lesser extent, political elite, raising in effect the prospect of the German Jewish symbiosis that never took place. She was an unusual author, writing letters exclusively. The vast range of her correspondents included the humble as well as the most eminent of the age. Taken together, her letters to them constitute an epistolary oeuvre of extraordinary significance.

The controversies surrounding Rahel in life continued after her death. She elicited the admiration as well as the scorn of many persons of note. For example, Thomas Carlyle, the nineteenth-century British historian, wrote that she was "a woman of genius, of true depth and worth . . . a woman equal to the highest thought of her century." He compared her favorably to another renowned and brilliant woman, Germaine de Staël, insisting that Rahel "has ideas unequalled in De Staël; a sincerity, a pure tenderness and genuineness which that celebrated person had not, or had lost."[1]

In an essay in the *Revue de Paris* (1837), Astolphe Marquis de Custine, a personal friend of Rahel's, also attempted to define her: "she had the mind of a sage and the heart of an apostle, and in spite of that, she was a child and a woman as any one can be."[2]

On the other hand, Heinrich von Treitschke, the eminent historian of the recently founded German nation with its hegemonic aspirations, did not view Rahel benevolently in his *Deutsche Geschichte im Neunzehnten Jahrhundert* (History of Germany in the nineteenth century): "How greatly the power of the Jews had risen in just a few years! Börne and Heine, Eduard Gans and Rahel set the tone among Young Germany [the literary movement]. . . . Cosmopolitanism and hatred of Christianity, corrosive scorn and the corruption of language, indifference toward the greatness of the history of the fatherland—everything was Jewish in this movement."[3]

Women, both Jewish and non-Jewish, viewed her in yet another light. For Fanny Lewald, a highly successful German Jewish novelist, the discovery of Rahel's published letters was a "revelation" from which she drew strength for her own struggle toward independence: "What had happened to me, what I had to suffer in the way of inconvenience, embarrassment and pain, Rahel Levin had known it all, had suffered it all, had conquered it all with her innate strength. She finally succeeded in achieving a position where she found what she longed for: the possibility for enjoyment and giving according to the inborn need of her nature."[4] For the early feminist socialist Lily Braun, Rahel Varnhagen was one of the "inspiring women" who "turn into agitators for the great ideals of humanity."[5]

This astonishing array of voices, to which many more could be added, is all the more unusual because Rahel was a woman undistinguished by birth, appearance, or special talent. She was endowed only with a superior intellect and a commanding personality, two qualities that set her squarely against the feminine ideal of her time. Her work as a salonnière and epistolary writer lay outside the canonical tradition. The likelihood of her falling through the cracks of recorded history like so many of her contemporaries was therefore considerable. That she fascinated and irritated throughout her life and continued to do so through her writings long after her death and into the present indicates the scope and daring of her ideas and aspirations.

The statements quoted above are interesting in another respect. Representing a range of attitudes and reactions concerning the emancipatory efforts of Jews and women, they disclose as much about the persons articulating them as about Rahel herself. Throughout her life Rahel, both as a woman and as a Jew, challenged established limits, either by opposing them outright or by simply trying to live in accordance with certain professed freedoms. Her life and thought therefore represented a continuous and active dialogue with the world around her. A portrait of Rahel Levin Varnhagen will thus have to take account of this discourse, showing her not in isolation but in a discernible social and historical framework. And it will have to assess her unusual oeuvre—spoken and written conversation—with its underlying utopian vision.

Though the fleeting world of the salon went largely unrecorded, Rahel herself established the foundation for her literary work by carefully preserving a large number of the letters written by and to her and preparing some of them for future publication. Here the role of her husband, Karl August Varnhagen von Ense, must be acknowledged. This "unseasonable democrat" was another thorn in historian Treitschke's side.[6] Varnhagen painstakingly collected, copied, edited, and published or prepared for publication a substantial part of the thousands of letters Rahel had written and received throughout her lifetime. After his death, his niece, Ludmilla Assing, continued his work. But even she faced censorship and persecution for attempting to disseminate the ideas of Rahel and Karl August Varnhagen. These forward-looking, humanist, and egalitarian ideas stood in stark opposition to the repressive and retrograde climate following the Vienna Congress of 1815 and continuing right up to World War I. Accused of treason, Assing fled to Italy, where she continued her work in exile until her death.

Rahel devoted her life and work to literature and the arts, philosophy and history, and the ostensibly lighthearted matters of sociability. With the publication of her writings, all of this assumed an intensely political meaning in the decades following her death. Neither she nor her husband probably would have been surprised at this. They were among the keenest observers and judges of the cultural and political developments of their time, and, equally important, they remained committed to rational and liberal thought and the belief in human progress. Throughout the nineteenth century and into the twentieth, Rahel continued to arouse the interest and admiration of liberals and the hatred of nationalists and anti-Semites, the latter reaching its peak during the time of Hitler.[7]

English readers familiar with Rahel Varnhagen have most likely come to know her through Hannah Arendt's controversial biography, *Rahel Varnhagen: The Life of a Jewess*, which first appeared in English translation in 1957. Written in the 1920s, when the emancipation of Jews in Germany had reached its apex as well as an impasse, it was not published until after the Holocaust. Arendt, who had just earned a doctorate in philosophy from the University of Heidelberg, keenly sensed the critical situation facing the Jews during the Weimar Republic. She even foresaw the end of Jewish life in Europe, although she could not have known the full horror of it. Analyzing the life of this most famous eighteenth-century Jewess with her unwavering belief in assimilation helped Arendt to reflect on her own position as an assimilated twentieth-century German Jewish woman.[8] For this reason, surely, it became an intensely personal and willful biography, notwithstanding Arendt's assertion that she wanted "to narrate the story of Rahel's life as she herself might have told it."[9] In her view,

Jewish assimilation in Germany failed, and the fault lay to some extent with the successfully acculturated Jews. Arendt believed that Rahel's efforts, therefore, were from the beginning misdirected. The study contains in its nucleus Arendt's later thesis of the fundamentally apolitical nature of the modern Jewish experience as well as her limiting paradigm of the Jew as either pariah or parvenu. By concentrating on Rahel's Jewishness, Arendt created a rather one-dimensional portrait of this very complex and self-aware woman. Relentlessly, she pursued the troubled and troubling aspects of the assimilation process. Rahel's other qualities, her resilience and strengths, her subtle social intelligence, her capacity for friendship, her many original and even radical insights, and, finally, her vehement protests against the curtailed existence of women, received very little attention.

Perhaps because Arendt's portrait of Rahel is so centrally informed by her own situation and predicament as a twentieth-century German Jew, it has remained the definitive biography in English and, to some extent, in German.[10] However, critical voices arose from the beginning. Even before its publication, Karl Jaspers, Arendt's professor and, after the war, her dear and trusted friend, expressed both admiration and reservations. She had sent him the manuscript for evaluation, and he responded in a very long and detailed letter, suggesting that she rework the biography thoroughly and present Rahel not merely in light of her Jewishness. He disagreed with her rendition on three major points. Without difficulty, he recognized the autobiographical connection: "this work still seems to me to be your own working through of the basic questions of Jewish existence, and in it you use Rahel's reality as a guide to help you achieve clarity and liberation for yourself." Second, he disagreed with her negative assessment of the Enlightenment: "everything you cite from 'enlightened' thinking is illustrated with negative examples . . . and then leads to pejorative presentations. But it was the greatness of the 'Enlightenment' — of what made Lessing what he is and, ultimately, Goethe, too — that carried Rahel." Third, he felt that her view of Rahel was "loveless." He observed: "Only on isolated pages does the depth of Rahel's soul become evident. . . . The great figure of this woman — who trembles and bleeds, without home and homeland, without a world and without being rooted in her one love — who is so honest, reflects ceaselessly, understands, misunderstands, and casts off that misunderstanding — . . . you let this figure speak, but not from her core, that is, not as this human being herself who is not in her nature a Jew but who passes through this world as a Jew and therefore experiences the most extreme things, things that happen not only to Jews."[11]

However, to consider Rahel in universal terms, as Jaspers suggested, was precisely what Hannah Arendt was no longer willing or able to do. By 1933 her position was clear and obviously the one that determined her interpretation of Rahel: "When one is attacked as a Jew, one must defend oneself as a Jew. Not as a German, not as a world-citizen, not as an upholder of the Rights of Man."[12]

But this Zionist-influenced anti-assimilationist position was anachronistic in its projection onto Rahel's time.[13] Arendt contended that Rahel learned nothing from history, "neither her own nor that of the country in which her family dwelt." She failed to consider that for Rahel and her generation history began anew with the Enlightenment and the possibility of assimilation. Instead, Arendt maintained that for Jews, history began seventeen hundred years earlier in Jerusalem, in other words, with the Christian era.[14]

One of the principal aims of the present study is to show that Rahel had an unusually keen and at times even prophetic understanding of the forces of history. Eighteenth-century Jews had good reasons for their optimism. The latest philosophical knowledge and the social and cultural transformations all around them presaged a bright future. Ironically, Hannah Arendt was unhistorical in demanding of Rahel the insights she as a twentieth-century Jew was just acquiring. Ultimately, the disagreements over the Rahel biography, of course, form part of the larger controversy surrounding Arendt's views on anti-Semitism and the German Jewish minority's interaction with the majority, precipitated by the publication in 1963 of her *Eichmann in Jerusalem: A Report on the Banality of Evil.*

The foregoing discussion reveals that Rahel Varnhagen's reputation has rested on her role as a salonnière and assimilated Jew, while her accomplishments as an author have been almost completely passed over. In literary histories, she is mentioned as one of the notable women of the Romantic period. As a woman, a Jew, and a letter writer, she did not fit into a narrowly defined literary canon. This situation did not change until quite recently. An initial impetus came from the publication of two new editions of her writings. In 1979 Friedhelm Kemp put out a four-volume edition that differed from earlier ones in that the selections also included, wherever possible, the letters of her correspondents, so that in many cases the reader could for the first time read the letters as the dialogue they originally constituted.[15] He also added critical annotations and informative afterwords. Even more importantly, in 1983, Rahel received recognition as an author in her own right with a ten-volume edition of her *Gesammelte Werke,* or collected works.[16] Most of these were reprints of the individual volumes published by Varnhagen and Ludmilla Assing between 1833 and 1875. Volumes 1 to 3 contain *Rahel: Ein Buch des Andenkens für ihre Freunde* (Rahel: A book of remembrance for her friends), volumes 4 through 6 hold the correpondence between Rahel and Karl August Varnhagen, and volume 7 the exchange between Rahel and her friend David Veit. Volume 8 features love letters in its first part and, in its second, the writings of the mystics Angelus Silesius and Saint-Martin with Rahel's annotations and commentaries. In volume 9, the editors printed letters and diary entries collected from various sources. Volume 10 contains scholarly essays, illustrations, documentary and interpretive texts by Rahel's contemporaries, a chronology, a comprehensive register with biographical data of Rahel's correspondents, and a bibliography, as well as an index. Both of these carefully and competently conceived editions permitted a shift in focus from Rahel the great personality and cultural figure to Rahel the writer of letters, aphorisms, and diaries.

The real catalyst for the renewed interest in this outstanding woman, however, was the rediscovery in the late 1970s of the Varnhagen Archive, one of the richest collections of source material on literary Romanticism and the history of the first half of the nineteenth century. The writings of Rahel and her correspondents make up a substantial proportion of these manuscripts. As part of the Prussian State Library's extensive and extremely valuable manuscript collection, these holdings were moved for safety's sake from Berlin to a Benedictine cloister in the village of Grüssau (Silesia) in 1941. In an ironic historical coincidence, Rahel's letters found their way to one of the monasteries she had herself visited as a young woman almost 150 years earlier. After the war, the entire deposition disappeared and was believed to have been permanently lost until it was detected, well preserved, almost completely intact, and cataloged some thirty years later at the Jagiellonian Library in Cracow, Poland.[17]

As a result of this rediscovery, increasing numbers of European and American scholars began to visit the archive beginning in the 1980s. It was not an easy journey, technically, intellectually, and emotionally. As Barbara Hahn and Ursula Isselstein have so poignantly observed, it meant retracing a journey hundreds of thousands of western European Jews had been compelled to make only a few decades earlier. For Cracow is only a short distance from Auschwitz; here the western Jews' journey came to an end as did the living traditions of millions of eastern European Jews. In many ways, then, Cracow is a fitting location for the Varnhagen Collection, for modern German Jewish history begins with these letters.[18] The struggles and disappointments as well as achievements recorded therein cannot but be seen in relation to their tragic end. Archival preocupations thus became intimately linked with twentieth-century history.

The scholars studying the letters of Rahel and her circle quickly recognized the immense historical and cultural value these papers held. They learned to decipher Rahel's notoriously difficult handwriting, no longer relying on and restricting themselves to Varnhagen's transcriptions as earlier researchers had done. They were nonetheless grateful for his documentation and biographical information on many of the obscure or by then forgotten correspondents. His careful identification and decoding of abbreviated or altered names and the large number of copies of letters he made in his very neat handwriting also proved helpful. Increasingly, the researchers came to recognize Varnhagen as a uniquely innovative collector, organizer, and cataloger. His farsightedness and conscientiousness are evident throughout the extensive collection.

Consulting the original autographs, however, opened up new perspectives on Rahel's life and thought as well as on her time and the many known and unknown persons with whom she had come in contact. The papers are especially interesting in regard to two groups with which Rahel was intimately associated: Jews and women. The letters, for example, contain a wealth of information on the process of Jewish acculturation, so much so that it is permitting us to rewrite important parts of this seminal period of German Jewish history.[19] The papers further document the existence of a unique circle of women friends—Jewish and Christian, bourgeois and aristocratic, and even some on the very margins of established society. Also of immense value are Rahel's epistolary exchanges with professional women who form part of this network, among them actresses, singers, writers, governesses. From the point of view of aesthetics, the letters prove to be an outstanding source on the strategies of writing by women and particularly, the complexities of the epistolary genre as used and developed by Rahel and her contemporaries.[20]

The new research soon made clear the need for a new and critical edition of unpublished materials. A group of scholars, including Barbara Hahn, Ursula Isselstein, Marianne Schuller, Consolina Vigliero, and Renata Buzzo-Màrgari, embarked on an ambitious transcription and publication project. A six-volume critical edition is being prepared, including three volumes featuring Rahel's correspondence with women friends, two volumes centering on her epistolary exchanges with the family, and one containing Rahel's diaries and other writings.[21] This means that Rahel is being recognized as a significant woman of letters worthy of serious scholarly efforts and no longer as merely a fascinating cultural figure. Thus a new chapter of Rahel research has begun.[22] It was greatly aided by extensive investigations into the history of European Jewry and the nature of prejudice and anti-Semitism coming out of the ashes of the Holocaust.[23] Further impetus came from feminist literary criticism. Although the newly transcribed materials constitute only a beginning, they are already yielding fresh insights and interpretations, thus deepening and in some respects revising the dominant picture of Rahel and her era. The present study benefits in important ways from my own research at the archive as well as that of many others.

One of the most interesting discoveries of this recent research concerns Rahel's share in the conception of *Rahel: Ein Buch des Andenkens für ihre Freunde* (Rahel: A book of remembrance for her friends) and, consequently, her status as an author.[24] Published a mere four months after her death, it became almost immediately her signature work. Varnhagen was always thought to have been the primary force and inspiration behind it. Rahel may have implored her friend Wilhelmine von Boye as early as 1800 to collect all her letters after her death and publish them. Her attitude toward authorship nonetheless remained highly ambivalent. While other women courageously ventured into the public sphere with their printed works, Rahel, throughout her life, published little and always anonymously.

According to the rediscovered autographs, however, Rahel took an active part in the preparation of both the *Buch des Andenkens* (Book of remembrance) and the *Briefwechsel zwischen Rahel und David Veit* (Correspondence between Rahel and David Veit), probably during the last five years of her life. Her diaries contain extensive lists of titles and contents in her handwriting that point to Rahel's diligent editorial activity. Together with a detailed note by Varnhagen, they indicate that these two works were the result of a collaborative effort, with Rahel as the leading partner and Varnhagen functioning more or less as her secretary. The two works embody two conceptional possibilities with regard to epistolary publications. The *Buch des Andenkens* presents letters and diary entries by Rahel in chronological arrangement, while the Rahel–David Veit correspondence features the letters of both partners and thus represents a dialogue. In the note, Varnhagen justifies his editorial practice by explaining the reasons for the occasional discrepancies between the printed text and the original handwritten one. When preparing manuscripts either for immediate or future publication, he usually read them over together with Rahel, and "she herself indicated what changes needed to be made for reasons of clarity as well as to avoid giving offense; at times, she left it up to me to make the necessary change or add her oral statements from a later time. In any case, every little alteration . . . is to be viewed as a result of our discussion or Rahel's agreement with it." He ends by stating emphatically that these "texts are Rahel's texts, altogether Rahel's" and merely executed and recorded by "her loyal friend and commissioned servant."[25]

These findings do not, of course, change Rahel's questionable authorial status, for even in *Rahel: Ein Buch des Andenkens* her name appears in the title only. The book itself is actually authorless and editorless, with only the lengthy introduction, signed by K. A. Varnhagen, serving as a point of reference or identification. In the other work readied for printing before her death, the *Briefwechsel zwischen Rahel und David Veit*, Rahel is identified as one of the two "authors" in the title. Once again there is no editor or author, and even the writer of the introduction remains unidentified. The title page informs the reader that the contents of the book are from the papers of the late Varnhagen von Ense. Ludmilla Assing, the person ultimately responsible for bringing the book out, is nowhere mentioned. Officially, then, authorship remained tenuous, subjecting the "works" themselves to considerable vulnerability. Only the loyalty of Varnhagen and, later, Ludmilla Assing guaranteed their survival and eventual publication.

The manuscripts, however, do tell us for the first time explicitly that Rahel thought of herself as an author, that she was intent on having her writings published, and that she held very specific views with regard to the form these publications should take. Her ideas were exceptional. At that time, women who published within the established literary norms had to navigate the narrow channel between asserting their own voice and submitting to the demands of a male literary establishment. Rahel opted for a different path altogether. The genres in which women writers succeeded best were the novel and lyric poetry. Rahel's talent, however, was essayistic rather than poetic. As her retold dreams show, she had no special gift for spinning a tale, and the very few occasional poems she wrote, as well as her attempts at translating some of her favorite German poems into French, also make clear that here was no lost poet. The letter and diary, both minor genres, were not only suited to her talent, they also permitted her to express herself freely and to adapt this expression to the various recipients of her letters without ever giving up her authenticity. At the same time, epistolary writing severely limited her readership. As Rahel herself became increasingly convinced that she had worthwhile things to say, and encouraged by Varnhagen, she grew less reluctant to publish.

Rahel's limited ventures into print during her life were from the beginning collaborative efforts. Whether these led to her eventual resolve to prepare major portions of her thousands of letters for publication remains a matter of conjecture. In any case, the cooperation between an extraordinarily gifted Jewish woman and her loyal and conscientious Gentile husband with his passionate interest in preserving individual historical testimonies of the time was a singular stroke of luck, never paralleled to this day. Rahel, the marginal person making use of a marginalized genre, succeeded in creating a work of great originality. In partnership with her husband, she also found an entirely novel way to preserve it and make it accessible for posterity.

Another important result deriving from this recent research concerns the posthumous reputation of Karl August Varnhagen. Rather well regarded during his life, Varnhagen became the object of a campaign of vilification following his death in 1858 and the publication of the first six volumes of his *Tagebücher* (1861–63, Diaries) by Ludmilla Assing. The diaries caused a sensation in Germany because in them Varnhagen espoused his liberal and democratic views freely and openly. His oppositional political orientation had already become evident from his correspondence with the great naturalist Alexander von Humboldt, which Ludmilla Assing brought to print in 1860.[26] The polemic against Varnhagen came from nationalist and anti-Semitic factions as well as Catholic circles. Rudolf Haym, a prominent and politically conservative scholar and critic, initiated the anti-Varnhagen discourse with a long and devastating review of the diaries that he turned into a biographical essay on Varnhagen.[27] He maligned him throughout with clever and pernicious attacks that were argued less on ideological and more on biographical and personal grounds. Haym's attack culminated in a summary judgment about Varnhagen's lack of integrity.

In his widely read *Deutsche Geschichte im Neunzehnten Jahrhundert* (History of Germany in the nineteenth century), the historian Heinrich von Treitschke, following Haym's lead, similarly called into question Varnhagen's character. Treitschke branded him "a traitor" and "the most vain and unreliable of all of Prussia's diplomats."[28] Others, equally unable to see the innovative aspects of the *Tagebücher* and other works, namely to record history as experienced by individuals in daily life, dismissed the author as a mere "gossip-monger," "a busy show-off and contact seeker," "an upstart." Varnhagen was further attacked in his capacity as a collector, editor, and compiler. He was said to have manipulated documents entrusted to him, to have altered or destroyed manuscripts, or to have excised parts from letters that portrayed him or Rahel in pejorative terms. This very negative image prevailed against the voices of other scholars, who, writing on Heinrich Heine and the literary movement Young Germany and working from archival sources, knew another Varnhagen.[29]

In her Rahel biography, Hannah Arendt portrayed Varnhagen in some of the most unfavorable terms, attacking him, as others before her, for his character and his editorial liberties and falsifications. Although ideologically far removed from the likes of Haym and Treitschke, she nevertheless repeated some of the same arguments against Varnhagen. Her harsh treatment of Rahel is to a large extent attributable to her contempt for her husband and to her effort to rectify what she considered Varnhagen's embellished and idolatrous image of his wife. She refuted Jaspers's picture of Rahel because it was, as she told him, based on Varnhagen's and therefore false. Having made extensive use of the Varnhagen Archive before fleeing Germany in 1933, she accused Varnhagen of having manipulated Rahel's legacy by making wholesale corrections in the letters, by expunging essential portions, especially those dealing with Jewish matters, and by coding personal names in order to make Rahel's associations and circle of friends appear less Jewish and more aristocratic and to show Rahel herself in a more conventional light.[30]

Correct about basic facts, Arendt nonetheless drew the wrong conclusions. As shown earlier, Varnhagen had indeed made certain changes in the printed versions, although not as many as Arendt implied. But his intentions were not to mislead the reader; the modifications were made with an eye to the repressive times and in deference to persons still living.[31] And, as the new research shows, with minor exceptions he faithfully indicated any alterations in the autographs or in accompanying notes. As it was, Rahel's and his writings were radical enough even in their tamer versions. Varnhagen was firmly convinced that a time would come when all of Rahel's utterings could be published, when "the greatest part of our conventional morality will no longer hold, when we smilingly shrug our shoulders over notions and rules which now govern us all. . . . Deceit and hypocrisy, now honored, will be despised; instead, truth and sincerity of which we must now be ashamed, will be honored. For such a time shall Rahel's writings be conserved."[32]

Arendt was equally unforgiving toward what she saw as Varnhagen's personal shortcomings. She considered him "empty," "vacuous," and "vain." "He was nothing and had nothing." Hence his mania to observe, to collect, to record.[33] At the same time, Arendt recognized precisely what made Varnhagen acceptable to Rahel—his willingness to listen to reason and his ability to understand, his kindness, and his rationality. These qualities became the basis of their friendship and marriage, Arendt conceded, without, however, revising her poor opinion of Varnhagen. There is no doubt that Varnhagen lacked the originality and creativity that made Rahel so unique and that this led to a certain idolatry of her, so that he at times cut a rather ridiculous figure. At a time when gender relations dictated that the man must dominate in all aspects of life, this marriage seemed wrong in every respect, so wrong that even today we haven't been able to free ourselves completely of this long-held attitude of surprise and disapproval.

We are still searching for explanations instead of accepting what the letters tell us in so many variations—that here was a marriage built on friendship, love, and mutual respect. The autographs, moreover, provide convincing proof that this outwardly dissimilar couple was among the first to engage successfully in an intellectual partnership. Whatever shortcomings this husband may have had, he was able to rise above the conventions of his time by admitting his wife's superiority and serving her as a loyal friend and partner. At the same time, the communicative sociability as initiated and practiced by Rahel—the gathering of noteworthy and like-minded persons who were also friends—played an important role in Varnhagen's later activities as a journalist, historian, and archivist-collector. This far-reaching network of oral and written communication is contained in the extensive correspondences or found its way into Varnhagen's diaries, memoirs, and biographies. Initially part of his ever growing collection, a good portion was eventually published by Varnhagen himself, by his niece Ludmilla Assing, and others committed to the cause of liberalism in Germany.[34]

Granting Rahel the status of an author does not make the presentation of her written work any easier. We have already seen how complex a development it underwent—from handwritten letters, sent on their uncertain journey, to collection and, finally, edited oeuvre. Further challenges arise because the work lies outside the canonical tradition. Rahel may have been a dedicated and prolific writer, yet she remains an author without an oeuvre in the traditional sense. Her writing was so closely related to life that a comprehensive study of her work calls for a chronological, even biographical, approach. At the same time, her life was outwardly so uneventful that any biography would tend to become an intellectual biography. Constrained as a woman and a Jew, she was forced to observe rather than act so that her writings amount to a distillation of insights gained over a lifetime. Besides her fascination with people, she was enthralled by ideas, especially those that promised to "move the world along" and make it a more congenial place for all of humanity. She considered herself a thinker, a *Selbstdenkerin*, and a critic: "That day alone is sweetened for me, when I come to know something new through or thanks to my own thinking."[35] But the results of her thinking have come down to us not as a whole but in fragments. This is, of course, the nature of epistolary writing: letters are lost or destroyed, sometimes as much as the entire side of a particular correspondence, philosophical ruminations give way to the urgency of mundane events, or the written conversation is incomplete because it is continued (or preceded) by an oral one.

More importantly, the fragmentary and incidental character acts as a constitutive element in Rahel's writings. A thought, observation, or insight contained in one letter may startle the reader, who then discovers it again almost unaltered in a diary entry or another letter. Such intellectual sparks are hardly ever treated exhaustively or systematically but stand side by side with a myriad of others, often quite unrelated, like a canvas dappled with a great variety of colors. They are written down as more or less brief essays and may even approximate the aphorism. At other times a thought, observation, or insight can be traced over a period of several years or even her entire life span, clearly showing a process of evolution and maturation. Thus, Rahel's inspirations, for which she was so admired, only appear to be born of the moment and spontaneously recorded; in reality they evince an inner logic and consistency indicating that they are the outcome of a sustained process of intellectual reflection and conform to a definite world view.

Another factor complicating the interpretation of Rahel's work is that it is not self-contained. It continually reaches out, not to an anonymous readership but to individual recipients whose sensibilities, intellectual capacities, or openness she took account of throughout the act of writing. The recipients in turn wrote back and therefore become, to a certain extent, a part of this work, thus necessitating their being introduced and identified. The study of Rahel and her work likewise cannot be self-contained but must encompass the large number of people with whom she was in contact. These included, besides her family and immediate circle of Jewish friends, the significant persons of her age: statesmen, poets, artists, scientists, and other outstanding men and women of aristocratic, bourgeois, or common origin, Jewish and Christian. Today of course, even the representative names of that era carry little meaning for the nonspecialist and particularly the non-German reader unfamiliar with all but the major events in German history and culture. This study will present them not as a mere compendium of names, but as conveyors of the variety and richness of Rahel's social and personal relations.

At the same time, unresolved conflicts and contradictions constitute an important aspect of Rahel's life, finding their way into the very core of her writing. Such dissonances were well known to the first generation of assimilated Jews struggling to find a place for themselves in the larger society—a society enlightened in theory more than in practice and therefore often hostile to Jewish aspirations. They are also typical of women attempting to break out of their confined roles. Rahel, with her heightened self-awareness, experienced the trials of Jewish assimilation and female emancipation with particular intensity. Careful attention to her statements will show that her views on Jewishness were much more complex than they appeared to Hannah Arendt and others, while her concerns for and opposition to the lot of women occupy a central place. Her status as a Jewish woman attempting to join mainstream society provides the key to many of her character traits. Believing herself to be a truly enlightened individual, Rahel despaired at her repeated exclusion by a narrow-minded and smug majority. Her sense of isolation and rejection joined a strong sense of self to produce laments and expressions of despair on the one hand and self-praise on the other.

In contrast to research on other writers, then, whose ideas are set down in a contained and relatively accessible body of work, a study of Rahel Varnhagen must first trace and assemble the wealth of ideas scattered throughout letters and diaries in order to identify important themes and their evolution. Her thought was often radical and ahead of its time, but on the whole, indebted and firmly committed to the principles of Enlightenment. Moreover, she remained receptive to new ideas and intellectually productive until the very end of her days.

A final difficulty, perhaps emblematic of all others, is naming this remarkable woman, not at all a straightforward matter. Selecting from her multiple names entails a confrontation with all the ambiguities and difficulties associated with being Jewish and female. Born in 1771 as Rahel Levin, she adopted during the 1790s the ethnically neutral surname Robert while traveling (probably to avoid the humiliating regulations Jews faced on journeys). In 1814 she was baptized as Friederike Antonie Robert, and through her marriage a few days later, she became Friederike Antonie Varnhagen von Ense. By then she was forty-three years old. For two thirds of her life, then, she was known as Rahel Levin or Robert and only during the last third as Friederike Varnhagen. To her old and close friends and acquaintances, she remained Rahel. And as Rahel, not Levin or Varnhagen, she entered history and literary history as well as the hearts of so many anonymous readers.[36] In this study the name Rahel is used, notwithstanding the trend in feminist criticism toward using surnames. For one, it will ensure the continuous identity of the author. Furthermore, the use of the first name expresses both the unique and intimate relationship between this unusual woman and her contemporaries and later readers as well as the limitations she faced throughout her life. Rahel, Bettine (von Arnim), Karoline (Schlegel-Schelling) — this is how the women of the romantic era were known. The use of the first name served as a mark of distinction but also clearly confined them to their place as women, no matter how outstanding their accomplishments.

The present study is an attempt to interpret Rahel's writings as they came to be created. It will consider them in relation to her life and the momentous political, social, and intellectual changes occurring around her and to present them as an integral whole. It will pursue the logic of her literary production without claiming to resolve its many conflicts and contradictions. By letting Rahel speak for herself through the many and often lengthy quotations, the author hopes to convey to the reader a firsthand impression of the vivaciousness and originality of this writing, fully aware of course of the difficulty and often impossibility of adequately rendering this language into English. Whether we are concerned with this eighteenth-century woman's commentaries on her time, gained from her keen understanding of history, or her insights into the human condition generally, we will find that her observations are topical, inspiring, and illuminating.

I

BEGINNINGS

A Jewish Girlhood in Eighteenth-Century Berlin

Rahel Levin was born in Berlin on 19 May 1771, the eldest daughter of Levin Markus, a well-to-do banker and jewelry merchant, and his wife, Chaie. The newborn child, the first after several miscarriages, was so small and delicate that there was little hope she would survive. She was wrapped in cotton wool and kept in a box for some time.[1] Against all expectation, the child survived and grew, soon revealing a precocious spirit. To be sure, illness, often of a psychosomatic nature, remained a constant companion and defining aspect of Rahel's life. Other children soon joined little Rahel. Markus Theodor, the second child and eldest son, was born a year later. After him, three more arrived: Lipman, later known as the playwright Ludwig Robert, was born in 1778, Rose in 1781, and Meyer, also called Moritz, in 1785. With these siblings Rahel maintained a close if not always harmonious relationship throughout her life.

The Jewish community of Berlin was of relatively recent origin. As part of an effort to replenish the population decimated during the Thirty Years' War (1618–48) and to fill the depleted royal coffers, King Frederic William admitted wealthy Jews to Berlin in 1670. They came from Vienna, where they were being expelled for ostensibly having poisoned the wells. In reality, the Christian merchants wished to rid themselves of their Jewish competitors. In the course of the next century, the small Berlin community grew, and about three to four hundred families, among them the Levins, prospered.[2] Within the state of Prussia they represented some 2 percent of the entire Jewish population. The economic differences between this tiny privileged group and the great majority of Jews were enormous. The latter was composed of four classes contending with varying degrees of poverty and deprivation. Artisans, rabbis, and officials (of the self-administered Jewish community) comprised about 8 percent and represented a kind of middle class. Then came the large group of petty tradesmen consisting of some 40 percent; household servants and peddlers made up the next group of about 20 percent, followed by a multitude of beggars and vagabonds who comprised another 30 percent. Although the Christian population was similarly stratified, each group was considerably better off than its Jewish counterpart.[3]

The affluent Jews enjoyed tremendous advantages over their poor coreligionists. Letters of protection (Schutzbriefe) issued by the king along with various privileges determined their status, markedly easing their material situation. They did not, however, exempt even the wealthiest of them from a myriad of regulations and levies. These stood in stark contrast, for example, to those governing the French Huguenots who, fleeing religious persecution in their Catholic homeland, were invited to settle in Berlin about the same time. The regulations pertaining to these immigrants, mostly artisans with specialized skills, were designed with their benefit in mind — to assist the immigrants in their new enterprises.[4] The Jews, on the other hand, faced obstacles at every step. They were denied the right of citizenship and excluded from all occupations where they could pose a threat to the Gentiles holding the monopoly. This meant that Jews were excluded from almost all the trades, at that time still under the control of the guilds, as well as from farming and all civil service posts. The letter of protection had its limits too. It granted the right of residence in Berlin but could be passed on only to the eldest son. Sometimes a second son could be added, if the wealth of the first amounted to at least a thousand *thaler* and that of the second to at least two thousand. Daughters were categorically excluded from these letters. The Berlin Jews were fortunate in their exemption from the degrading duty of paying tolls for themselves and their wares at one of the two gates through which they were permitted to enter the city. However, they were obliged to pay fees of ever varying amounts for every occasion — births, weddings, funerals, the construction of their houses, and especially the letters of protection. And finally, although no longer confined to a ghetto, the Berlin Jews were still held collectively responsible for any debts, bankruptcies, thefts, and other crimes within their community.

The elaborate regulations underwent periodic revisions without, however, abolishing the Jews' exceptional status. Such was the case in 1730 under King William I and again in 1750 under King Frederick II. In both instances, it was the sovereigns' self-serving political and economic interests that determined the policies toward the Jews. The spirit of tolerance and humanistic ideas, for which Frederick II especially was praised, was notably absent in these regulations. In fact, the so-called enlightened king was particularly adept at devising new schemes for filling his treasury for his wars of conquest. Thus Jews were required to buy a certain amount of china from the not very profitable Royal manufactory without being able to choose the objects. In this manner, the philosopher Moses Mendelssohn came into possession of twenty large china monkeys. Distributed throughout his home, they must have served as a constant reminder of his inferior status. Berlin's reputation as an enlightened city did not accord with its treatment of the Jews. Count Mirabeau, for example, the French revolutionist and promoter of a constitutional monarchy who lived in Berlin in 1785 and 1787, was horrified. He aptly termed the Regulations of 1750 "a law worthy of a cannibal."[5]

The Edict of 1750 further restricted the occupational opportunities available to Jews by barring them from the dry goods trade, thereby channeling them even more directly into the narrow and risky world of banking. Very wealthy Jews were also permitted and even encouraged by the government to start or expand fledgling industries. But these were hazardous ventures as well in a state whose economic base was still almost entirely agricultural. Taken together, these policies had the effect of increasing the already grave economic and social disparities within the Prussian Jewish communities. While the great majority of Jews lived in constant danger of economic ruin, and of these a sizable proportion were actual paupers, a very small number of Jews who were particularly useful to the state acquired great wealth and enjoyed special privileges.[6] Levin Markus was among them. These men's good fortune depended on their business acumen as often as on their willingness to engage in risky ventures, as the following example illustrates. During the Seven Years' War (1756–63) Levin Markus joined a small group of other, for the most part still wealthier, protected Jewish merchants, among them Itzig, Gumperz, Isaac, and Ephraim, for the purpose of minting the Prussian money. The Christian merchants increasingly refused this commission as being too dangerous. In particular, the Jewish entrepreneurs were charged in 1760 with the manufacture of counterfeit money, consisting of silver-plated copper rather than solid silver coins. Although the order, along with secret instructions regarding the composition of this devalued money, came from King Frederick himself, the Jews were blamed for it. A popular ditty about this new money illustrates a widely held belief: "Outwardly bright and inwardly dim, outwardly Frederick, inwardly Ephraim." In many cases, the great risks led to extraordinary gains. In addition to their savvy, the Jews' long-standing experience in banking, their international connections, and strong communal ties proved highly advantageous. The poet Heinrich Heine probably had in mind these very successful and ambitious Jews when he observed: "Regarding the founders of our modern financial dynasties, we may perhaps utter the more prosaic word: that the first banker had been a lucky scoundrel" (*Lutezia*, 1843). Moses Mendelssohn, too, advised his friend, the poet Gotthold Ephraim Lessing, to use caution when dealing with the Ephraims. Lessing was at that time working as secretary to General Tauentzien, who, in 1760, was put in charge of overseeing the Prussian coinage.[7] Consequently, we may safely assume that when the king granted the general privilege to Markus Levin in 1763, this was not out of goodwill but in recognition of valuable services rendered.

The general privilege gave Levin Markus the same rights as the Gentile merchants. It also permitted him and his entire family to reside in Berlin. His position therefore was about as secure and legitimate as it could be for Jews at the time. This must have enabled him also to survive the turbulent years, marked by inflation and high taxation, following the Seven Years' War. The Levin children were fortunate in growing up in comfortable, even luxurious, circumstances. Their home was spacious and elegant. Reminiscing about their childhood, Markus wrote in a letter to Rahel of "performing ballets in [their] stocking feet on the gobellins" (tapestry carpets) of the well-heated living room on Saturday mornings when the parents were still asleep.[8] The family could afford to spend summers at the popular baths. The children periodically accompanied the parents on journeys, most often to the trade fair in Leipzig. Moreover, their childhood coincided with the period of Jewish emancipation in which the elder Levin enthusiastically participated. Like those of other successful Jews, Levin Markus's enterprises in merchandising, banking, and money lending brought him into increasing contact with the outside world. His clients included aristocrats, actors, and musicians who, given the temptations and the need for representation in the capital, tended to live beyond their often modest means. Their pecuniary difficulties brought them to Jewish houses, many of which were already imbued with a spirit of openness, modernity, and worldly sophistication. Business dealings were often turned into social gatherings with the entire family participating. Thus began the social relations of progressive Jews with artists and the aristocracy. Young Rahel frequently joined these informal affairs, gaining experience as a hostess and practicing one of her outstanding talents, the art of conversation. If other daughters attracted admiration through their "exotic oriental" beauty, Rahel fascinated because of her intelligence and wit.

But material comfort, intellectual curiosity, and sociability constituted only one side of the Levin household. The other was much more negative, owing to the lack of harmony within the family. The cause lay in Levin Markus's difficult character and the patriarchal family structure he used to his full advantage. The family dynamics were related poignantly by Henriette Herz in her memoirs. Six years older than Rahel, she became the earliest of the famous Berlin salonnières. In 1781 while accompanying the Levins on a journey to the Leipzig trade fair, she had occasion to observe the father. She described him as one of the most ingenious and witty despots, and for this very reason capable of being especially hurtful. "His greatest pleasure was displeasure. His will was the highest law, and under this iron will his whole family suffered, doubly so Rahel who also bore the pain inflicted on her good, gentle, but intellectually somewhat limited, mother."[9] Henriette observed carefully, as a letter by the sixteen-year-old Rahel indicates. It is addressed to her brother Markus, who was undergoing commercial training with an uncle in Breslau. She reminds him to be sensible, as evidently he had been the cause of some displeasure. Like a grown-up she analyzes the situation and her parents. She concedes that their mother was weak, but that she had also suffered a great deal, and that more grief was in store for her if the father came to know about the complaint.[10] This early letter already reveals important characteristics of the later Rahel: her great understanding of human frailties, her deep empathy for those least able to defend themselves, and her tireless efforts at conciliation.

Rahel's intelligence and her quick wit pleased her father, and she became his favorite child. But his doting love was not to her benefit. Neither did she receive the necessary understanding or nurturance from her mother, who rather favored the eldest son, Markus. The unusually bright and sensitive child was therefore left to fend for herself and, moreover, as the eldest, also felt compelled to mediate the familial conflicts. Many years later she analyzed the effects on her character formation of her father's tyrannical rule and the role she assumed within the family. She singled out two inherently positive traits that, in her view, had become so pronounced as to be character flaws:

These two qualities of mine, however, are: too much gratitude and too much consideration for human feelings. I would sooner reach for my own heart . . . and hurt it than offend another person or even see an offended one. And I am too grateful because I always fared badly and always immediately think of helping and forgiving; and also because *I* alone always helped; this latter has become quite passionate and mechanical. . . . All this is: because . . . nature has given me one of the finest and most strongly organized hearts on this earth; because I have no personal charm . . . : because also my rough, strict, violent, moody, genius-like, almost mad father, overlooked this naturally strong heart and broke, *broke* it. Broke my every talent for action without being able to weaken [my] character. But now the latter works forever the wrong way, like a plant which grows toward the earth: the most beautiful qualities turn into the most hideous.[11]

This is one of many probing exercises at self-analysis and one of the very few references to her father. Rahel developed a personality that in many respects overcompensated for her father's faults. Her desire to please and her consideration for others at times reached pathological proportions, exposing her to further hurt and insults but also assuring her moral superiority. Sociable and gregarious as she was, Rahel was concerned with what she called her lack of charm. But she saw its cause not so much in her undistinguished outward appearance, as her later biographers insisted, as in those exaggerated character traits that she perceptively considered part of the paternal legacy. The metaphor of the wrongly planted tree was originally used by Karl August Varnhagen to characterize his future wife's tenuous position within society. She immediately recognized how very fitting it was and appropriated it.

The family was liberated from capricious paternal authority in 1790, when Levin Markus died. For Rahel, then nineteen, it was too late. Even from the perspective of the grown-up, those early years did not take on a gentler patina, but remained a distinctly painful memory: "A more tortured childhood until age eighteen one cannot experience," the thirty-six-year-old wrote.[12] But the younger children benefited, as Rahel now took over their care and education, guiding them with more consistency as well as with reason, imagination, and gentleness. Overall, the situation improved considerably, although conflicts persisted. Markus, just eighteen years old, became the head of the family, even though everyone relied on Rahel for advice and support. He had extricated himself from the immediate family and achieved independence by marrying early. Markus also took over the father's business and assumed responsibility for the family funds. This meant that, although the inheritance was divided equally, Rahel became financially dependent on her younger brother until her marriage in 1814.

Educational Opportunities

Information about Rahel's education and schooling is scanty and haphazard. Throughout her life she insisted that she learned nothing, that she was "an ignoramus." Compared with her contemporaries, the brothers Alexander and Wilhelm von Humboldt, for example, with whom she became acquainted as a young woman and maintained contact until the end of her life, this may well be true. Their Huguenot mother made sure that the two gifted boys, left fatherless at an early age, received the very best education. The paternal title of nobility made them eligible for a career as higher civil servants. Both brothers spent a part of their lives in government service, but their most important accomplishments were the fruits of many years devoted to intellectual pursuit. Alexander became the world-renowned naturalist and explorer, while Wilhelm is known today as the great humanist, linguist, and reformer. Destiny did not look so favorably on the Jewish girl, Rahel Levin, comparably gifted and well-to-do. She was excluded not only from all educational institutions but also from most professions.

Nevertheless, Rahel's education was not quite as neglected as her remarks suggest. It was aided greatly by the transformations taking place within the Jewish community at large. Prompted by the Haskalah, the Jewish Enlightenment movement, Jewish thinking underwent a gradual process of secularization accompanied by increased receptivity to German culture. This was particularly true of the well-to-do Jews of Berlin. As mentioned earlier, relations between Jews and Gentiles were no longer limited to business dealings and contacts with the government but were increasingly of a social nature. Jews, whenever permitted, joined reading circles, then a popular form of social intercourse, and they began to frequent the theater. For the latter they developed a passionate interest, understandably so, since the German stage represented a forum for progressive social and political ideas. Literature, philosophy, and science thus played a seminal role in the rapprochement of two social groups that had been living in fairly strict isolation from each other.

Learning, of course, was a long-established and revered tradition among Jews, although it was devoted almost exclusively to religious or Talmudic studies. Increasingly, however, young Jews demanded initiation into modern thought. The philosopher Moses Mendelssohn (1729–86) was neither the first nor the only one of these pioneering scholars, although he did achieve the greatest prominence. Born and raised in Dessau, he began studying the Talmud as a young boy. When his teacher moved to Berlin, young Moses resolved to follow him there. He was only fourteen when he arrived one day on foot at one of the two gates at which Jews were admitted to the city.[13] Asked what he wanted in Berlin, he answered simply that he wanted to learn. Initially, his studies remained entirely traditional. But contacts with more worldly Jews awakened his interest in other philosophical theories and recent scientific discoveries. Secretly he began to learn German, then still proscribed by the rabbis. Soon he added the study of Latin, mathematics, and music. When he was twenty-five, he was writing philosophical treatises and literary criticism. And by the time he was thirty-five, he had established himself as the representative leader of the Berlin Enlightenment movement. His friendship with two similarly enlightened Gentiles, the poet Gotthold Ephraim Lessing and the publisher Friedrich Nicolai, was quite unprecedented and served as a model and inspiration for the kind of relations now possible between Gentiles and Jews. Mendelssohn's exemplary life and work were of far-reaching significance for the process of assimilation. Additionally, his translation of the Pentateuch (the first five books of the Hebrew Bible) into exquisite German helped a large number of Jews master the language, further promoting Jewish attempts at acculturation.

Buoyed by the positive changes all around, the next generation accelerated the assimilatory process inaugurated by the previous one. And only two generations later, Germany possessed in Heinrich Heine (1797–1856), a Jewish poet, and in Felix Mendelssohn-Bartholdy (1808–48), a Jewish composer, artists of the first rank. Opportunities for a modern education improved particularly for boys. In 1778 the Jewish Free School opened its gates to poor children, founded by the wealthy and progressive merchants Daniel Itzig and David Friedländer. Its curriculum, a radical departure from that of the traditional *cheder*, included German, French, and Hebrew along with basic mathematics, writing, drawing, and geography. In order to prepare themselves for a productive life, the students also learned bookkeeping and other commercial subjects. For the well-to-do sons, among them Rahel's brother Ludwig Robert and her friend and correspondent David Veit, attending gymnasia (high schools) and universities was already a matter of course. Difficulties relating to their Jewish origins arose for the most part only later, when these young men attempted to find appointments in their professions.

Formal education for girls, however, was still out of the question. Besides being trained in household chores and sewing, they were taught reading and writing, usually in Hebrew script, and learned a smattering of French and German. For the rest, however, they were dependent on the willingness of their parents to engage tutors for them and on the intellectual stimulation of their more educated brothers, friends, and husbands. As most of these men subscribed to Enlightenment thinking, they could not in good conscience refuse to share some of their knowledge with the young women in the household or to supply them with the books being talked about.

The most detailed descriptions of the educational opportunities available to the daughter of an open-minded Jewish family in Berlin during the latter half of the eighteenth century are contained in Henriette Herz's memoirs. She learned German, Greek, and Italian. She also took up Sanskrit, Turkish, and Malay. She received dancing and, upon requesting them, piano lessons. One of her great passions was to participate in amateur theater productions. She read passionately, fetching novels and plays from the lending library. Evenings she often read aloud to her father, who shared his daughter's love of literature. To prepare her for impending wifely duties, she was sent to sewing school. After her marriage at age fifteen to the physician Marcus Herz, she acquainted herself, under his guidance, with modern physics. At the same time, she became a devotee of the new German authors, especially Goethe. The memoirs further reveal that Henriette also knew Hebrew, for she instructed Wilhelm von Humboldt in this language. And she must have learned English, because she mentions translating two English travel books and Mary Wollstonecraft's *A Vindication of the Rights of Woman* into German. Undoubtedly, Henriette Herz was of superior intelligence and, above all, linguistically very gifted. However, she lacked the erudition and originality of thought as well as the emotional depth for which Rahel was so admired. She herself seems to have been aware of these differences and generously conceded that Rahel represented "the highest blossom of the new spirit."[14]

Since the well-to-do Jewish families were closely associated with each other, Rahel must have enjoyed a similarly privileged and eclectic education. Both her parents were already able to read and write in German, although their expression remained formulaic. Like many in his circle, the father was an avid theatergoer and seems to have appreciated art and music, interests he imparted to all of his children. An oil portrait of him commissioned from one of the foremost Berlin artists of the time, Daniel Chodowiecki, gives an idea of the degree of acculturation achieved by Levin Markus: dressed in eighteenth-century fashion, beardless, with powdered hair or a wig, firmly holding an ornate staff, Markus reveals self-confidence, resoluteness, and no traces of his Jewish origins (see fig. 3). Similarly, a painting of Rahel and her brother Markus from about 1785 by another well-known artist, Johann Christoph Frisch, portrays the children as adults, dressed in Gentile fashion, together with the attributes of their newly found culture: Rahel is standing next to an open keyboard instrument with the music displayed; Markus is sitting on a stool beside her, holding pen and paper (see fig. 2). The mother, of whom no portrait exists, seems to have been much more tradition-bound, although she was many years younger than her husband. Like other married women of her generation, she still wore the customary headdress and observed the Jewish holidays. It was the father who broke with Jewish tradition and religious practice; he no longer went to the synagogue, and he saw no need for religious instruction for his children.[15] Most likely, he oversaw and supported Rahel's quest for a modern education.

We know for sure that Rahel grew up speaking and writing Yiddish, utilizing Hebrew script. She also learned German and French along with their respective scripts. Additionally, she received music and piano lessons, which must have been very thorough, for in 1829 she wrote in connection with the rediscovery of the music of Johann Sebastian Bach: "My musical education consisted of nothing but the music of Sebastian, and all the Bachs, and the entire school, thus we, from *that* time, are very well acquainted with it all."[16] Her letters inform us that in the 1790s she possessed and thus also played the two "double sonatas by Mozart," piano scores from his opera *Don Giovanni* and from Gluck's *Iphigenia in Tauris,* and *Ariadne in Naxos* by Georg Benda, a contemporary Berlin composer. In the 1790s we find her looking for a teacher of composition. Rahel became an accomplished pianist and a perceptive critic of music composition and performance. Like Henriette, she received instruction in social dance. She loved dancing, especially waltzing, then a new and daring dance. And, like Henriette, she must have been eager for any book she could lay her hands on. Finally, Rahel, too, learned the traditional womanly activities, such as sewing, embroidery, and household tasks in combination with the very real responsibilities for the care and supervision of her younger siblings.

The details about Rahel's and Henriette Herz's upbringing along with bits of information conveyed by similarly situated girl friends, among them Dorothea and Henriette Mendelssohn (the philosopher's daughters), show us that the daughters of well-off Jews were being included in the emancipatory process. Their education, unsystematic and haphazard though it remained, was vastly superior to that of Gentile bourgeois girls. It was in fact oriented on and compared favorably with that of aristocratic women. The parallels become evident when we consider Chodowiecki's series of ten etchings, in which he depicted the daily life of a lady, each portraying a different activity: The Visit, The Household, Sewing, Embroidery, The Art of Writing, Reading, Drawing/Sketching, The Promenade, Singing, and Music. The intent behind this educational program was to combine the useful with the beautiful or pleasant. Though not institutionalized, this kind of education carried the advantage of being flexible and adaptable: while often superficial, it could also become thorough and encompassing, depending on the pupil's talents and motivation, circumstances permitting. Rahel and many of her girl friends seemed to have been fortunate in that their parents indulged their quest for knowledge and provided them with lessons and tutors. Like their brothers, these girls had no difficulty understanding and adopting new ideas from the Enlightenment and Humanism as mediated through contemporary literature and philosophy. They embraced these ideas wholeheartedly because they concurred with their own aspirations and hopes. These young women's deep commitment to Enlightened Humanism and their love of the arts later lent intellectual substance to their salons and justified their fame. Undoubtedly, Rahel was the most outstanding and committed among them.

Although schooling for boys had always received a great deal more attention in Jewish society, female education that went beyond mere practical training to include knowledge of literature and religion was not entirely without precedent.[17] Given the outstanding significance that education or *Bildung* assumed for the assimilating Jewish men and women, and given also the very scant knowledge we have on the subject of female education, it is well worth considering here the traces of an earlier tradition of learning among Jewish women. Quite likely, Rahel's and her contemporaries' successful efforts at education did not develop within a vacuum. Some of the old ways were passed on to these girls, even as they were losing their former appeal and relevance. In the sixteenth and seventeenth centuries, as printing became cheaper, books specifically addressed to Jewish women began to appear. It was a development that had its counterpart in Christian society. Many of the books were translations of biblical texts into Yiddish; others contained passages from Jewish law, moral tales, and rules of conduct; still others consisted of collections of commandments for women. By the seventeenth century, "worldly" narratives became increasingly popular; they derived mostly from medieval literature and were adapted for a Jewish readership. Since this literature was written in Yiddish, it was intended primarily for women. In contrast, men devoted themselves to reading and studying Hebrew texts. But women did more than buy and read these books. As printers, publishers, and authors they were closely associated with the actual production of this literature.

The high educational level of earlier Jewish women is further documented by the discovery of a collection of forty-seven letters written in 1619 by women in Prague and sent to Vienna (without, however, ever reaching their destination). These letters reveal that the average Jewish woman could not only read and write as well as conduct her husband's or her own business, but also that she was knowledgeable about most aspects of Jewish tradition. She was able, for example, to appreciate the complexities of a legal dispute, the charm of legends and history as well as the inspiration gained from biblical exegesis or the ethical necessity of the commandments. So far, Glückel of Hameln's (1664–1724) famous memoirs provide the best illustration of a Jewish woman's accomplishments. As a trusted and competent advisor to her husband and, after his death, as a businesswoman on her own, as a teller of biblical, moral, and secular tales, and, finally, as a chronicler of her family's history, Glückel of Hameln stands as the model of a seventeenth-century educated Jewish woman.[18] These examples suggest that prior to the onset of emancipation and assimilation, women were well integrated into their communities' spiritual and intellectual life, which has all too often been portrayed as the exclusive domain of men. Moreover, Gentile or "worldly" culture was not quite as foreign to the inhabitants of the ghetto, and its walls, therefore, not quite as impermeable as they are generally believed to have been.

Two points follow from the above observations. First, Rahel and her contemporaries were not the earliest educated or even secularly educated Jewish women, although they immersed themselves much more thoroughly in German culture than their predecessors. They achieved their intellectual sophistication primarily through personal initiative and perseverance. But it was ultimately their forward-looking fathers who provided them with the opportunities to learn, while, previously, women themselves seem to have established an informal and alternative educational network. Second, given the extensive published Yiddish literature, both religious and secular, it is conceivable and even probable that Rahel herself read at least some of it as a child and benefited from its richness, even if she never acknowledged any such influences. Her thinking at times bears a striking affinity with Jewish religious thought.[19] It is revealed, most notably, in her pronounced rationalism and her insistence on looking for causes and their consequences. Her lifelong search for a social order based on unambiguous lawfulness, too, was consistent with Jewish thought. And so was her view that the world's inherent law and order was an expression of divine will. Since these ideas meshed so closely with those of the Enlightenment, Rahel may not have been aware that, perhaps, she owed more to her Jewish background than she was prepared to admit.

Education for Rahel was, of course, a lifelong endeavor, an attitude consistent with Jewish and Enlightenment thinking. Her letters suggest, however, that the most important intellectually formative period occurred when she was in her early to mid-twenties. At the same time as she established herself as a salonnière and epistolary writer, she also made her most sustained efforts at self-education. Her letters inform us that she took up the study of Italian and English while continuing to improve her command of German and French. She pursued her interest in music by taking lessons in violin and, as already mentioned, the principles of composition. The letters reveal furthermore that already as a young woman Rahel was unusually widely read in classical and European literature and in recent and contemporary German literature. She had, for example, read Homer's *Odyssey*, the dramas of Shakespeare, Dante's *Inferno*, Rousseau's *La Nouvelle Héloïse*, and the writings of the young Germaine de Staël. Many of these works she was able to master in their original languages.

Rahel's knowledge of literature, however, was not merely extensive and encompassing. It was clearly oriented around Enlightenment thought. Among German authors, she esteemed above all Gotthold Ephraim Lessing (1729–81), who, in his drama *Nathan der Weise* (1779, Nathan the wise), had created the first positive—and somewhat overly noble—Jewish protagonist in German literature, patterned after his friend Moses Mendelssohn. She admired Lessing as a courageous, incisive, and independent thinker, a man who dedicated his life's work to the pursuit of reason, truth, and tolerance. Another representative of the Enlightenment frequently mentioned by Rahel in her letters was Christoph Martin Wieland (1733–1833). He edited the first German literary magazine of note, *Der Teutsche Merkur* (The German mercury), and prepared the way for German Classicism with his elegant, life-affirming, and often erotic narratives. With his novel *Die Geschichte des Agathon* (1766, The story of Agathon), he created the prototype of the German Bildungsroman. Rahel was also familiar with Schiller's major dramas, *Die Räuber* (1782, *The Robbers*), *Kabale und Liebe* (1784, *Intrigue and Love*), *Don Carlos* (1787), and later also with *Maria Stuart* (1801, *Mary Stuart*), *Die Jungfrau von Orleans* (1801, *The Maid of Orleans*), and *Wilhelm Tell* (1804, *William Tell*). But she remained always somewhat weary of Schiller's idealism as well as his dualistic thinking. She much preferred Goethe's dialectical approach. As we shall see, it was this author's writings that assumed a momentous significance for her. Goethe was then not yet the Olympian figure he became in later years. Granted, he had caught the literary limelight with his storm and stress drama, *Götz von Berlichingen mit der eisernen Hand* (1773, *Götz of Berlichingen with the Iron Hand*), and his epistolary novel *Die Leiden des Jungen Werther* (1774, *The Sufferings of Young Werther*). But his classical plays, *Egmont* (1788), *Iphigenie auf Tauris* (1787, *Iphigenia in Tauris*), *Torquato Tasso* (1790), and his pathbreaking *Bildungsroman*, *Wilhelm Meisters Lehrjahre* (1795–96, *Wilhelm Meister's Years of Apprenticeship*), had not had the same impact as his youthful works. Rahel grasped their significance immediately and, in her salon, became Goethe's early interpreter and most enthusiastic advocate. In his writings she found portrayals of much of what she herself experienced, esteemed, hoped for, and reflected upon. She recognized in Goethe a kindred soul.

Rahel also immersed herself in the works of the younger luminaries of the Romantic movement, with whom she was for the most part also personally acquainted. Among these were the brothers August Wilhelm and Friedrich Schlegel (1767–1845 and 1772–1829, respectively), known as much for their critical as for their literary works. Closely associated with them was Ludwig Tieck (1773–1853), author of novels, fairy tales, and novellas, all of which were characterized by scurrility, irony, and an often demonic undercurrent. Tieck's association with the theater was instrumental in reforming and invigorating the German stage; he was also responsible for bringing Shakespeare to Germany. The theologian Friedrich Schleiermacher (1768–1834) was another intimate member of this circle, as was Wilhelm von Humboldt.

Rahel did not restrict her reading to fiction; she was equally interested in the theoretical aspects of literary production — literary criticism and issues of aesthetics — as well as philosophy. Her letters refer to Rousseau's "Letter on Music," Lessing's *Theorie der Fabel* (*Theory of the Fable*), and his correspondence with Ramler and Nicolai as well as a biography on the admired author. She read the literary magazine *Die Horen*, edited by Schiller and Goethe, and immersed herself in a major philosophical work, Johann Gottlieb Fichte's *Wissenschaftslehre* (*Science of Knowledge*). She was a thorough and actively engaged reader who considered literature and philosophy as nothing less than guides to life and self-knowledge.

A notebook preserved among her papers bearing the title *Excerpts* gives additional insight into her intellectual pursuits as a young woman as well as her method of learning.[20] It contains passages from her readings, mostly short texts that impressed her as particularly valuable and poignant. There are quotes in German and French by Wieland and Rousseau, a somewhat longer extract by the encyclopedist Denis Diderot on the education of women, and one by the essayist Michel de Montaigne on public education. Additionally, we find epigrams by the seventeenth-century German poet Friedrich Logau, rediscovered by Lessing, as well as Italian canzonettas and ever more Goethe quotations, especially from his tragedy *Torquato Tasso*. Besides the encompassing number of authors whom Rahel admired and respected, there are some of equal importance not mentioned by her. These include the representatives of the Empfindsamkeit movement (Pietism and

Sentimentality), represented by the writers Friedrich Fürchtegott Gellert and Friedrich Gottlieb Klopstock and the theologian and physiognomist Johann Kaspar Lavater. This is significant, for these men were of utmost importance for writers and thinkers of the generation that preceded Rahel, including Goethe.[21] Enthusiasm of this kind, and even sentimentality, had little appeal for her. She was and remained truly a child of the Enlightenment and of Rationalism, and, although she was a contemporary of the Romantics, sharing many of their preoccupations, she distanced herself from their irrationalism and otherworldliness.

The fruits of these considerable efforts at self-improvement are revealed in the wealth of knowledge she acquired as well as her modern ideas on the purpose and methods of education. These were probably prompted as much by her responsibilities for her younger siblings as by her personal idiosyncrasies regarding learning, specifically her inability to learn passively. Her own theory of education stressed active participation and practical application. In 1794 she wrote that she would "make every effort to find the means" for children to "acquire their talents" more easily. If at all possible, she would take them to the countries whose languages they were learning. The idea of developing their talents, however, had to come from the children themselves. She would never force children to study who felt no urge to learn. She was convinced that such coercion would do no good and that children ought to study "in order to be able to think better, to expand their knowledge, to grow, and, in any event, to make themselves useful . . . in short, to satisfy the great thirst . . . which I would never attempt to give to anyone but all the means to quench it. . . . I would only *force* the children to learn a thing so perfectly that they could earn their daily bread with it, and the closer to a trade this is, the better I'd like it, a trained, useful cashier, master builder, gardener, a good carpenter, a competent farmer."[22] Concluding her reflections with questions of a speculative nature, as she was apt to do, she wrote: "when are they [the children] educated, when are they finished? when do they begin to act on their own? when are they supposed to be happy (to ask even more foolishly)? Therefore: I force them into nothing, their *free* will is their only dowry . . . to interfere as little with it as possible is the only thing we can give to children."

Rahel's philosophy of education did not concern itself with the separate question of female education. The occupations she mentions excluded the possibility of female participation. She was as yet unable to think in terms of a coherent plan for improving the lot of girls and women. Experience, however, enabled her to recognize certain harmful educational practices.

She took a stand against the then current system of rote learning and mere accumulation of factual knowledge in support of the kind of knowledge that would benefit society as a whole. Rahel's notions of education differed in important ways from the educational policies Wilhelm von Humboldt developed and instituted when, in 1809, he was appointed minister of culture and education. He set the course of German education well into the twentieth century. Like Rahel, he subscribed to the idea of an inclusive and unified humanistic philosophy of education pertaining to all disciplines; but he oriented the new humanistic gymnasium on his understanding of classical Greek education, dissociated from all practical work and social activity and therefore elitist and devoid of a sense of social responsibility.[23]

The emphasis on an ethical and socially oriented education led Rahel some years later to formulate her ideal of an educated individual: "An educated person is not one whom nature has treated lavishly; an educated person is one who uses the talents he has kindly, wisely, and properly, and for the highest purpose . . . who can look firmly at where he is lacking and realize what he is lacking. In my mind this is a duty and not a gift; and constitutes for me solely an educated human being."[24] For Rahel the meaning of education went beyond the acquisition of knowledge to include the patient, active, and expansive development of the self and all its potentialities. It corresponded closely to the concept of *Bildung* as it developed in Germany at the end of the eighteenth century. Though not easily defined, this notion of education permeated the literary and philosophical works of the time. It was realized most perfectly in Wilhelm Meister, the protagonist in Goethe's masterful and thoroughly optimistic Bildungsroman *Wilhelm Meister's Years of Apprenticeship*, a work Rahel read intently throughout her life.[25] She earnestly strove to live up to this ideal: the evolution of the self through effort, experience, love, and wisdom. It was the high level of *Bildung* as much as her brilliance and wit that brought her recognition and admiration from friends and acquaintances.

Ultimately, however, Rahel was right in insisting that her education was inadequate, her own great efforts and the considerable opportunities available to her notwithstanding. As she put it, she "had not gone through the systems" like the men of her generation, and she was well aware of the consequences. She exhibited the typical characteristics of self-taught persons—insecurity, shyness, and a lack of systematic thinking on the one hand and, on the other, intellectual independence and originality. Furthermore, her studies envisioned neither a definite goal nor competence in a profession. There were no ready-made roles for her to step into and no tasks to engage in outside the confines of family and home. If she nevertheless succeeded in turning her role as hostess and her private correspondences into something akin to a profession, namely that of salonnière and epistolary writer, this was once again due to her very own ingenuity and perseverance. For Jewish men, the rewards of a modern education were evident, for one might then escape from the often hated occupations in commerce and finance. Furthermore, the new professions, medicine, law, and the arts, offered intellectual satisfaction as well as recognition from coreligionists and the more open-minded segments of Christian society. They therefore pursued their newfound goals eagerly and soon found themselves at the head of the German intellectual elite. The Jewish intelligentsia, which contributed so fundamentally to German achievements in the arts and sciences up to 1933, had its origin in the enthusiastic embrace of a humanistic education and the ideal of *Bildung* in the latter half of the eighteenth century. For Jewish women the rewards of learning were less tangible and, consequently, their accomplishments all the more remarkable. To be sure, the new education greatly enriched and enlarged their understanding of the world and brought escape from the narrow lives most of their mothers still led. Their salons even gave them a sense of participating in the larger society. However, education and *Bildung* did not free them from their dependent and confined status as women. Their motivation derived exclusively from their love of learning. They thus realized most successfully what, according to Enlightenment interpretation, the twelfth-century Jewish philosopher Maimonides (Moses ben Maimon) praised so highly: "learning for learning's sake." Rahel, even if unconsciously, united both Jewish and Enlightenment thought on the highest level and passed it on in her salon and through her letters.

YOUTHFUL HOPES, ACCOMPLISHMENTS, AND REALITIES

The richest and most optimistic period of Rahel's life coincided with the last decade of the eighteenth century. The early years of the nineteenth, on the other hand, already bore many of the signs of limitations she would have to come to terms with, as both a woman and a Jew. Over the course of this decade and a half, Rahel established her first and widely renowned salon (the second she held with her husband, Karl August Varnhagen, during the 1820s) and started her extensive network of correspondences. She became an expert interpreter of the works of Goethe and of literature generally. She also undertook several journeys and lived through two love relationships.

Rahel's First "Salon"

With youthful optimism and little concern over her "erroneous birth," as she termed her stigmatized heritage, Rahel, now in her early twenties, set out to construct a life for herself.[26] In doing so, she pursued two objectives that would remain vital to her until the end of her days: one, to overcome some of the constraints imposed on her as a woman and two, to promote social integration for herself as an assimilated Jew as well as for other marginalized groups. In the family's drawing rooms she began to assemble a circle of friends and acquaintances who, as she believed, shared not only her interest in literature and the arts, but also her commitment to more egalitarian social relationships. The family members and immediate Jewish circle were very much included in this undertaking. In many respects, Rahel's "open house" or "society," as this institution was called in Berlin, evolved from her father's earlier social gatherings. It differed, however, in two important respects. It was no longer associated with the conducting of business affairs. More importantly, Rahel, from the beginning, intended these evenings to be more than just friendly get-togethers. In the early 1790s she was as yet not able to formulate her goals very well. Beauty and a refined society were important, but even more so a certain spirit that she worked hard to create and that she modestly described as "a capable good will . . . not invisible" to visitors.[27] The Levin home, in the words of one of her guests, was simple yet comfortable and in its own way also "plentiful and exquisite." Line, the old and somewhat curious maid of the family, served tea and sometimes took the liberty of voicing her own opinion.[28] Rahel herself, however, was clearly the center and spirit of these gatherings.

The same visitor, identified as Count von Salm, described in lively detail an evening at Rahel's. Although stylized, idealized, and written after Rahel's death, his expansive account provides insight into what contemporaries found so captivating about this young woman and the society she assembled around her. It also reminds us of the importance sociability assumed at the time. Besides being known as the century of Enlightenment, the eighteenth was also the "sociable century."[29] Participants in the many venues of sociability—secret societies, associations, and reading circles, as well as the salons—were seeking more egalitarian human relationships. In combatting the rigid class barriers still in effect in Germany, sociability contained the potential for social change. Rahel's "open house" was very much a part of this progressive development and must be viewed within this larger context, especially because it went a good deal further in its efforts at overcoming class distinctions than most other social organizations.

Count von Salm described Rahel as "neither tall nor beautiful, but of a fine and delicate build and a pleasing facial expression; a trace of endured suffering . . . gave this expression something deeply touching; but her pure and fresh complexion, combined with her dark and lively eyes, betrayed a wholesome strength that dominated her entire being. From these eyes a glance fell upon me, a glance, which penetrated my innermost self, and to which I would not have liked to present a guilty conscience." Salm further relates that Rahel "was considered a girl of extraordinary intelligence, clever as the sun, and kindhearted at the same time; thoroughly original; she understands and feels everything, and whatever she says, is often in an amusingly paradoxical way so strikingly true and profound that one repeats it to oneself years afterwards, still thinking about and marveling at it." The count was also full of admiration for the "freedom and grace" with which the young hostess was able "to stimulate, to enlighten, to create enthusiasm! No one could withstand her sprightliness. And all the things she said! I felt as if in a whirlwind and could no longer distinguish, what in her wonderful, unexpected utterings was wit, profundity, good thinking, genius, or curiosity or caprice. I heard colossal pronouncements from her, true inspirations, often in a few words, which flashed through the air like lightening, and pierced the innermost heart. She spoke words of admiration about Goethe which surpassed everything I had ever heard."

Clearly, Count von Salm was as impressed with Rahel's human qualities as with her brilliant mind. The care and sensitivity he took in conveying the young woman's special appeal are typical for this period of emerging individualism, when the acquaintance with a notable human being was considered something of an event. Moreover, he was delighted with the company he met at Rahel's that evening. He was one of a number of noblemen present, among them Gustav von Brinckmann (1764–1847), who had brought him to the gathering. Brinckmann was for many years active as a Swedish diplomat in Berlin as well as in Dresden, Paris, and London. He was thoroughly at home in German culture and literature and even wrote poetry in German. The two gentlemen were joined by Peter von Gualteri (1764–1805), an officer and adjutant to the then reigning King Frederick William III, and a Major von Schack. After a while the very popular actress Friederike Unzelmann made her entrance. The poet Friedrich Schlegel, already famous for his scandalous novel *Lucinde*, was there, immersed in conversation with another writer, Ludwig Robert, who was Rahel's favorite brother. In the course of the evening, the latter happily complied with a request to present some of his new poems. Since they were mostly satires and parodies, Rahel was not very pleased. She opposed personal satires because, in her view, they contained something inherently "malicious." Additionally, during these early years, the young hostess was intent on establishing the art of conversation as the primary intellectual activity at her salon and thus discouraged readings, performances, and other diversions. It was for this reason also that she limited herself to serving simply tea, although it must be remembered that tea was then a rather exclusive beverage. Another famous person making his entrance that evening was Friedrich von Gentz (1764–1832), the statesman and publicist. Initially an admirer and follower of Kant and Rousseau as well as a supporter of the French Revolution, Gentz turned increasingly conservative. After 1815 he was closely associated with Count Metternich, the architect of the Period of Reaction which held Europe in its grip until the Revolution of 1848.

One of the last to arrive that evening was Prince Louis Ferdinand (1772–1806), a nephew of King Frederick II and the highest-born visitor to grace Rahel's society. Unusually handsome and charmingly unconventional, he was a very welcome guest. But, like other members of the high nobility, he led an essentially marginal existence, unable to find a meaningful role for himself in this age of democratic revolution. Though a libertine in his personal life, his public actions betrayed political conservatism. He was gifted, sensitive, distraught, and very much in need of Rahel's empathy and her "straightforward attic truths," as she called the advice she gave him. She was apt to receive him in the privacy of her room under the roof, reserved for her more intimate friends, where the prince could also be heard improvising on the piano. Other less prominent people, relatives, and close friends of their own Jewish circle completed the social gathering that night.

It was a typical "refined" society as Rahel envisioned it, of mixed social background and differing interests and philosophical orientation, governed by wit, intellectual sophistication, and an attitude of tolerance—a society that compared favorably with those one would encounter in Paris or Vienna. Count von Salm describes the lively conversation, how it moved easily from person to person and from subject to subject. "The talk was of the theater, of Fleck [the actor], of Righini, whose operas at the time met with the greatest applause, about August Wilhelm Schlegel's public lectures which even the ladies were attending. The most daring ideas, the keenest thoughts, the cleverest wit, the drollest games of the imagination followed in casual and general sequence." The conversation was "unforced" and "unintentional." Everyone participated in a "natural manner and no one was obtrusive, people seemed to enjoy listening as much as speaking." The observing count was impressed with the spontaneity and vivaciousness of the evening. He seemed neither troubled or surprised by the range of guests assembled nor by the tone or content of the sprightly conversation.

But not everyone was always as tolerant. The romantic poet Clemens Brentano, who visited Rahel's salon in 1804, also admired her wit and kindness. But as a young man with a decidedly conservative orientation, he was no friend of emancipated women or Jews. His description of Rahel and her company, as conveyed in a letter to his future wife, the writer Sophie Mereau, is rife with ambivalence:

Yesterday I visited the famous Mademoiselle Levi, who has a not unpleasant tone in her society, it could be very agreeable if the conversation were not so slovenly; she is over thirty years old, I would have guessed twenty-five, rather short but graceful; she is without pretension, permits the conversation to take any turn, even to the point of uncivility, to which she reacts with merely a smile, she herself is extremely kind and yet strikingly witty. That Prince Louis Ferdinand and Prince Radziwill visit her causes much envy, but she doesn't care any more than if they were lieutenants or students, if these had as much spirit and talent as those, they would be equally welcome to her.[30]

Different visitors thus recognized similar qualities in Rahel, most notably her keen intellect and her striking wit on the one hand and her kindness and tolerance on the other. But they assessed them and her intentions differently, depending on their open-mindedness or conservatism. Wilhelm von Humboldt was another guest who harbored conflicting feelings toward Rahel, with regard to both the goals she pursued and the position she had achieved for herself in this small social circle. And this in spite of the fact that he had frequented Jewish homes from an early age and, after the Prussian defeat by Napoleon in 1806, actively supported the reform movement, including the civil emancipation of Jews. He liked seeing Rahel because, as he remembered many years later, one almost "never left her without . . . taking away something of substance which prompted further serious and often profound thought or which was emotionally moving."[31] At the same time he reproached her for her "lack of discrimination" in choosing her society.

What these men objected to was Rahel's disregard for social hierarchies. However, this was precisely what made her assemblies unusual and a deliberate force for progressive change. Hers was a truly mixed society, composed of men and women, Christians and Jews, of noblemen, civil servants, and poets, actors, singers, and other theater folk. It was a society where social rank counted for very little, but intelligence, talent, and character meant a great deal. A conversation between Rahel and the philosopher and theologian Friedrich Schleiermacher illustrates the young salonnière's intentions and the objections they called forth perfectly. Brinckmann recalled to Varnhagen:

When [Rahel] once reproached Schleiermacher that he visited her so seldom, and this one answered jokingly: "If only you did not keep such bad company . . ." she replied with a smile: "But that is precisely your mistake. A thinker must be able to make something of everything, in his own way. Would you yourself, with your powerful mind and all your excellent talents, have become such a great scholar and erudite man, if you had not read very many bad books. Not through these books, but by considering and working through their stupid and dull contents have you developed your specific genius. . . . Why don't you judge my bad company in the same way? Just ask Brinckmann, I have finally taught him to read and leaf through all kinds of people."[32]

People were the objects of Rahel's study — to be read like books, individually and in groups, highborn and lowborn, accomplished and weak, prejudiced and vain, or selfless and noble. The entire range of human motivation, emotion, and activity furnished the material for this lifelong project.

Rahel was quite aware that she possessed a special social talent. She defined it many years later in a letter to Clemens Brentano, thereby unwittingly countering many of the points in his earlier critique (which was unknown to her):

I have an infinite love for society and always have, and am quite convinced that I was born, destined and equipped by nature for it. I have infinite presence and agility of mind in order to comprehend, to answer, to treat. I am very understanding of personalities and circumstances of all kinds, I understand fun and seriousness, and no subject matter is . . . foreign to me to the point of making me uncomfortable . . . I am modest and yet reveal myself through speech and can be silent for very long and love all things human, [I] *tolerate* almost *all* people.[33]

Rahel's was not the only "open house" in Berlin. In all, the Prussian capital counted at the end of the century at least nine such circles presided over by Jewish women.[34] Of these, Henriette Herz's gatherings were the earliest and Rahel's the most brilliant. Henriette's husband, Dr. Marcus Herz, had provided an initial setting when, in 1779, he presented at his home lectures on the philosophy of his former professor, Immanuel Kant, which many notables attended, among them the brothers Humboldt and members of the royal family. By 1784 Henriette began to receive guests of her own in the adjoining drawing room and thus established the first "literary salon." The eldest daughter of Moses Mendelssohn, Brendel Veit, later known as Dorothea Schlegel, also opened her home to friends and acquaintances of both Jewish and Christian background, although hers was reputed to be an informal reading circle rather than a salon. The Jewish women were sought out not only for their intellectual sophistication, poise, and charm but also for their kindness and personal warmth.[35] The informal and intellectually stimulating assemblies at their homes offered a welcome alternative to the staid and protocol-laden social events of the aristocracy and the court as well as the tedious card-playing evenings popular in most bourgeois homes. Although a mixed society could be found in all the "open houses," Rahel more consistently transgressed against the rules of etiquette and convention by treating her guests according to her egalitarian and humanistic principles. Tolerance was for her not just a beautiful principle but something to be practiced in daily life. She remained unimpressed by criticism such as Brentano's and Wilhelm von Humboldt's, relying instead on her own definition of nobility and virtue: "I would exchange my best friend for a scullery-maid if I considered her more noble and ethical than him: (and I *have* done it; recently)."[36]

Besides the visitors introduced by Count von Salm, a number of others require mention here, as they all contributed to the distinctiveness of Rahel's gatherings and also became correspondents. Many remained part of her circle of friends for many years; others fell short and even joined the early anti-Semites. Quite a number achieved prominence as artists or intellectuals. The most exceptional among these was probably Wilhelm von Humboldt, mentioned several times already. Although Rahel respected him for his intellectual brilliance and was proud to have him as her guest, she also harbored ambivalent feelings toward him. With his wife, Caroline, she was for many years on intimate terms. Friedrich Schleiermacher, also mentioned earlier, attended, as did his student Count Wilhelm zu Dohna. Two other noblemen who admired Rahel were the young Wilhelm von Burgsdorff and the older Prince de Ligne. The latter was in the service of Austria and a much respected author. Among the many artists of the time to be found at Rahel's were the opera singer Maria Marchetti, the actor Johann Fleck and his wife, Sophie Louise, also a successful actress, the sculptor Friedrich Tieck (Ludwig Tieck's brother), and the architect Hans Christian Genelli. The writer Jean Paul Richter, another devotee, visited when in Berlin. Another famous visitor was Madame de Staël, who had heard so much about Rahel that she insisted on making her acquaintance when she came to the Prussian capital. Rahel's friendship with two nonconformist and open-minded countesses, Josephine von Pachta and Karoline von Schlabrendorf, also dates from this period. And finally, there was Pauline Wiesel, the mistress of Prince Louis Ferdinand, who became Rahel's most unconventional friend and rebel soul mate.

Many of Rahel's personal friends came from her own Jewish circle. Dorothea and Henriette Mendelssohn, Nettchen Markuse, Wilhelmine de Boye, Friederike Liman, the sisters Sara and Marianne Meyer (later known by their married names Sara von Grotthuß and Marianne von Eybenberg), Esther Gad as well as David Veit were among those who most genuinely admired Rahel. As Jews they shared many of her goals and ideals and could therefore best appreciate her accomplishments and the obstacles she faced as she made her inroads into Gentile society. These Jewish friends remained loyal to each other throughout their lives, despite long periods of geographical separation or loss of contact.

Interestingly, they as well as the family members receive very little attention in Count von Salm's description, although some of them at least must have been present on that representative evening, as they formed an integral and essential part of these gatherings. Count von Salm seems to have slanted his account in favor of the glamorous and eminent. Recent archival research has cast new light as well as new doubt on the accuracy of this by now canonical report. Although all the persons mentioned were Rahel's guests and even friends and genuinely admired her, the composition of the society on any given evening may not have been as described. Other unpublished testimonials suggest that the evenings at Rahel's were more modest and less intellectually brilliant. Moreover, unpublished letters by Brinckmann, who was a frequent guest and friend, and one who followed the social experiments of Rahel and other Jewish women with keen interest, reveal his persistent anti-Jewish prejudice, which, like so many others, he saw no need to abandon. In time, Count von Salm's report evolved into a myth about the "Berlin salons." It contributed to interpretations of those salons as more auspicious and historically significant than they likely were and also implied that outstanding Jews and prominent and truly enlightened Gentiles were successfully integrated. By contrast, none of the women who received guests in their homes attempted a similarly encompassing description of their activities, and neither did they ever use the term *salon*. They must have been conscious of how tentative and vulnerable their experiments were.[37]

The tenuous situation of Jews is further shown by the absence of reciprocity. Though the grand and the powerful could be found at Rahel's, she herself was not considered part of high society. Because she was Jewish, she was not accepted in the homes of most of her highborn guests. They often referred to her as "the little one" or "little Levi," terms that betray an attitude of amiable condescension. They appreciated Rahel's open house for its free and cosmopolitan character as much as for its enlightened and tolerant spirit, but they felt no urgency to open their own doors to this new cultural phenomenon. This sad commentary on the state of even the more progressive segments of German society brings to mind again the utopian dimensions of Rahel's and the other open houses of Berlin.

Not surprisingly, the Berlin salons never attained the significance of the more politically oriented ones of Paris, whose tradition reached back into the seventeenth century. Although the French salons shared many of the features already identified with those of Berlin, notably greater social integration and the prominence of women, and were for these very reasons also looked upon with disapproval by many, they functioned as an established social institution. The salonnières themselves were drawn for the most part from the aristocracy or high bourgeoisie, while many of the guests were not only eminent but also in a position to influence the course of political events.[38] The Berlin salons, by contrast, were a much more modest as well as fragile undertaking, initiated and led by women from neither the top nor the center but clearly the margins of society. Having assimilated into German culture, these Jewish women no longer accepted their outsider status and began in their own small way to transform the lofty concepts of Enlightenment thinking into reality.

As noted earlier, many contemporaries of the Jewish salonnières attributed transformative possibilities to these freer social associations. Friedrich Schleiermacher was among the first to recognize and explore the utopian potential of enlightened sociability as he encountered it in the Jewish salons, and the special role women played in creating it. In 1799 he published anonymously a detailed if speculative treatise on the subject, entitled "Attempt at a Theory of Social Behavior."[39] Parts of it he later incorporated in his work on ethics. He drew his insights from his experiences at the salons of Henriette Herz and Rahel Levin. Schleiermacher declared free sociability, bound or determined by no external purpose, as one of the first and noblest needs of all educated human beings. Such social relations, he stated, provided the individual with opportunities to go beyond his own limits to become acquainted with other and foreign worlds, so that by and by no human manifestation would remain unknown to him and even the strangest characters and circumstances would become familiar ("friendly and, as it were, neighborly") to him. This task was accomplished by means of freely associating rational people engaged in mutual education or *Bildung*. Freed from the constraints of the "lowly" business world, a person could enter a completely intellectual world, where he could cultivate his mental faculties to the fullest capacity. Free sociability allowed for the temporary stabilization or harmonization of competitive social forces as well as for transcending them. The guiding principle of Schleiermacher's deliberations was the advancement of awareness and tolerance through a process of social interaction. It was in this uninhibited interplay of, at times even contending, social and intellectual forces that he saw the potential for progress.

So far, Schleiermacher's characterization accurately reflected the aims of the Berlin salonnières. However, he was quite explicit in assigning free social interaction to a separate realm—that of leisure—which was removed from both the bourgeois or professional existence and the domestic sphere. Various coercive forces governed bourgeois or professional life, from which the individual then sought recovery during his leisure time. Since women had no part in this bourgeois sphere and were equal to men only as educated individuals, Schleiermacher declared them as ideally suited to become the founders of this superior sociability. In positing separate male and female spheres, Schleiermacher betrayed his indebtedness to the then evolving gender ideology. He relegated the activities of women to the realm of leisure and the beautiful, which stood in contrast to the useful. In doing so, he drew parallels between sociability and art: both contained their purpose within themselves. Schleiermacher thus objectified and aestheticized sociability in the same way that Kant had done for art when he called for the "disinterested contemplation of the work of art." In locating free sociability in a separate realm rather than in everyday reality, however, Schleiermacher weakened its potential for real change.

The Berlin salonnières conceived of their societies in very different terms. Since, as Jews and women, they were themselves the objects of an actual process of social transformation, they treated social gatherings, their ease, wit, and sophistication notwithstanding, as a kind of testing ground. This was particularly true of Rahel, who saw no benefit in insisting on discretion or neutrality and, in addition, seems to have elevated self-exposition to a principle. Karl August Varnhagen recalls how, as a young man newly introduced to Rahel's gatherings, he was at times perturbed by the inexorable candor with which she admitted to and explored her own strengths and weaknesses.[40] Rahel challenged the society that did not really accept her by inviting it to her salon. She challenged it further by making herself the object of the deliberations when she saw the need for it. This was surely what Schleiermacher meant when, in his essay, he referred to the playing out of competitive social and intellectual forces. However, as the representative of one of these competing forces, Rahel could hardly have considered her assemblies with "disinterested contemplation" or as dissociated from "bourgeois life" or reality, as Schleiermacher proposed.

Although Rahel did not leave a coherent "theory" comparable to that of Schleiermacher, her ideas concerning the purpose and meaning of sociability can be found throughout her letters. They reveal not only the seriousness with which she regarded and cultivated human relations but also her thoroughly egalitarian thinking and her insistence that men and women were equally responsible for improving the world for all of humanity.

Sociability, in Rahel's view, was an integral aspect of human existence: "Sociability. Actually that which is most human among human beings! the essence and point of departure of all that is moral! Without companions, without comrades during this earthly existence, we would ourselves not be persons, and any ethical action, law, or thought, [would be] impossible: impossible, without the premise that to another—the image of a person—is the same as to us, that *he is* what *we are*. Therefore, whoever ruins sociability, harms it, harms me; whoever damages it, damages me: my innermost self."[41] Rahel joined the old notion of man as a social being to the much newer one of the brotherhood of man. And by inserting herself into the equation, she made explicit the close link between the social and the personal spheres, and that the well-being of one was not possible without the well-being of the other.

Rahel thought of sociability in terms of a creative endeavor and thus related it to artistic activity as well. But, unlike Schleiermacher, she saw and demanded that art and therefore also sociability be purposeful rather than disinterested, that it offer guidance and insight into the state of human affairs: "In all of life as in art, its practice and contemplation, ever more relations must be set forth (this alone means living), not because we live more this way: no repetition could achieve that. But with each particular relationship something new is created; and for this reason alone its increase is desirable, invigorating, joyful, noble, real."[42] The creative aspect of human relations was predicated on treating each person as unique, equal, and an end in itself.

In Rahel's view, the desire for a better society emanated from the individual's lack of freedom and autonomy which precluded the realization of one's potentialities. Thus she admitted toward the end of her life that we are all "vassals. . . . Our innermost being even is coerced (gezwungen)" but confronted this unsatisfactory situation with an eternal wish to be whole: "our desire for a holy, free, unharmed state. *Must* we not desire this? Are we not ourselves this very desire?"[43] Rahel saw a dialectical relationship between individual happiness or self-realization and social justice. In typical eighteenth-century fashion she conceived of self-realization in terms of a duty as much as a right: "Man is a work of art . . . given to himself as a task. Material, artist, and workshop [are contained] within ourselves."[44] This notion relates closely to Rahel's ideal of the educated individual, as discussed earlier.

As a member of a marginalized group within a rigid class society, Rahel very clearly grasped the historical significance of changing social relations. The strict feudal code governing all aspects of human relations was beginning to give way to a freer, more egalitarian mode of interaction. In her salon she made every effort to move this transition along. Her gatherings therefore were very much part of everyday reality, for Rahel's commitment to egalitarian thinking prevailed over various aspects of elitism. At the same time she had no illusions regarding its efficacy. Salon society in Berlin never comprised more than about a hundred people. It could therefore serve at most as a model for progressive change among the privileged. In no way did it or the many other societies and associations, which similarly favored more inclusive social relations, represent a microcosm of changes occurring in the society at large. Nevertheless, the salons of Berlin, and Rahel's in particular, planted the seeds for a tolerant and egalitarian society. Additionally, they were important as a venue for further Jewish assimilation and as female accomplishments in the public or at least the semipublic sphere.

Besides promoting social equality and integration, the Berlin salons played an important role in the dispersal and promotion of literature.[45] Writers habitually frequented the Jewish open houses, where they were sure to find intelligent and stimulating conversation and sometimes had occasion to read from their works. Their presence as well as that of other intellectuals ensured that the newest publications were acknowledged, read, and discussed. Moreover, since books were not easily acquired at that time, they were often exchanged among friends and acquaintances. Gustav von Brinckmann's excellent library, for example, provided a welcome resource for salon visitors.

The late eighteenth century was in so many ways a time of transition from which literature and the author, especially, were not exempted. The salon reflected these changes particularly well in that it brought together old and new types of authors. Gustav von Brinckmann and Prince de Ligne, for example, represented the older type of author, the "dilettante" or "virtuoso," connotations with which they proudly identified. Both terms did not yet suggest the negative image of "dabbling," but meant that writing was but one of many activities in which the privileged and financially secure aristocrat or bourgeois engaged. Friedrich Schlegel and Jean Paul, on the other hand, exemplified the new type, the free-lance author, who had to prove himself in the marketplace. Since in Germany the marketplace was slow to establish itself and copyright laws were not yet accepted or respected, most of these writers led very precarious existences. Ludwig Robert, for example, could launch his career as a professional writer only with the backing of the family wealth and by considerably reducing his living standard. Through her liaison with and later marriage to Karl August Varnhagen, Rahel helped such authors, both male and female, establish connections to publishers or recommended them outright.

Finally, Rahel's assemblies were important because, through her profound insights into the writings of Goethe, she helped promote an appreciation for his mature works. Because they were so novel and demanding in both form and content, many readers reacted with disapproval or a lack of understanding. Rahel proved to be an effective interpreter and thus, her assemblies also functioned as a forum for literary criticism.

Rahel, the Writer of Letters

For Rahel, letters had a purpose similar to that of the salons—the cultivation of human intercourse and, if possible, friendship. In contrast to the quite innovative role of salonnière, at least as far as Jewish women in Berlin were concerned, Rahel the epistolary writer could draw on a long tradition of female letter writing. In the eighteenth century, it was quite acceptable for a woman to carry on extensive personal and even "learned" correspondences. Women were acknowledged to be excellent letter writers and to have played a significant role in the evolution of this genre. The letters of Madame de Sévigné (1626–96), written over a lifetime and published as early as 1734, served as a model to many younger writers. The cult of friendship, with which women were so closely associated, encouraged letter writing among the bourgeois classes. Women's letters dealt with everyday life and were characterized by spontaneity, immediacy, and emotional depth. They thus differed radically from the formalized, bombastic, and turgid style used by men for official purposes. In their letters, women pioneered a language capable of expressing an individual's emotional and intellectual world. Men quickly realized the possibilities this new mode of writing offered. They in turn began to make use of the private letter for the purpose of exploring their inner lives in relation to their daily experiences and even cultivated qualities and sensibilities previously spurned as feminine.

Increasingly, the art of letter writing was considered an essential aspect of a person's education, and children practiced it from an early age using sample letters. People took great care in composing their letters, for the arrival of a letter was no small event. The author knew that his or her epistle was likely to be read not only by the person it addressed but passed around or read aloud to members of the family as well as friends and acquaintances. Letters were judged with regard to content and style. Especially good letters were often copied and even published, particularly if they came from people of renown. Personal letters were thus rarely private in the strict sense but more often and more accurately semipublic in nature.

Admittedly, letters served primarily as a means of communication, but they were also read as a key to the writer's character and an indication of her or his educational accomplishments or *Bildung*. This meant that, although the range of topics was by definition limitless, many of the concerns and preoccupations of the age found their way into personal letters. Letters typically reflected the period's mania for the knowledge of human nature, the fascination with moods and introspection, the appreciation of the beauty and wonder of nature, and concerns over social injustice and suggestions for overcoming them. Naturalness as well as openness and truthfulness were also considered essential qualities of the well-written letter.

The enchantment with personal letters and the importance assigned to them is revealed by the statements of some of the most prominent men of the time. The philosopher and man of letters Johann Gottfried Herder demanded that the letter transmit not merely "cold news"; he wished for it to be "an imprint of the soul" or, as Schiller put it, a person's "physiognomy." Heinrich Heine, in one of his romantic moods, asked that it be the "heart's blood in an envelope." Gotthold Ephraim Lessing viewed it in more rational and traditional terms, as a substitute for oral communication, as a "conversation" or "chat." In a letter to his future wife, he lovingly reprimanded her for not writing: "And do consider that man does not live by smoked meat and asparagus alone but, what is more, by a friendly conversation, spoken or written."[46] And Goethe, while introducing a slightly critical note about the lack of discretion, summed up the whole mood of the time very well when he reminisced in his autobiographical work *Poetry and Truth*: "there was then such a general lack of reticence among people that one could not speak or write to any individual without the feeling that various others were being addressed. A person would examine his own and others' hearts, and because the Taxis[47] postal system was reliably swift, the seal secure, and the postage reasonable—and such communications were of no interest to the authorities—this moral and literary exchange was soon widespread."[48]

Not surprisingly, epistolary writing also exerted a decisive influence on literature generally. The expressive possibilities that personal letters had pioneered, including carefully drawn character portrayals and the exploration of inner moods, thoughts, and feelings, gave rise to a new genre, the epistolary novel. The model work, Samuel Richardson's *Pamela* (1740), was originally meant to be a collection of sample letters. But in combining these with a story, Richardson created the first modern epistolary novel. Others followed, most notable among them Rousseau's *La Nouvelle Héloïse* (1759, *Julie, or, the New Heloise*), Sophie von la Roche's *Die Geschichte des Fräulein von Sternheim* (1771, *The Story of Fräulein von Sternheim*), and Goethe's *Die Leiden des jungen Werther* (1774, *The Sufferings of Young Werther*). Common to all of them was the fact that the depiction of the protagonist's sensibilities took precedence over action or plot.

Additionally, philosophical and historical treatises and especially literary criticism were often presented as letters or even correspondences, as they were particularly suited for didactic purposes. Prominent examples from that time are Moses Mendelssohn's *Briefe über die Empfindungen* (1755, *Letters on the Sentiments*), Lessing's *Briefe die neueste Literatur betreffend* (1759–63, *Letters Concerning the Newest Literature*), which also contain contributions by Mendelssohn, and Schiller's *Die ästhetische Erziehung des Menschen* (1795, *The Aesthetic Education of Man*).

The above overview shows the immensely important role that letter writing played in the intellectual life of the time. Nevertheless, at the very moment that literature appropriated the possibilities offered by epistolary writing for its own purposes, the letter as an autonomous genre was demoted to secondary status. Goethe and Schiller, in redefining literature along classicist lines, declared drama, prose, and poetry as the three major genres. They also set forth a new (Kantian-inspired) aesthetic ideal—the autonomous, self-contained, and objectified work of art. The letter, which was inherently dialogic, subjective, and deliberately purposeful in its intent to communicate, to explain or convince, could not fulfill these demands. Letters continued to play an important role throughout the nineteenth and into the twentieth century but were regarded more as an auxiliary genre. Increasingly they assumed historical and documentary significance and were rarely appreciated for their literary value alone. Rahel's letters, too, were viewed primarily from this perspective. Their immediacy and close association with her life further encouraged this approach. However, since her writings consist almost exclusively of letters, and she herself viewed them as literature, they will be considered in terms of their literary as well as their documentary value.

Rahel is unique among epistolary writers in that she made the letter her almost exclusive literary means. Poetic passages, aphorisms, literary criticism, explorations of philosophical questions and social problems, essays on the art of acting, dance, painting, and music, reviews of musical and theatrical performances, even diary entries, found their way into her letters. Moreover, hers were always real, that is, not fictitious, letters. According to her own estimate, their number reached well beyond ten thousand and thus surpassed those written by "Voltaire and his kind."[49] Excerpts from them, especially reviews, literary criticism, and aphorisms, appeared in various journals and magazines during her lifetime, beginning in 1812. But Rahel always insisted on anonymity, never overcoming her ambivalent attitude toward authorship. In 1816, for example, she wrote to Ignaz Troxler, a friend and the editor of the magazine *Schweizerisches Museum* (Swiss museum), which featured selections from her letters that year[50]: "About me, my dear friend, you can say anything but my poor name! To me, it is as comfortable as a dark dress which gives the illusion of also keeping you warm; if it came to light, I would feel cold, I could no longer wrap myself in it, and would stand revealed and quite embarrassed."[51] At the same time, anonymity provided her with the freedom to experiment with and evolve her own modes of expression. She was well aware that the newness of her situation, as she saw and reflected upon it, and the specific temperament and sensibilities it generated, required other, less definite categories than those favored by the established literary canon, her deep admiration for Goethe, the accomplished master of language and form, notwithstanding.

Toward the end of her life she summed up what she considered her accomplishments as a writer, clearly conveying the idea that her letters were more than documents or traces of her life. Rather, she viewed them as "results," as "the yield of silent and ignored pains of long standing, of tears, suffering, and thinking; of the joys of solitude and the tedium of being disturbed. Pearls which a half century cast up from a storm-tossed human soul, treasures like those contained in the great sea: if it does not confine them to an affected garden pond where their destiny is stagnation: without failure: even if not immediately noticed and admired by the ignorant."[52]

These words, dynamic and unwieldy as always, betray Rahel's commitment to authenticity and truthfulness as well as her insistence on accepting the challenge of life in all its facets instead of withdrawing from it. They also indicate how closely associated living and writing were for Rahel. She readily acknowledged the letters' historical and documentary value. But by referring to them as "results," "pearls," and "treasures," she also stressed their aesthetic or literary quality. Her letters then, like the work of other creative individuals, represent Rahel's evolution as a human being, an intellectual, and an author. They also show her refusal to sharply separate life and art because of her strong belief that the beauty and truth of one domain was valid also for the other.

When Rahel began writing in the early 1790s, however, theoretical questions of this kind hardly concerned her. Her letters, from the start, evince the spontaneity, vivaciousness, and intellectual versatility characteristic of women's epistolary writing. The choice of topics also shows them to be very much within this tradition: they dealt with literature and literary events; they contained character portraits and descriptions of nature; they reported on daily life; and they quite ignored or betrayed naiveté about political events. Numerous references indicate that Rahel was familiar with the epistolary tradition. She mentions the letters of Ninon de Lenclos, Madame de Sévigné, Voltaire, Mirabeau, and Lessing, among others.

She wrote, as she tells it, since the age of twelve or thirteen, "notes (billets) and letters to her siblings which provoked much laughter and comment." Although she believed that all thoughtful people wrote like her, she was also conscious of certain difficulties. These she attributed to the fact that "*the others* . . . were so strange and couldn't quite understand what I was saying, and also because I was not able to say it very well." As for the rest, she assumed that people "were and thought like me. I stayed with this opinion—too long for my own good—[and] saw each diverging case as an exception."[53] At the same time, as she reflected on how spontaneous and natural writing was for her, she also questioned her initial naiveté by referring to a problem she faced repeatedly throughout her life—the failed communication. Rahel, who was uniquely capable of understanding and empathizing with others, was herself often misunderstood. Yet she felt a deep need for people to see her as she wished to be seen. This desire was, of course, closely bound up with her plea for social acceptance. In 1795 she expressed it with the help of one of her striking metaphors: "If only I could disclose myself to people the way one opens up a cupboard; to show with a single motion the contents neatly arranged in their shelves. They [people] would surely be satisfied; and, as soon as they saw it, also understand it."[54] This was her lifelong desire and the reason for her many self-presentations as well as the meticulous care with which she responded to letters. Her words betray a degree of inner self-confidence that contrasted starkly with her precarious social position.

Dialogue and, by implication, communication and mutual understanding are surely the most distinguishing features of letter writing. Rahel not only fulfilled these requirements most faithfully but also demanded them of her partners. In her letters she tells a great deal about herself, her thoughts and feelings, her emotional and physical states; but the letters also reveal the deep empathy she willingly extended toward others, her spontaneous readiness to help, console, guide, or merely entertain or share a happy moment. Dialogue provided the basic motivation for her writing, which, for this reason, was never self-contained but always addressed to someone. The first to recognize this was the writer Jean Paul. He declared her an artist but one who could only write if she wrote to someone.[55]

The explicitly dialogic quality was one outstanding feature of Rahel's writing. Another was the wealth of her ideas and the great variety of topics as well as the depth, acuity, and originality with which she expounded or reflected upon them. Even though she led an essentially uneventful life in Berlin, her correspondents couldn't stop praising the richness of the thought and insight in her letters. David Veit, for example, with whom she carried on an intensive epistolary exchange for almost a decade, wrote: "Your letter alone, dear Rahel, was worth the journey."[56] In 1793 Veit was on his way to Göttingen, where he was to complete his medical studies. On his way there he had stopped in Weimar, where he had the great fortune of meeting the literary luminaries he and Rahel revered so much, Goethe, Wieland, and Herder. Dutifully he reported to Rahel his impressions in a long letter full of details, a letter which also initiated the correspondence. Rahel's reply impressed him so much that he put it on the same level as the actual experience. Friedrich von Gentz was even more rapturous, as illustrated by his letter of 1803: "Angels in Heaven! Is there a language on earth in which one can write to you? — Is it possible to answer *such* letters? . . . What depth of pleasure and what depth of instruction glances at me from your letter. . . . Yes! if I could write like you! or rather, if I was capable of *that* with which you substitute writing! Your letters are not *written* at all: they are living persons."[57] Gentz copied all of Rahel's letters in order to be able to read them over and over again "with enjoyment," as he found her handwriting difficult to decipher.[58] Veit, too, declared his correspondence with Rahel as "wild and madly necessary."[59]

Gentz referred to a third characteristic of Rahel's writing—her language. In part, the peculiar liveliness and immediacy of her expression was a result of her consciously cultivated dialogic style approximating the spoken language. If the letters are read out loud, the difficulties created by broken off or otherwise incomplete or disconnected sentences, faulty or idiosyncratic punctuation or word order, or inconsistent orthography mostly disappear. Ultimately, however, Rahel's use of language is related to her social situation. Although Veit repeatedly attempted to guide Rahel toward a more standardized German, he finally came to the following important realization: "In your letters . . . every word looks like you have invented it for your own use." He further explained: "You look at [each word] as if anew; and use it as if for the first time, in its relations to other concepts, etc." Therefore it often acquires a new "meaning which it should rather have. You try to eliminate whatever is arbitrary in language and make it necessary or natural."[60]

Rahel herself considered her linguistic peculiarities a deficiency, especially during these early years. She couldn't understand why she who was so sensitive to language did not succeed in using it more gracefully. She was further distressed about not being able to improve: "Even my taste, my judgment is improving, and yet I speak worse than the most common woman. . . . Everyone can write and speak better, with far dumber thoughts. . . . I appreciate every 'and,' 'well,' 'then,' the least little word; [I] recognize so nicely the differences among poets and writers, [I] am able to characterize them, to classify them, much better than others, and yet [I] am unable to smooth out, to improve."[61] Rahel could not achieve that which she admired so much in Goethe's writings, and later also in her husband's: the controlled and measured use of language, which allowed for a carefully crafted paragraph, the paced development of thought, and the balanced description of feelings.

Rahel's writing was not smooth or balanced. Her sentences and words burst forth in torrents; in order to capture the moment or the situation she was describing in all its intricacies, she enumerated and specified, drew parallels and comparisons. She took recourse to foreign words, coined neologisms, underlined a word or part of a word as many as three, four, seven, and even seventeen times. Margins are mostly missing, the lines running past the edge of the page. As she herself put it, when she wrote to people it was "as if the heavy, full horizon of my soul thunders forth."[62]

By the time she was in her late twenties Rahel had reached a degree of self-awareness and social insight that enabled her to perceive her linguistic peculiarities for what they really were: a reflection of the newness of her social and cultural experience—marginal, experimental, and unguided by tradition. Thus she wrote to the Romantic writer Friedrich de la Motte Fouqué in 1801: "Language is not at my service, not even my own, German; our language is our lived life; I have invented my own [life], I therefore could make less use than many others of the existing phrases, that's why mine are often rough, but always genuine."[63]

The life that Rahel the Jewish woman "invented" for herself at the end of the eighteenth century was that of an intellectually active woman engaged in spoken and written dialogue. Communication was vital to one eager to leave the century-old isolation of the Jews behind and join the society at large. In her "open house" and in epistolary writing she recognized possibilities for the kind of communication that would pave the way for more genuine human relations—a prerequisite for her integration. She seized upon these, exploited and further heightened them in a way that no one had done before her. Although she employed the spoken and written word for similar purposes, she was also careful to distinguish between them, insisting, for example, that a letter should not represent a conversation per se but be the portrait of a conversation. Mostly, she preferred the immediacy of the spoken over the written word.

Viewed from a historical perspective, both the salon and the letters occasioned and reflected important social developments in late eighteenth-century Germany or, more specifically, Prussia and Berlin. If the salon represented an attempt to realize an enlightened society, the letters provide insight into the discrepancy between the professed principles of tolerance and humanistic thinking and their failings in real life. Thus, the letters recorded that which can no longer be reconstructed due to the volatile and impermanent nature of oral communication in the salon.

2

THE EARLY LETTERS

From the very beginning, Rahel showed herself to be a very diligent and eager correspondent. Writing was for her a serious intellectual activity, demanding concentration and quiet surroundings. For women, these were luxuries they could rarely count on. Not surprisingly, Rahel's letters are replete with complaints about interruptions. Other difficulties impeding a smooth writing process were the lack of a properly prepared quill—in one letter she writes of making do with a piece of wood—poor quality paper, or the challenge of fashioning an envelope. Nonetheless, she often managed to write several long letters in one day. At other times, the writing process was extended over several days.

Rahel's correspondence during this early period falls into several groups. The most outstanding and encompassing epistolary exchange is undoubtedly that with David Veit. Additionally, Rahel exchanged letters with many of the frequenters of her salon, among them Gustav von Brinckmann, Prince Louis Ferdinand, and Friedrich Gentz, thus laying the foundation for her far-reaching correspondences with notable persons. Family letters constitute another important group, as do those she exchanged with her women friends. And finally, there were the love letters. The following discussion will take up each of these groups separately.

RAHEL AND DAVID VEIT

The correspondence between Rahel and David Veit is for several reasons especially instructive. Although it was not published until 1861, recent studies have shown that Rahel herself prepared it for future publication, just as she had the *Buch des Andenkens*. It follows a different conception from the latter, however, in that Rahel decided to include both sides of the correspondence. This is a clear indication that she was conscious not only of the high quality of Veit's letters but also of the uniqueness of this written dialogue between two young people, both of whom were firmly and enthusiastically committed to Enlightenment thinking. David Veit and Rahel were not lovers but friends, who treated each other with utmost esteem, candor, and consideration. The correspondence is therefore one of friendship and intellectual exchange.

Rahel and David Veit were of the same age and came from similar backgrounds. They grew up in forward-looking Jewish families who nevertheless exerted considerable pressures and constraints on their children's development. Rahel repeatedly characterized their common difficulties and anguish with the words from Goethe's *Torquato Tasso*: "Only the galley slaves know each other." Both young people participated in this correspondence with great earnestness and with the clear intent of achieving intellectual clarity. Characteristically, they answered each other's letters point by point and often discussed complex questions and problems over the course of several missives. Moreover, they frequently reflected on the manner and purpose of their written communication. Thus, this youthful correspondence can be regarded as one of the few that fulfilled Rahel's demand for reciprocity.

Their mutual agreement, however, was far from being spontaneous or automatic. Rather, it was the result of considerable effort on the part of both writers. For, although Rahel could count on Veit's ability to intuitively grasp and appreciate much of what she related and confided, she also knew that he was in many ways quite unlike her. In fact, so different did he appear to her that initially she dared not even hope for "our present agreement, because it seems to me that things occur very differently within us . . . if not actually in a contrary manner. . . . Therefore our friendship appears to me a real victory . . . the product of two . . . rational beings who, however they may twist and turn, will unfailingly meet again at the truth, to which they always turn, which they seek in great earnestness."[1] Rahel's trust in the power of reason is unmistakable and reciprocated by Veit in his own manner. For example, he communicated to her his delight at certain thoughts of the contemporary Jewish philosopher Salomon Maimon (1753–1800). In particular, he appreciated Maimon's distinction between the enthusiast and the philosopher: "both are untiringly in search of the first causes of human knowledge; only, the philosopher seeks the data . . . for these causes in experience, while the enthusiast believes that they too can be found within the human soul."[2] Rahel and Veit intuitively sided with the philosopher, being careful always to test their thoughts and theories against their personal experiences and observations. They thus avoided, in spite of their youth, falling prey to the seduction of enthusiasm and sentimentality typical of their times. Furthermore, Rahel's perceptive assessment of the significance of this correspondence and friendship is indicative of her considerable historical consciousness. Even at the time of writing, she viewed it — as we would today with the benefit of historical insight — as the written discourse between two truly enlightened individuals, capable of overcoming differences through reasoned argument, a tolerant attitude, and truthfulness.

In view of the considerable trust Rahel felt toward David Veit, it is hardly surprising that she confided to him her youthful hopes and expectations as well as the unhappiness caused by frictions at home and discouraging experiences in her social interactions. In particular, she protested against the limitations imposed on her as a woman. At this stage, she seems to have been affected by these much more consistently than by anti-Jewish prejudice; the extent of the latter she acknowledged only gradually. Against her female state, on the other hand, she launched a vehement protest: "How can you be so cruel," she accused Veit,

and remind me that I ought to or must see this; don't you know that I am consumed, completely consumed, like something which ceases to be? Is it possible for a regular person to accept the pavement of Berlin as the world? . . . and is it a woman's fault that she *too* is a human being? If my mother had been kind and hard enough, and had only been able to suspect how I would turn out, she should have smothered me at my first cry in the local dust. A *powerless* being who gets no credit for sitting at home, who would have Heaven and Earth, men and beast against her, if she wanted to get away . . . and who really must stay home, and who has to swallow all kinds of reprimands, if she makes *mouvements* which are noticeable, which are made with *raison* because it is really not *raison* to agitate; because if the glasses, spinning distaff, gauze, sewing things are dropped, then everything goes to pot (so haut alles ein).[3]

Behind the outrage and desperation, conveyed by the strong language and the breathlessness of the sentences, barely separated by commas and therefore seemingly endless, Rahel's analytical mind is at work. She gives a poignant characterization of the diminished life her family and society assigned to her: the tacit assumption that a woman should suppress her natural yearning to see the world and remain at home, busying herself with tedious feminine tasks. Her friendship with Veit must have made the disparities between the opportunities available to men and women especially apparent. Both of them were young, gifted, ambitious, and filled with a zest for life. But only Veit could follow his aspiration to prepare for a profession at the university (newly open to Jews), to travel, and to be received by notables, such as Goethe, Herder, and Wieland. Only he could exert a certain control over his destiny while hers was determined by forces completely at odds with her interests, talents, and inner needs. As she so succinctly put it, she was a "powerless being," physically and intellectually constrained and restricted in a way that, in her view, condemned her to immobility. Rahel was to invoke this image of being immobilized again also with regard to her Jewishness.

Rahel's aspirations to live fully and without familial and social restraints represented only one source of her difficulties. The other emanated from her superior intelligence, deemed equally unbefitting to a young woman. Family and friends were both impressed and disconcerted by her keen intellect and wit. As a young girl, she had evidently delighted in displaying her cleverness and her gift for quick repartee. But as she matured, she began to make a distinction between wit and intelligence. The former took on a negative connotation due to its customary critical edge, while the latter became positive because it entailed thoughtfulness and empathy for human frailties. Those around her, however, were reluctant to recognize this new tolerance. This is how Rahel saw the situation: "'They cannot forget that once I wanted to be cleverer than they', they cannot forget that at fourteen I was witty; they hate me because they fear me; they fear me because they think I am clever (their common word); but they don't know that I have an intelligent thought in my head."[4] Rahel therefore continued to "do penance for old sins," as she put it. The sense of being misunderstood and an outsider thus accompanied her from the outset and was continuously reinforced even by those most familiar with her.

In other respects, however, Rahel was surprisingly willing to conform and adapt to social demands. She accepted the new feminine ideal of the time and the special sphere accorded to women by Enlightenment and Romantic ideology. Although women did not gain in terms of social or political rights, their possibilities for intellectual, artistic, and personal development increased greatly. According to Goethe, Schiller, Friedrich Schlegel, and many others, women were now recognized for their greater kindness, their integrity, their unselfishness. They were considered the models and embodiments of a higher humanity and morality, and the muses to man, the artist and creator. This expanded horizon appealed to the young Rahel as well as her women friends, newly released from the isolation and much greater constraints of traditional Jewish life. They seemed quite willing to embrace this ideal, which in reality confined them again to an auxiliary role. In one of her letters to Veit, Rahel took Goethe's famous words and applied them to the plight of women: "Right on, Veit, praise me as a *woman*, that's what I like most. That's what everyone wants to deny me most; because they do not understand me; and one does like to be understood. You know that I cannot abide classes and don't like to be restricted to one, except to that of human beings. Nevertheless, one does belong to one, and 'Noble be man, helpful and good', especially woman, say I, and therefore, let it show that I belong to them; because what else can they [women] do? We must make the best of that which we are able to do."[5] Although a tone of resignation is detectable already in these words, it would be several years before her failed love relationships taught Rahel that the new feminine ideal as she understood and pursued it was unrealizable.

Jewish matters do not occupy a central place in this correspondence. In fact, they are mentioned quite infrequently, often in passing. Nevertheless, the few instances where Jewishness is discussed by either Rahel or Veit are crucial and show that both of them followed Jewish affairs with a keen interest. In the early 1790s, perhaps buoyed by the visible progress all around them, they maintained an essentially optimistic if realistic outlook. At that time Rahel refused to accept a Jewish fate. Thus, in that first and much admired letter to Veit, in which she responded to his accounts of meeting with Goethe, Wieland, and Herder and chafed against the restrictions imposed on her as a woman, she defiantly stated: "I shall never accept that I am a Schlemihl and a Jewess."[6] In examining Rahel's and Veit's attitudes toward Jews and Jewishness, it is well to recall their situation at the end of the eighteenth century. As members of a tiny minority that, as a result of the new spirit of tolerance as well as economic and social changes occurring throughout the century, had achieved a certain respectability and considerable wealth, their belief in assimilation was well justified. Within this privileged group, however, the opinions were divided in regard to the desirability of assimilation as such, the pace and direction this assimilation was taking, or how best to improve the Jewish civil status in Prussia. The orthodox, notably rabbis and community elders, vehemently opposed assimilation. Then there were those who were convinced that reform of what they considered to be outdated ceremonial laws and rituals was necessary in order for Jews to participate more freely in the society at large without having to abandon their faith and allegiance. Among these were many prominent Berlin Jews, including David Friedländer, Joseph Wolff, Lazarus Bendavid, and, of course, Moses Mendelssohn.[7] Finally, there were the enlightened universalists who favored complete integration through assimilation and even conversion to Christianity.

Rahel and David Veit belonged to the last group. Their remarks on Jews and Jewishness are as critical as they are discriminating. They also indicate that Jews were seldom permitted to forget their blemished status. Insults and slights occurred quite frequently and may explain why such matters are referred to only briefly or allusively in the letters. Such negative experiences did not, however, result in a more positive identification with their Jewish origins. Rahel had distanced herself from Jewish traditions to the extent that she could make fun of them or openly go against them.[8] She perceived her Jewishness in largely negative terms—as humiliation that she wanted to put behind her and therefore adamantly insisted that one had to "get out."[9] However, both Rahel's and Veit's attitudes were quite unrelated to the Jewish self-hatred one often encountered at the time. They never denied their Jewishness and they maintained their strongest and lifelong friendships with other Jews. They also were well aware and proud of many qualities that distinguished the Berlin Jews especially—their wit, their erudition, and their generosity. But they had little patience for what they considered obsolete customs and laws that excluded them from mainstream society. Moreover, they recognized that not all efforts at assimilation were commendable. Veit, for example, reserved his sharpest judgment for assimilated Jews who reproduced Gentile pretensions and class prejudice within their own circle.[10] This resolute stance also indicates that he and Rahel not only viewed their own community, whose faults and weaknesses they knew intimately, but also the Gentile world, which they wanted to join, with critical eyes. In all instances, the two young people's judgments were guided by humanistic and egalitarian principles.

The discussion about Moses Mendelssohn, especially, which occurs early in the correspondence, shows that Rahel's and Veit's motivations were neither opportunistic nor self-serving. Rahel had known the philosopher since she was a child. The two families had lived not far from each other and maintained close contact. And Rahel's friendship with the eldest and youngest of Mendelssohn's daughters, Brendel (later known as Dorothea Schlegel) and Yente (Henriette), was especially close during their years in Berlin. Rahel and Veit admired and respected Mendelssohn and were well aware of his significance for the emancipation of Jews. Like them, he was intent on bringing the Jews out of their social and spiritual isolation into the mainstream of humanity. He did this by reconciling the Jewish Haskalah with Enlightenment thinking. If the two young people's deliberations nevertheless have a critical edge to them, this is attributable less to their youthful sense of superiority than the claims of a new generation.

The deliberations were prompted by the publication in 1793 of *Gotthold Ephraim Lessings Leben* by his brother, Karl Gotthelf Lessing.[11] As already noted, the friendship between the three bearers of humanity, Moses Mendelssohn, Gotthold Ephraim Lessing, and Friedrich Nicolai was illustrative of the enlightened spirit governing relations between Jews and Christians in Berlin. Since Mendelssohn was also a friend and advisor to Lessing's brother, the latter, as compiler of his famous brother's biography, included passages written by Mendelssohn. Veit recommended the book to Rahel, urging her to read it, as it was fascinating not only in regard to Lessing but also because it revealed much about Mendelssohn.[12] Rahel replied a month later, saying how much pleasure she derived from the book, although she criticized the biographer's style and use of platitudes.

She then turned her attention to Mendelssohn's contributions: "Mendelssohn's dedicatory epistle is very beautiful: *mais elle se ressent un peu* [it smacks a little], like so much of his [writing], of oriental morality tales and therefore sounds precious."[13] Veit promptly wrote back, assuring her that as far as Lessing was concerned they were in complete accord. Turning to Mendelssohn, Veit granted that the philosopher did "indeed affect an oriental posture" but then went on to explain: "but you mustn't forget that he retained this posture for good reasons. . . . He wanted to show that a Jew, with the spirit of his fathers and educated entirely according to the dictates of the Orient, can attain the highest freedom; he wanted to show by example, what the Jew can achieve as a Christian *and* a Jew; he was always intent on swimming between both parties; sometimes, of course, even the best trained swimmer is not up to the task, and breaks out in cold sweat. How much praise and how much blame are contained in this opinion, I need not explain to you."[14] The two parties Veit referred to are the Jews and the Christians, although Mendelssohn was at pains to maintain good relations also between opposing factions within the Jewish camp, such as the orthodox and the enlightened mentioned earlier.

Veit's assessment of Mendelssohn's intentions and options betrays considerable historical knowledge and insight. The discussion takes up and reformulates the question of whether a despised minority must of necessity prove itself morally superior in order to gain acceptance. Mendelssohn embodied this principle through his exemplary life and his rigorous moral standards. To Rahel and Veit such a stance was no longer normative. Their understanding of the meaning of Enlightenment, rather than being based primarily on strict and abstract philosophical tenets, was informed by a freer and more flexible individual morality conveyed by the new literature.

Moreover, the Enlightenment goals of Rahel and Veit differed from those of Mendelssohn. He strove for recognition and respect while they demanded full integration into a society that they knew was in many ways faulty and retrograde but seemed well on the way to being enlightened.

Veit concluded the discussion on Mendelssohn with the following words:

About Mendelssohn [I will say] nothing further than that he was precious in his earlier writings, [his letters] on the Sentiments; but his Letters on Literature! but Jerusalem! but the Morning Hours![15] by God! (you see, I am even swearing and getting all worked up). He alone could present lucidly the finest speculations, without detriment to thoroughness; and even *after* him (in Germany, the time *before* him is not worth mentioning), nobody succeeded as he did. He, who in his early writings wanted to be theologian and *bel esprit* could not help succumbing to affectation. If you consider, however, that he was a Jew who created a forum for discussing German philosophy (der die deutsche Philosophie zur Sprache brachte), this is truly amazing.[16]

Rahel replied promptly, assuring Veit that she agreed with him. In part, she conceded to Veit's opinion because he showed himself vastly better acquainted with Mendelssohn's work.[17]

In addition to these intellectual discussions, Rahel and Veit also recounted their personal experiences as Jews. In one letter Veit reflected on his situation as a Jewish medical student in Jena, where he had moved after a year in Göttingen. He observed that in Jena, where he saw "no Jews and enjoyed the same advantages as the other students and [suffered] no insults," he tended to think and speak about his Jewishness all the time and was often surprisingly depressed about it. This puzzled him, especially, because in Berlin he would not give it a thought for months at a time.[18] In her reply, written in an unusually upbeat mood, Rahel chided him for giving in to such despondent feelings and then offered a perceptive analysis of her friend's preoccupation, contrasting his situation in Jena with hers in Berlin: "In Berlin, [the problem of] Jewishness is solved with every person in his own way, although not in totality, and one rarely or never risks facing discussions or other harshness. In Jena, however, everything is still 'enveloped in the dust of the wilderness (through which Moses had led them)', there one must always be afraid of the [first insult]; you know this is the most disagreeable thing about it and that which you really fear; whatever one fears, one tends to think of often, without the thing instilling this fear in us actually happening."[19] These lines convey how clearly Rahel understood her people's situation in Berlin and elsewhere. In the Prussian capital, where they formed a sizable and prominent community, Jews belonging to the educated and assimilated elite could expect social acceptance on an individual basis. Jews as a group, however, remained an unsolved political, social, and cultural problem. Socially and culturally they found themselves in a period of transition, while politically they remained without civil rights, locked into their exceptional status. Ostensibly, Rahel's figure of speech refers to the biblical Moses. But it is equally valid when associated with the Moses who led his people out of the wilderness into the Age of Enlightenment. Admittedly, it was Mendelssohn's influence that was to a large extent responsible for the vastly improved situation of Jews in Berlin.

Only four months later, however, Rahel radically revised her cheerfully confident perspective. In a most heartbreaking lament she confided to Veit her anguish over being Jewish: "I have a strange fancy: it is as if some supramundane being, just as I was thrust into this world, plunged these words with a dagger into my heart: 'Yes, have sensibility, see the world as few see it, be great and noble, nor can I take from you the faculty of eternally thinking. But I add one thing more: be a Jewess!' And now my life is a slow bleeding to death. By keeping still I can delay it. Every movement in an attempt to staunch it—new death; and immobility is possible for me only in death itself. . . . I can, if you will, derive every evil, every misfortune, every vexation from *that*. . . . This opinion is my essence."[20] We do not know what occasioned this outcry. But once again, as she had done with regard to her female state, Rahel evoked the image of being condemned to immobility to indicate not only her suffering but also her helplessness vis-à-vis a situation over which she had no control. Both times immobility signified the impossibility of living life. In the first instance the image was one of being "consumed," of "ceasing to be." In the second, Rahel employed an even more heartrending and vehement metaphor—that of "slowly bleeding to death." Keeping still implied passivity or resignation in the face of any insult, injury, or injustice, something that was impossible for someone as deeply committed to truth and fairness as Rahel. Veit was deeply moved: "I assure you that I cannot read your letter without great effort, as I cannot read twenty pages of Werther at a time; and it is doubtful that anyone has ever written more pitifully and truthfully about Jews than you."[21]

That Veit saw similarities between Goethe's epistolary novel *The Sufferings of Young Werther* and Rahel's confession is not surprising. In the letters of Werther, Goethe successfully pioneered the new language of subjectivity in which he had the passionately sensitive, melancholy, and life-weary protagonist explore and pour out his soul. Although *Werther* captivated the readers of his time primarily as a story about thwarted love, the fictitious letters also rail at a rigid social order. As a member of a disadvantaged minority, Veit was only too familiar with such undeserved impediments and thus receptive to this aspect of the work as well. He read the book over and over, making a veritable study of it, and he did the same with Rahel's letter, as the present tense of "I cannot read" suggests. Like Goethe's Werther, Rahel opened her innermost soul in this letter, at the same time creating a language for expressing the specific hurt and humiliation that many Jews were experiencing but for which they had not yet found the words.

Many leading Jews, and Moses Mendelssohn in particular, habitually spoke out against the injustices perpetrated against their coreligionists. Mendelssohn's most moving statement, moreover, was of a very personal nature. In 1780 he wrote: "Here in this so-called tolerant land, I nevertheless live so constrained, so limited in all respects as a result of true intolerance, that I must imprison myself in a silk factory all day long for the sake of my children. Sometimes I take a stroll with my wife and children in the evening. Papa! the innocence asks, what is that fellow calling us? Why do they throw rocks after us? What did we do to them?—Yes, dear Papa! another one speaks, they always pursue us in the streets and curse us Jews! Jews! Is it such an insult for these people to be Jewish? And how does this affect other people!—Woe, I cast down my eyes and sigh to myself: Mankind! Mankind! how did you let it come to this?"[22] Although Mendelssohn openly related his difficult situation (as a Jew he was forced to earn his living through commercial activity) and the insulting experiences, he did not reveal how he dealt with them either personally or as a father. In the letter, he remained aloof and objective, forever the teacher-philosopher, more ashamed for than offended by his fellowmen's unenlightened behavior. Mendelssohn's letter was addressed to a young Benedictine monk, Peter Adolph Winkopp, a man not necessarily familiar with the extent of disparagement Jews continually faced. Since Rahel was writing to a fellow Jew, the specifics of the situation were not only unnecessary but also uninteresting. New and therefore highly interesting, however, was the subjective viewpoint, the precise description of how the inner self was affected by hatred and contempt—a self, moreover, considered unique by all standards, noble and equipped with a superior sensibility and intelligence. Veit understood both the truthfulness and woefulness of Rahel's self-depiction.

Veit concluded his response to Rahel's lament by informing her about his intention to convert to Catholicism during his planned trip to Italy. After that, he intended to go to France, "where I need not make use of my baptismal certificate. My family shall never come to know, even if I were to return to Germany. True, we are lame and yet must walk, and that's why I want to go to France, where the only good wooden legs are being manufactured just now; that's probably all the Jews can expect of the Revolution."[23] The allusion to lameness came from Rahel's letter; after her emotional outcry, she quickly checked herself and began to argue rationally, as she imagined Veit might. To this purpose, she used the example of a man with a lame foot who could be reproached for making too much of his infirmity because he was otherwise quite healthy. But, Rahel argued, he is made to feel this one misfortune two and tenfold because of the way the world reacts to him. For, instead of alleviating his suffering by helping him (which would be the reasonable reaction in a just world), people ignore it and even despise the man for being so awkward. "And the lame man, forced to walk, shouldn't be unhappy?"[24] Thus, Jewishness turns into a handicap and blemish as a result of the Gentile world's attitude.

Rahel's inclination was to demand understanding and empathy instead of callous insults on the bumpy road to assimilation. As a woman she did not have the options availabe to David Veit, the man with a prestigious profession. He looked toward France, where at least some of the ideals of the Enlightenment had found a political reality. There, the Revolution had given Jews their citizenship, and they could become practicing surgeons, an occupation denied to them in the German lands.[25] Rahel, too, considered conversion at this time. However, for reasons we do not know, they both refrained from taking this step. Veit never converted and Rahel only much later, prior to her marriage to a Gentile. They seemed to have remained faithful to an assertion Rahel made quite casually early in the correspondence: "[If] the morality and happiness principles cannot help . . . [then] one will have to make do with the great necessity principle and, because nothing *else* can be done, wrap oneself respectfully in one's cloak and remain a Jew."[26] In other words, the demand for happiness and the new morality were legitimate only if they permitted faithfulness to one's self.

The reflections on Jewish matters culminated with both Rahel and David Veit admitting to persistent difficulties and rejection. The Gentile world's opposition to their quest for assimilation was both institutional and personal. Among the approximately thirty-five hundred members of the Jewish community of Berlin, very few were as unconditional in their demands for equality and integration as Rahel and Veit. This meant that they experienced their fate as individuals and sought personal solutions to the problems of discrimination. Their attitudes alternated so often between optimism and dejection because no discourse existed among like-minded Jews that could have provided a more general perspective. Not until 1820 did a group of young men form an association, the *Verein für Cultur und Wissenschaft der Juden* (Society for the culture and science of the Jews), with the aim of "gaining insight into the Jewish world."[27] In view of this situation, the insight and understanding Rahel and David Veit extracted from their varied experiences are impressive and revealing indeed.

Rahel's unusual social sensibility is revealed not only in her observations on Gentile-Jewish relations but extended to all manners of social interaction. The character portraits popular at the time and scattered throughout her letters illustrate this particularly well. The following two portraits, one of the family servant and one about her aristocratic friend Gustav von Brinckmann, shall serve as examples. They require some effort on the part of the reader, as they were written to someone familiar with the persons and the specifics of the situations depicted. But difficulties also arise because of Rahel's compulsiveness to include every detail or afterthought.

Rahel's description of the servant sheds light on her attitude toward the lower classes as well as the atmosphere within the family. "Our servant is an honest, obliging, respectful, fairly unintelligent and uncouth and inelegant fellow; if he were refined and elegant, he wouldn't respect us, would be more snug and not so obliging, also because he wouldn't have so much fear, and he wouldn't fit into our entire household; furthermore, he is, like all servants, a little deaf." She admits that although everyone agrees that an elegant servant would not suit the family at all, there were nevertheless plenty of reasons to be angry with him. And, of course, the "most impatient one explodes the most often, and that's my sister-in-law; but I take his side . . . Marcus comes to my support . . . Mama also comes around quickly, and in the end is even pleased with her steady children who are not so taken by the flighty but are content with honesty. I even impress the children [of Markus]—in all sorts of manner—I explain to them the condition of the servants, how it could happen to them any day, how they [the servants] know nothing and have learnt nothing, and how unseemly it is to aggravate someone's vexation. . . . Thus he is secure with us and is really getting better all the time."[28]

Rahel uses the Brinckmann characterization to show Veit and others that "I am not totally dazzled by people with whose good qualities I seem to be very much taken."[29] The sketch drawn by the twenty-two-year-old Rahel reveals indeed not only her keen insight into human nature but also her capacity to see through the elegant world in spite of her admiration for it. Thus, she was aware that the apparent equality with which she was treated by various aristocrats was really inconsequential. According to Rahel, Brinckmann, in contrast to Veit, was a friend who didn't "take care" of her because he failed to suggest books she should read or to loan her some from his well-stocked library. This is because, "as obliging as he may look as a result of his running about, he is nothing but a philosophical man of the world: which in my view means that he is a person who has reflected enough to know that one must be courteous, obliging, and pleasing and that people want and need nothing else, and that, for a variety of reasons, it is right to treat them so. . . . [He is a person] who has considered the most important and beautiful matters and then arranged his thoughts in nice rows and put them away securely." At the same time, Brinckmann, according to Rahel's analysis, is a person who isolates himself from many things or who, with the most assured carelessness, forms entirely distinct opinions for himself. Rahel understood that Brinckmann was open-minded, well-intentioned, and unprejudiced enough to seek her company, but he had not freed himself from arrogance and condescension.

Deliberations about societal problems and trends, society's impact on the individual, as well as ways in which the individual or a minority reacted to and could affect social structures and cultural patterns—these varied topics constituted an essential aspect of the epistolary exchanges between Rahel and David Veit. In addition, their common love for literature, as the discussion of Rahel's education already suggested,[30] provided an endlessly fascinating topic. In fact, Veit's initial letter, with its detailed and lively account of Weimar and its luminaries, set the stage. Among the many authors, past and present, Goethe occupied an exceptional position. No other writer was mentioned, discussed, admired, and quoted as often. Lessing came second, at least during these early years. As noted earlier, Rahel was among the few who readily grasped the significance and meaning of Goethe's classicist works. Her favorite works included the ones that were published during the years she came of age: the dramas *Iphigenia in Tauris, Egmont, Torquato Tasso*, the Bildungsroman *Wilhelm Meister's Years of Apprenticeship*, and his lyrical poetry. She recognized that Goethe, to achieve his poetic vision, needed to essentially redefine each genre anew, and she appreciated each work's intricate symbolic structure and character development. Goethe became her lifelong avocation and source of study, from which she drew consolation, strength, and inspiration and also found confirmation for her own thoughts and feelings. The significance of his work was such that "the main features of her being are illuminated through her reverence for and apperception of Goethe."[31]

Thus, in September 1796 she sent Veit Goethe's poem "Idyll," which was to appear in the next *Musenalmanach* (Almanach of the muses), and remarked: "I am not silent about it because I want to, but because I must. I am becoming ever more sensitive; and Goethe and I are so mingled within me that I feel with his words—as wrong as this is—rather than think. Yes, yes, it continues to go *crescendo*: he knows what I want to say, he can *say everything*. He is a god! . . . Don't think I am raving only because of the idyll. No, we read Iphigenia yesterday, and Tasso before that. This Iphigenia! Now I really appreciate it."[32] In the next letter, she took up *Wilhelm Meister*, of which she had reread all the parts in the course of the summer, "in [the spa of] Töplitz, on the Geiersberg, in Dresden, and in all the inns, and in Berlin."[33] After discussing some of the characters in the novel, she drew her conclusions: "How masterful of Goethe to both describe his characters and have them speak as distinct individuals and not ever renounce his [own] distinguished and cultivated language. How masterfully Laertes is portrayed with a few traits . . . what a profound and delicate glance into the most ordinary human being. Friedrich, however, in the last part, he had to have *heard*; even *he* [Goethe] cannot invent this [kind of speech]. Altogether he must have listened often: and been able to gain the confidence of all sorts of people. In addition to his unique way of seeing, of this I am convinced."[34]

The criteria according to which Rahel judged literary works were primarily psychological and sociological. She expected literature to take up and provide insight into the conflicts of the time and thus demanded a realistic portrayal of the contemporary world and a range of believable human characters with their individual hopes and predicaments, talents and limitations—what she called *Menschenkenntnis* (knowledge of human nature). Goethe's aesthetic ideal of mimesis, combined with his beautiful language and the encompassing scope of his poetic vision, fulfilled these expectations. In his works Rahel the outsider found a model that confirmed her own utopian vision of a society of refined and enlightened individuals. This explains her assertion that Goethe "knows what I want to say" or that she feels "with his words."

Rahel applied the same realist criteria also to Goethe's female characters. Like so many women of her time she admired them, partly because at this point she largely identified with the feminine ideal projected in these characters, but partly also because Goethe portrayed women as complex and deeply feeling human beings. They contrasted favorably with the template-like female characters in most other works, permitted to move only between virtue and vice. Many of Rahel's friends and acquaintances saw similarities between her and Goethe's female characters. Veit, for example, thought that she combined the tragic Aurelia's intellect and heart with the lighthearted Philine's spiritedness.[35] Rahel agreed that she often found her own words in Aurelia's. At the same time, she admitted that this was even more true of Lessing's words. She then repeated her conviction that Goethe could not have invented Aurelia's thoughts and speech any more than he had Friedrich's but must have actually heard them from a woman.[36] This (admittedly) idealized realism constituted part of Goethe's greatness for her.

At the same time, Rahel distanced herself from Aurelia's melancholy, maintaining that: "If I had been *completely* happy once in my life, like Aurelia, and in this happiness had forgotten myself to the point of [bearing] a child, I could never again be completely unhappy. What do you expect? The moment of ripeness cannot last; and then I could not have been *entirely* wrong about a person to whom I have given myself. . . . In any case, this is how I think about woman's happiness." Rahel further reasoned that a fallen woman, such as Aurelia, should "get up with decorum and candor and seek to restore herself."[37] For the displaced Mignon, however, yearning for the "land where the lemons bloom," the outsider Rahel expressed special sympathy, finding her also "the most interesting" of the large cast of characters.[38]

Several things follow from Rahel's reading of these characters. One, she reserved a particular interest for women's plights and possibilities — be this in literature or real life. In Goethe's works, she evidently found answers not only to her quest for identity as an emancipated Jew but also as a woman. But she was far from identifying only with female characters, recognizing herself just as often in male figures and recognizing her thoughts in the words of male writers. That the latter counted among the first minds and talents of their age only attests to Rahel's superior and daring intellect. Second, even as a young woman, Rahel did not hesitate to differ with so cherished an author as Goethe. Her intellectual independence is evident in her opposition to Aurelia's submission to a tragic and infamous fate. The same letter also contains a rather sharp rebuke of one of the tales in Goethe's *Unterhaltungen deutscher Ausgewanderter* (1795, *Conversations of German Refugees*), the subject of which was the French Revolution.[39] Third, literature and life existed for Rahel in close proximity to to each other, notwithstanding her great artistic sensitivity. Such a view indicates once more the immense significance social outsiders like Rahel drew from the literature of the time and particularly from Goethe's conceptions of a tolerant and enlightened society. She made this explicit with the following statement to Veit: "Goethe and life are still one for me; I immerse myself in both."[40] Life provided the foundation of art while art was given the task of elucidating life's labyrinthian ways. At the same time, literature was not meant to function as a refuge or escape but as a means to self-knowledge and renewed involvement in the affairs of the world.

Rahel was furthermore familiar with the major aesthetic debates of the time. Two literary reviews that appeared in the fall of 1794 and were much debated and admired by the educated and literary-minded aroused her keen interest. She presented her comments to Veit in great detail in a letter amounting to more than twenty printed pages.[41] One of the reviews was by Friedrich Schiller on poems by the then popular Friedrich Matthison and the other by Wilhelm von Humboldt on Friedrich Heinrich Jacobi's novel *Woldemar* (1779, 2d vol. 1794). Rahel was rather displeased with Schiller's review because she considered his criteria too narrow. He was setting up literary models to be imitated, whereas she thought that it was up to the artist to select the appropriate artistic form for conveying a topic and ideas. While Schiller expected the artist to imbue the work of art with his spirit and dismissed all other methods as mere mechanical narration or even worse, imitation, Rahel argued: "But simply narrating is sometimes poetic and *simply* copying most poetic of all in a work; done at the right time this is great and demands as much knowledge of human nature (*Menschenkenntnis*) as bringing sentiment and ideas into the description of a landscape."

With Humboldt's review, on the other hand, Rahel was delighted.[42] He had analyzed the novel's characters primarily in terms of their social and psychological authenticity. This approach corresponded closely to hers, and Rahel therefore praised his *Menschenkenntnis*. Humboldt's review, however, did not cause her to change her mind about the novel itself. She felt that *Woldemar* was written too much according to a scheme. It presented a philosophical system instead of unusual characters who would reveal the philosophical framework if one cared to analyze them. And although an author should intend to prove something, the work of art should not always tell what it wants to say but show it. Since she was convinced that Humboldt could have written his review about any reasonably good work, she regretted that he had not chosen a work by Goethe.[43] Rahel recognized that the difference between Jacobi and Goethe marked a literary turning point. While Jacobi still arranged his characters within bourgeois life according to the Enlightenment system of virtue, Goethe was already concerned with depicting the problematical aspects of these very ideals. He created outstanding and noble characters who nevertheless fail to attain fulfillment or success as a result of the circumstances in which they found themselves.

Moreover, Goethe's didacticism was much less explicit and largely free of the trite moralism that characterized so much of Enlightenment literature. Humboldt, who came to know of Rahel's views through Veit, stated that they were by far the best assessment yet about *Woldemar* as well as his review.[44]

Rahel knew that her views would be a valuable contribution to the ongoing literary discourse, but she remained in the background, participating only indirectly through Veit. Humboldt, for example, was kept in the dark about the identity of the person who made the comments he admired. Several remarks in Rahel's letters to Veit reveal the reason for her modesty: she was afraid of becoming known as a "learned woman" or, what was even worse, a "female pedant" (Pedantin). This fear may also have been, at least in part, the reason why Rahel insisted throughout her life on her "ignorance." And although she was only too conscious of the disadvantages of her haphazard schooling, her modesty was to a certain extent also a pose, intended to protect her from the reputation of being "unfeminine." Only in her letters to Veit did Rahel present her ideas openly and forthrightly. Only to him did she admit that, in addition to being his best and constant friend, she was also his "learned friend."[45]

CORRESPONDENCE WITH
GUSTAV VON BRINCKMANN AND FRIEDRICH GENTZ

Rahel's way of corresponding with the nobleman Gustav von Brinckmann was altogether different. Brinckmann was some ten years older and famous to the point of being infamous for the length and frequency of his letters. People joked that he lived in order to write letters. Since Rahel had sized up the "philosophical man of the world" accurately, she showed herself from an angle that would please him. In her letters to him a light and playful, almost gallant, tone prevails, especially in the early years of their correspondence. Thus, she answered him from the spa of Freienwalde, where, in the summer of 1794, she was undergoing a course of mineral waters: "And you claim to be a friend?! in no case are you delicate and concerned about your friends' health: how can you burden me during an exhausting cure, to investigate whether you are in love. Yes, you are. There you have it, your shock (Schreck)."[46] Even though she adjusted tone and manner to his taste, she always remained true to herself and sincere toward him. If he underestimated her knowledge or her power of perception, she reprimanded him playfully. For example, in response to Brinckmann's poems, which he sent her for an evaluation but not without including a great many explanations, she wrote: "such beautiful poems and such bad assumptions, so offended!—and yet obliged to say thank you—as I must."[47] She was equally sanguine about his praises of her. Rather than succumbing to his flattery, she responded with a careful analysis of its meaning:

that you present yourself as so very weak against me and consider me so far above yourself means that you make me into an idol and yourself into a living human being, to whom it pleases, among other things, to collect, to admire, to fear, to pray. If the little house god is not made of gold or marble, however, and believes his own adulation. . . . he becomes his own fool as well as that of the others. I have dedicated myself . . . to *one* god *entirely*, and whenever I have been saved, it was he who saved me, the truth. From you too, it shall save me this time: because it is the truth which compels me and advises me to be sincere toward you.[48]

The correspondence with the older aristocrat did not allow for the thorough and painstaking discussion of questions and problems that characterized the intimate dialogue with David Veit. In her letters to Brinckmann, Rahel tended to offer the results of her thinking and observations and thus exhibited her special talent for aphoristic writing. In other words, she formulated her personally experienced social disparities and incongruities in general terms. Thus, when Brinckmann was suffering from a toothache and she wanted to visit him to cheer him up but was not allowed to for propriety's sake, she wrote to him: "In order to prevent a *bad* girl from acting stupidly, a *good* girl is to be curtailed."[49] Likewise, she characterized her difficulties with her first lover, Karl Count von Finckenstein, and the society around her, in the most sparing of words: "My love actually amounts to nothing, believe me—the traitor hands me only a thin blindfold and none to the others for me."[50] The actual difficulties are left vague, but the situation as such is precisely rendered: the lover is quite openly disloyal, while society disapproves of her liaison with him. Both statements pertain once again to her disadvantaged state as a woman. But in contrast to the vehement outbursts in her letters to Veit, from whom she could expect understanding and empathy, her statements to Brinckman are veiled, terse, urbane, although pregnant with meaning for anyone willing to read attentively.

Surprisingly, women and their situation formed a frequent topic of deliberations and one that shows Rahel's social sensibilities particularly well. Together with the views expressed in the letters to David Veit, they provide insight into Rahel's thinking on the subject when a young woman. They reveal that she was alternately torn between vehement protest and a willingness to accept social strictures up to a point. When passing judgment on women, she carefully weighed the options available to them against socially imposed constraints: "A refined, educated, and intelligent woman does not *become* dull and silly: she can, however, be weak and dependent and usually is . . . the more refined a woman is the sooner she puts up with all that she must put up with . . . and a completely amiable woman must furthermore have courage and self-reliance in order not to become . . . that which she must seem to be and also not seem to be that which she is supposed to seem."[51] Rahel provides Brinckmann with a glimpse into the very complex strategies she felt women had to develop in order to gain or preserve society's approval while at the same time protecting what was essential for their own self-esteem.

Rahel also confided to Brinckmann her views that men and women related differently to each other: "It hurts us [women] more to give up a woman than a man. We never believe to hold *him* securely—even though we love him more—we never tell or show *him* quite everything—even though he rules over us more—and in the end—trust . . . in another person is the most we are able to offer."[52] Although often critical of women, Rahel also knew that women made the more trustworthy friends. Rahel reached the limit of her compliance with society's demands when it came to marriage. Although she very much wanted to marry, and even more to fall and be in love, the price was too high for her because within marriage the inequality between men and women became institutionalized. She thus countered Brinckmann's suggestion that she marry: "Marry, you say. I cannot marry; because I cannot lie. (Don't think I am proud of it: I cannot like some people cannot play the flute.) Otherwise I would do it now. I would like to make it my task and maxim to make a man happy who loves me with all his might."[53] This must be seen as another reference to her tenuous relationship with Finckenstein, which she was at the point of breaking off. By not being able to lie, she meant that she could not pretend to honor a man who did not measure up to her expectations.

This letter, dated 9 March 1799, marked a turning point in the correspondence. The sprightliness and wit of earlier years gave way to greater earnestness and solicitude. Brinckmann had been assigned to a diplomatic post in Paris, where he became acquainted with Mme de Staël, about whom he wrote extensively in his letters. From Rahel's answer, we also gather that he felt "orphaned, sad, and discouraged." In her reply, Rahel was unusually tender and forthcoming. She thanked Brinckmann for his impressions of de Staël, and she empathized with his personal difficulties.

She returned his trust in her by revealing her own unhappiness over the growing awareness that her relationship with Finckenstein was doomed. But although she openly admitted to this failure, she did not convey the full extent of the hurt and humiliation. Vis-à-vis Brinckmann, she retained her composure, while her language took on a poetic coloring: "Je suis rassi[s]e [I am calm], *but, sad!*, and in good spirits, *deeply* wounded, and elevated above this and myself."[54] The real despair she confided to her sister and her women friends, as we shall see, and to her diary. There we can read: "Slave trade, war, and marriage!—and they wonder and merely patch up things."[55] All three institutions appeared to her equally unjust and anachronistic in that they denied individuals and whole groups their rightful humanity. In the course of several years spent in close association with Gentile society, Rahel's optimism and faith in progress had received some sobering blows. She was beginning to realize that overcoming social barriers proved much more formidable than previously suspected—especially for her, the Jew, the woman, the individual of undistinguished birth who was nevertheless brilliant.

Any attempt to define Rahel's social status in terms of her outsiderness, however, would both oversimplify and misrepresent what she eventually came to call her "paradox." She was both a social outsider and a privileged exceptional individual, a Jew and a woman of genius. Men of accomplishment especially were fascinated by her. Friedrich Gentz, who came to know her more intimately during the waning years of the century (although their correspondence did not begin until 1803), called her "the first being in this world," "teacher," "oracle," and "friend." These are not attributes bestowed on a woman destined to become a wife and mother or even a lover (although in the same letter Gentz refers to what their sexual union would have meant for both of them).

Such adulation may explain why the bond between Rahel and the admiring men who attended her salon, despite its considerable intimacy, remained primarily one of intellectual friendship. Rahel's perceptive way of analyzing psychological and social phenomena impressed these men as new and compelling. They were themselves conscious of living in an age of transition, and Rahel helped them understand themselves and the times better. For them, she combined feminine sensitivity with masculine erudition and thus confounded their own ideology, in which the feminine and masculine spheres were neatly separated. Once again, it was Gentz who expressed this most poignantly, when he wrote to her: "You are an *infinitely productive* creature, I am an *infinitely receptive* one; you are a great *man*,

I am the first among *women*."[56] After meeting Rahel in Carlsbad, Goethe characterized her as a "beautiful soul." According to his scheme of things, however, beautiful souls were those female characters who were excluded from marriage and motherhood, notably Iphigenia. In many ways Rahel agreed with these androgynous definitions, as she herself often characterized herself as both *Freundin* and *Freund* (female and male friend). Flirting with androgyny, however, was a game permitted to men only; women in similar circumstances stood in immediate danger of losing their femininity.

THE LOVE LETTERS

There was one young man, however, who fell in love with Rahel during these waning years of the eighteenth century: Karl Friedrich Alexander Count von Finckenstein. They were introduced to each other in the winter of 1795–96 at the Royal State Opera, Unter den Linden, during a performance of a work by Righini. They immediately immersed themselves in a discussion on music, an interest that formed the initial basis for their mutual affinity. Finckenstein was a lover of music and of church music especially. He also was an active member of the Berlin Singakademie. He was slightly younger than Rahel, very blond, and very proper in his behavior. Unlike his cousin Wilhelm von Burgsdorff, with whom Rahel was also well acquainted, he was, despite his aristocratic upbringing, socially not very adept. Rahel responded to the shy and somewhat awkward young man with the delicacy that was so uniquely hers and later invested the relationship with her customary passion and sincerity. Marriage to Finckenstein would have greatly improved her social standing as well as furthered her integration into Gentile society. Class prejudice largely prevailed, however, and Rahel must have experienced few happy moments. Although they were engaged to each other, she was not accepted into Karl's family and social circle, which meant that she could not accompany him to the balls, the concerts, or the visits that he insisted were part of his duties. Instead, he was drawn into her circle. Even when she was absent from Berlin, Karl spent much time with her family and her friends. For Rahel's sake, the relationship was kept clandestine, although everyone knew and talked about it. The couple spent relatively little time together, as Finckenstein lived mostly on the family estate in Madlitz and later was posted in Rastatt and Vienna. Rahel spent the summer months of 1796 in Carlsbad and Teplitz following a prolonged illness in the spring. Karl was in turn prevented by illness from coming to Berlin in the fall of that year. The following summer Rahel again traveled to the spas of Bohemia. It was during this time that the strains in their relationship became marked.

The correspondence as it exists is not very helpful in reconstructing the story of a love that Rahel came to see as deeply humiliating. For obvious reasons, the good moments, where harmony and agreement prevailed, went largely unrecorded, as they were spent in each other's company. Furthermore, the correspondence is one-sided, with eighty-six letters by Finckenstein and only five by Rahel extant.[57] Since the latter all date from the final year of their relationship, they are, as she herself called them, "desolate" love letters, full of queries, reproaches, and protests over his treatment of her, with the exception of the last one, which was her farewell letter. His letters, on the other hand, amount to continuous rather bland, even stereotypical, reiterations of love. Whenever her letters were loving and solicitious he was happy. Her reprimands, worries, and expressions of disappointment he tended to ignore. Above all, Finckenstein's letters reveal his deep attachments to his family and to Madlitz, the lovely country seat surrounded by an exceptionally beautiful English garden. Situated in the Mark, a barren region in eastern Prussia, it contrasted starkly with the general poverty of the surrounding villages. Life at Madlitz was quite self-contained, devoted to the study of art and literature and especially to music. Visitors tell of the fine musical offerings they enjoyed and the charm and hospitality of the family.[58] Karl was thus amply compensated while separated from Rahel. Moreover, in this almost idyllic atmosphere he had no need for the social and intellectual challenges of a brilliant Jewish woman.

Ultimately, the relationship failed because of the family's reactionary attitudes as well as Karl's inability and unwillingness to stand up for himself. He was incapable of the kind of courage that great passion commands because he was incapable of such passion and very much in need of encouragement. Thus, he wrote that first summer: "I need you. I don't know, but I am so dejected although there is nothing actually wrong with me, nothing excites me, nothing engages my feelings. It is so unbearably still and dark within my soul, and so I thought a letter from you would bring me some of that consolation I usually found with you, when my soul was not well and I only had to rush to you to become content and happy again. . . . A letter from you must make life bearable again."[59] His missives are replete with what she had done for him. She had "opened his eyes" about himself, and this earned him also the respect of others; she had "given [him] his sense of self" and "motivated" him.[60] In one of his last communications, he wrote: "You have perfected my education (Bildung). . . . You have given character and form to my person by giving life and movement to all that lay dead and still within me."[61] He confided all his self-doubts and weaknesses to her, some of which were grounded in the circumstances of the times, most notably the increasingly superfluous role of the nobility: "Everyone but I has his purpose in life."[62]

Sometimes Karl would rally and make an effort to be resolute: "Don't consider me weaker than I am, and believe me that I can prevail if I really want something."[63] However, his innate passivity, his indifference, and his love of comfort prevented him from carrying out even minor plans, let alone from resolving the situation as a whole. Rahel repeatedly accused him of lacking the courage to flaunt even meaningless social conventions. Mostly, she urged him to be strong, true, and not to "stand with each foot on a different shore. Cross over. I can no longer act for you."[64] Eventually, she had to admit to herself that Karl was incapable of appreciating her. Social convention and prejudice proved stronger than her extraordinary personality. She broke off the relationship, at the same time turning the responsibility for action over to him: "I shall utilize the years during which you are away to become unacquainted with you. You can no longer persuade me. *Be* something, and I shall recognize you."[65]

Subsequently, it becomes clear that marriage was never seriously considered by Karl or by his friends who were also visitors at Rahel's salon, notably, Wilhelm von Burgsdorff and the architect Hans Genelli. But while the men succumbed to convention and prejudice, Rahel's two aristocratic women friends, the countesses Josephine Pachta and Karoline von Schlabrendorf, sided with her and human decency. Pachta wrote to Rahel as early as 1797 that she regretted not having been able to speak to Finckenstein alone. She urged Rahel to remind him of his pledge to her [Pachta]: "not to solemnly promise anything but rather to keep all the more faithfully . . . what he already promised—even if the words he had used were different from those employed before a court of law. Or did he think that the words 'I love you' did not contain the most holy commitment to a union which excluded any other? If he hadn't understood this, he should admit it . . . and learn that you can destroy (töten) a human being with words to which you have given a false meaning."[66] Rahel's other intimate noble friend, Karoline von Schlabrendorf, provided her with the opportunity to go to Paris and thus escape Berlin for a time.

As happened so often after an emotional crisis, Rahel succumbed to a serious illness, and the Paris journey did not take place until the summer of 1800. Before leaving, she charged the friend of her youth, Wilhelmine von

Boye, to collect all her letters after her death and to have them published, because it is "an original story and poetic." She also confided to her: "I am on my way. . . . You see, I who never wanted to *had* to retreat. I must *leave* everything that I know, that I love, that annoys and offends, challenges and pleases me!—For nothing. Without any hope. It is a kind of death of which it contains the pain but not the ominous and sublime. I must die but I shall not be dead. . . . Like Posa I have *lost*. And yet [I] would not like to belong to those individuals who do not put themselves at stake. *Everyone* I loved mistreated me. They do not know it: I won't tell them; that's why I am leaving."[67]

In Paris she was a stranger and permitted to feel like one. She lived near Place Vendôme and met often with the Humboldts. She also made the acquaintance of a young handsome merchant from Hamburg named Wilhelm Bokelman. For Rahel, this relationship was a lovely interlude, for which she was infinitely grateful. It was governed by an amorous atmosphere in which neither made any demands or claims on the other. Rahel wrote some of the most beautiful and delicate love letters to Bokelmann after they went their separate ways. To her sister Rose, however, she confided: "I don't like to write . . . it makes me very sad. . . . It is not one of those sadnesses that will go away; [not one] in which clouds break the beam of light and darken the landscape in an agreeably melancholy fashion. No, the landscape itself is destroyed, and my eternally heavenly mood can only cast bright glances upon it. The sadness remains [as will] insight, earnestness; it is over. . . . Outwardly, I am as I was, almost as agreeable, as you know me [to be], and shall almost remain so."[68]

The following spring Rahel traveled from Paris to Amsterdam, where Rose now lived, having married Carel Asser, a Dutch lawyer. From there she returned to Berlin in the company of her mother. The following year she became aquainted with the handsome secretary to the Spanish Legation, Don Raphael d'Urquijo. Both fell head over heels and passionately in love with each other. But this love was to be even more devastating for Rahel than her first. Urquijo was not prejudiced in the way that Finckenstein was; instead, he was subject to intense jealousy. As Karl August Varnhagen stated many years later: "For the Spaniard, jealousy was the dogma of love."[69] Rahel tried to appease and reassure him by cutting off most of her social relations and by withdrawing to the country. But he continued to suspect her. The breakup came after one and a half years. Rahel had postponed it again and again and never got over it completely. She continued to see Urquijo—he came to her as a refugee in Prague, or when he was in debt or faced other problems—and she helped him. He was said to have married a woman who deceived him but whom he trusted blindly.[70]

The correspondence between Rahel and Urquijo, carried on mostly in French, once again exists in only rudimentary form. In 1808 Rahel sent the letters to Varnhagen, who had begged to read them. The greater part of them subsequently perished during the Wars of Liberation. Varnhagen admired them deeply, saying that they expressed a fullness of life that similar writings by Goethe and Rousseau only rarely surpassed: "Night after night I sat reading these pages, I came to know things of which I had no idea or rather, which lay dormant within my consciousness."[71] Rahel, who was somewhat reluctant to let Varnhagen see the written testimony of her "greatest ignonimity," tried to explain herself: "Once I lived totally for another human being. I loved him to the point of folly! because he, his *appearance*, was the present and the future to me—and in a sense this remained true—also, I never thought of leaving him. But that too was wrong: . . . I was not loved by him; and he knew nothing about friendship."[72] She also asked Varnhagen to consider that Urquijo never told her that he did not love her, that he was forever with her; only he did not believe her love but excited it to the point of frenzy with his jealousy. " 'Je t'aime, mais je ne t'estime pas' [I love you but I don't esteem you], he told me a thousand . . . times. . . . 'Je t'estime, mais je ne t'aime plus' [I esteem you but I don't love you anymore], he said during the last month: and so I murderously (mordgewaffnet) seized my own heart with my hand; and parted; as from life. For I knew, it was like black death: and wrote . . . : I *choose* despair, which I do not know! The murdering went on for a long time. And a *wasteland* arose which was more terrible than pain, laceration, and missing the lover. Scold me. . . . But consider this . . . that nature had endowed him with a charm . . . a charm for me, against which the brightest consciousness . . . could not work fast enough."[73] This is how Rahel wrote five years after the painful experience.

Rahel's experiences were of course not unique. Unique was and is the testimony of her suffering and humiliation as well as her special circumstances. For reasons that elude us, she did not undergo the traditional arranged marriage, unlike Henriette de Lemos-Herz and Dorothea Mendelssohn-Veit-Schlegel. The loss of tradition signified not only freedom in the positive sense, which Rahel surely welcomed, but also the increasing absence of an organizing social network for various occasions. As a result, Rahel could look to no one's support in this life-determining matter. Although highly critical of the institution of marriage, she nevertheless did not wish to remain single and dependent on her brothers for the rest of her life. A woman could achieve respect and social standing only through marriage. Her mixed society, where, as she believed, the like-minded gathered, therefore provided the best chances for a marriage. It was a path that many other educated and acculturated young Jewish women were taking at that time.

The most notorious case was probably that of Moses Mendelssohn's eldest daughter, for whom he had carefully selected a husband, Philip Veit, a decent, generous, but pedestrian and traditional Jewish man and merchant. Dorothea persevered in the marriage for fifteen years, bearing two sons, until she met the young poet Friedrich Schlegel, nine years her junior. With the help and support of Friedrich Schleiermacher and Henriette Herz, she eventually obtained a divorce and lived with Friedrich in Jena and Paris until they were married in 1804. Friedrich Schlegel's scandalous novel *Lucinde*, depicting the boundless commitment of two lovers to romantic love, only inflamed and prolonged the shocking episode. Dorothea, however, after years of "enslavement" in a sterile relationship, had simply followed her heart. In so doing, she refuted her previous life of denial and sacrifice and pursued an entirely new goal—happiness—or, as she put it, "self-satisfaction."[74]

Rahel held comparable expectations. With characteristic intensity, she committed herself to this new phenomenon of romantic love, through which women—and men—were supposed to reach their greatest fulfillment and human potential. She refused to compromise, to give in to the lies, pretense, and hypocrisy she observed in so many marriages. Her demand for mutuality within a love relationship was rooted in Enlightenment thinking, specifically in the notion of natural rights, rather than in the more radical writings demanding the civil and political emancipation for women. She appears to have been unaware of the three seminal texts of the time: Mary Wollstonecraft's *A Vindication of the Rights of Woman* (1792), Olympe de Gouges's *Déclaration des droits de la femme à la reine* (1791, *Declaration of the Rights of Women*), or even Theodor Gottlieb von Hippel's treatise *Über die bürgerliche Verbesserung der Weiber* (1792, *On Improving the Status of Women*).

On the contrary, when, in 1808, Rahel attempted to gain some objectivity over her devastating experiences, she referred explicitly to the ideology of romantic love: "For a long time now I have been wanting to analyze, identify, and portray in all its contortions and withdrawals *this* lie, upon which the best of our age pride themselves, and which constitutes in part the entire new European love, so that it may never again live; but as certainly and truly as my mind has grasped it, it does not possess the powers to analyze it in a Fichtean manner or to portray it as Goethe would have (Goethisch vorüberschreiten zu lassen)."[75] Rahel's failed loves exemplify the almost inevitably disastrous consequences for women committed to a notion of personal emancipation that neglected all social and political factors. The new ideology of love took on a disproportionate significance for Rahel—and other women then and into the twentieth century—because it represented a possibility for actively intervening in one's destiny. Rahel struggled against her growing realization that once again, instead of being recognized by her lovers as a sovereign subject, she was not much more than an object condemned to passivity and subject to rejection.

THE CORRESPONDENCE WITH WOMEN FRIENDS

At this time, Rahel also initiated her extensive epistolary exchanges with women. Recent archival research has revealed that the letters Rahel exchanged with women comprise close to a third of her entire correspondence and thus constitute an essential aspect of her communicative network.[76] An unusually large proportion of these women were professionals—actresses, singers, authors, governesses. It was Rahel and Karl August Varnhagen's vision and sense of history that ensured the survival of a large number of these letters and other papers, including unpublished manuscripts, and their integration in what eventually became the Varnhagen Collection. A good number of Rahel's letters to these friends have been incorporated in the *Buch des Andenkens*. Some of her correspondents' letters have appeared elsewhere, as part of the correspondences of the women's husbands or the famous men with whom they exchanged letters.[77] But the greater number still awaits publication and promises a wealth of new information into the lives of women, the culture of the time, Jewish history, and last but not least the writing strategies of women.

Initially, the women Rahel corresponded with came from two social groups—Rahel's own Jewish circle and the nobility. Later on, the network became more varied and more extensive. The early correspondences were also the longest lasting, with many extending over decades. Rahel's friendships with Jewish women were founded on their common background and specific experiences as Jewish women. Her friendships with the countesses Pachta and Schlabrendorf also built on their mutual ordeals as women, women whose rebellion against their lot was based on their deep commitment to Enlightenment thinking.

Not surprisingly, affairs of the heart played an important role in the young women's letters. They knew each others' disappointments in marriage, the expectations, complications, and sufferings of love. They discussed family matters, the qualities and problems of their common acquaintances and friends, and they never tired of expressing feelings of affection, love, and concern for each other.

At other times, however, intellectual and public matters—a discussion of art, literature, or music or an analysis of social conditions—constituted the primary topics. An early letter by Dorothea Schlegel, then still known as Brendel Veit, is an excellent example. She was spending the summer of 1792 with her relatives in Strelitz, not far from Berlin, from where she paid a visit to the nearby principality of Rheinsberg. Here Heinrich von Preußen, brother of Frederick II, owned an exquisite castle. Dorothea attended a performance by a French opera company of Glucks's *Iphigenia in Aulis*, about which she gave a witty and very knowledgeable account. The last third of this long letter, however, Dorothea devoted to a detailed critical assessment of the social conditions at Rheinsberg and an indictment of the parasitic feudal system she encountered there. In no uncertain terms, she expressed contempt for the "senseless" power and wealth of the prince:

his house, his garden, and everything he can overlook from *his* window is abundant and splendid; [but] you go one house beyond, only around the corner, and you'll find not a roof that's intact, not a street that's clean, not a child that's dressed decently. Poverty and misery everywhere; and even this wretched existence is precarious; with his life theirs end too; and [caused] by a thousand superfluous things which they must provide him with, while they don't have the bare necessities. The land on which he capriciously built a palace, is poor, all around there is nothing but deep sand and only the roads which *he* uses have been made to flourish at great expense. Cursed aristocracy! . . . An opera like this costs more than rebuilding a ruined little house, in which peace and wealth could reside.[78]

She ends by saying that she now understood the French, and how an entire people could rise up against the luxuriating tyrants who insisted on playing these eternal symphonies to avoid hearing the cries of misery.

Dorothea was thoroughly outraged at such systematic injustice and ex-ploitation for the purpose of ostentation and waste. Rheinsberg was small enough for her to perceive the connections between the poverty of the general population and the unproductive wealth of one prince. In the last sentence she addressed her friend directly: "Forgive me my ardor, dear *aristocrat*—you should only see Rheinsberg." Evidently, Rahel, much younger and more impressionable, seemed to her rather too well disposed toward aristocrats at this time, so that Dorothea felt entitled to this gentle reprimand.

Such instances are the exception, however, for it was Rahel who had the original and pertinent insights as well as fundamentally democratic attitudes. In general, the tone in the letters written to Rahel is one of admiration, affection, and even wooing. Her Jewish friends, especially, readily accepted Rahel's superiority while her aristocratic ones treated her as an equal.

THE FAMILY LETTERS

If Rahel's letters were generally characterized by spontaneity, liveliness, and her own peculiarly original language, sprinkled with neologisms and foreign words, this was even more true of the letters destined for the various members of her family. In them she expressed her moods and mood changes even more readily and jumped even more blithely and abruptly from one topic to another. Often she used the insolent tone typical of Berliners. At other times, she exuberantly expressed her affection and longing for her family. Her annoyance, too, she communicated openly and bluntly: "You are all by nature as bad as I am by design when I aim to be bad. Most of all you, Rose! What mood, what condition, what occupation can keep you from writing to me. I know them all; you have time enough."[79] This is the beginning of a letter Rahel wrote from Paris in the winter of 1800, when she was trying to regain her bearings after the Finckenstein affair. It is the older sister speaking to the younger one as well as to the brothers, for whom she had cared since the father's death, playfully reminding them of their duty toward her. The letter continues with some further reproaches, with laments about her unhappiness and lack of good fortune, with questions about her little nieces, Fanny and Hanne, followed by suggestions regarding the children's schooling and how to treat the incoming second teeth. Rahel then moves on to her and the family's larger circle, inquiring about her women friends, actors and actresses she knows and admires, the theater, the whereabouts of Prince Louis Ferdinand. She expresses regret over the death of the philosopher Maimon and the lack of notice taken of the passing of this remarkable man. She also includes some thoughts about their friend Gualteri, adjutant to King Frederick William III, whom she liked for his sensitivity.

But again and again she returns to the family, wishing for news about their daily lives:

And what is the *hackneyed rascal*, the *polisson* [scamp] Moritz doing? Is his vest and his things still so ill fitting, does he still lose all his gloves, is he funny and witty? write me something about him sometimes! And—our poet [Ludwig Robert], does he still go in bare feet and his *Schanzlöper* [coarse woolen coat] *till* noon and *into* the afternoon? is his poem growing and getting polished? does he read? does Moritz still speak such beautiful German? and—!!!—is Mama happy now to be living *small* and *alone*? [this was presumably a reference to the diminished social life as a result of Rahel's absence, which the mother welcomed] . . . is she well? . . . Do give! as long as you are in Berlin, something to the flower woman; then I shall be back; and tell her that.[80]

These lines are indicative of the lively relations within the family; they betray a deep affinity as well as conflicts among the various members.

Particularly noteworthy among the family letters of this early period are those Rahel wrote during a visit to Silesia in August 1794. She herself attributed great importance to them, reminding her recipients to be sure to save them, not only because they also served as her journals (she could not possibly write everything twice), but because they were done "par inspiration du moment." Her constant concern was that she would not find the time to write every day and that "later, one impression after another will be lost."[81] We have seen earlier how much Rahel wanted to travel. However, this was a journey that, at least initially, she was not keen on. As a result of the mother's predilection for economizing, it was made by "ordinary" rather than the more comfortable and luxurious "extra post" that Rahel had been used to since childhood. Her companions were her mother, her sister Rose (then just thirteen years old and probably for this reason called the "beast"), and an elderly Jewish scholar who served as the obligatory male companion. This man's uncouth behavior and unsavory manners, especially, turned the journey into a veritable endurance test for Rahel.

In contrast, the travels Rahel undertook to the spas of Bohemia (or the ones she envied David Veit for) were made in the company of like-minded persons and led to an enlightened society. In Töplitz, Carlsbad, and Pyrmont the sophisticated and educated congregated during the summer months, so that Rahel could count on seeing many of her friends and acquaintances from Berlin as well as meeting new ones. Thus, in addition to the treatments she underwent for health reasons, these stays also had their pleasant side. Rahel not only enjoyed the stimulating social and intellectual life, she continued to pursue her goal of assimilation. The more lighthearted sociability at the summer spas worked to her advantage. People seemed willing to disregard for a brief time the carefully guarded conventions and class barriers that normally separated them from each other. The fact that Rahel was taken to the ball by the Prince de Ligne, that she immersed herself in the writings of Goethe with Count Wilhelm von Burgsdorff, that she had the opportunity to meet Goethe in 1795 and Beethoven in 1811, and, finally, that it seemed equally acceptable for her to be living with her Jewish friend Friederike Liman, the actress Friederike Unzelmann, or the Countess Josephine Pachta—all point to Rahel's considerable freedom and acceptability within this society.

The journey to Silesia, on the other hand, led to Rahel's relatives in Breslau. This meant a return to a more traditional Jewish world and, as such, a journey backward in time. The initial shock this encounter precipitated in the sophisticated young woman from Berlin is evident from her first letter: "With what words shall I say that which I would like to communicate to you with a single scream." This is how Rahel began the description of Breslau and her uncle's house to her brother Markus and the others at home. She was aghast at what must have been a fairly self-contained *shtetl*, with houses crowding in on each other and "billions of Bohemians, and what kind?! like we never see them in Berlin." The term *Bohemian* seems to have been a designation the Levin family used among themselves when referring to traditional Jews. Rahel speaks of the "Frankfort Bohemian street," of "Bohemian hair," and of "yelling . . . from . . . so many Bohemian mouths." Fearing that curious eyes might read the letter before she could entrust it to the mail, she switched to French. Although the aunt had met them in a beautiful carriage, which raised her hopes, their descent down a narrow and teeming street to a "cursed house" deprived Rahel of the "rest of her good humor." Used to a spacious, airy, and even luxurious home in Berlin, she found herself in a house full of small rooms, featuring many doors but few windows. She was expected to share one of these tiny rooms with her mother. And though it was clean enough, it smelled of oil and looked out on a "disastrous and ugly courtyard." Moreover, one could hear every word spoken throughout the house, and below there was a stable with a "wild horse on a chain that pawed the ground all night." After describing her surroundings, Rahel elaborated in great detail on the behavior and dress of a little niece, or what she called a "middle thing," a relative who was also a servant. This young girl showed Rahel around. After all their things were "thrown" into their chamber, the mother packed them into three wardrobes, while Rahel sat completely discouraged on a chair, hoping that she "would wake up after all and find the whole thing a bad dream." But this was not to be. When she asked about the clavichord she had been promised, she was told that there wouldn't be one, although she might get a forte-piano the following morning. Rahel insisted on going to get it right away, in part to escape the crowded house. Her younger brother, Liepmann (later,

Ludwig), who was then undergoing commercial training with the uncle, accompanied her and also showed her around. Again she openly admits her disappointment at seeing "*nothing* but Bohemians in *all* the streets and workmen and the like." The sights and sounds she encountered gave Rahel the impression of having arrived in the famous Frankfort ghetto, which she had never seen but about which she must have heard enough to form a very unfavorable opinion. Rahel ends the account of her first day in Breslau with a further tale of woe that she nevertheless renders in a humorous way: "At the same time, a colony of fleas was happy on my body which they had chosen for their island of freedom and equality, the freedom they seized and they ran and bit equally hard, they must have at the very least celebrated the establishment of the Republique." Unable to change her clothes, Rahel finally fainted during prayers, "due to fleas, tiredness, boredom, sadness, and shock, but *especially* because of the fleas."

The real shock, however, came the following morning when Rahel was awakened with what she at first took for Jews quarreling as their voices competed with the noise of "countless chickens and geese and turkey hens and ducks" in the little courtyard. Only after some time did she realize that she was overhearing the early morning prayers in the synagogue her uncle had recently established at his house: "I get up and look and hear only too clearly that it was a memorial to *Him* that the Bohemians shout every morning in mystical language which they call Holy, all the way to his palace in the clouds; don't think that this is exaggerated. I could hear and repeat . . . every holy word . . . and Mama also knew exactly what they were saying. . . ." Unable to bear it, Rahel fled to her uncle's rooms, where she felt somewhat more secure and comfortable.

We may empathize with the discomfort and disappointment of the privileged young Rahel. At the same time, her intolerant and vehement response comes as something of a surprise, as the reader by now knows her as a person of magnanimity and empathy toward those less fortunate. Her intense reactions suggest that Rahel's desperation may have been motivated by something rather more complex than what we would define today as culture shock.

In time, Rahel adjusted to the situation. She came to appreciate the kindness and generosity of her aunt and uncle. And she recognized that both of them were highly regarded by fellow Jews as well as many influential Gentiles in the city and the surrounding areas. Moreover, she was indebted to her aunt for a beautiful journey to the Silesian mountains. She saw new places and was introduced to interesting people. Thus Rahel began to view the trip in terms of the then popular educational journey (Bildungsreise). In her letters, she repeatedly assured her siblings in Berlin that "I shall become clever after all."[82] The journey received further legitimation through Zöllner's *Letters from Silesia*, an informative and thorough account about the region written from the point of view of the enlightened traveler. Rahel consulted the work for information on places she should see or had already visited, but her letters show no actual traces of this two-volume tome. Instead, she communicated and relied upon her own observations and experiences or, as she put it, her "genuine story of the soul and the events."[83]

Rahel had a special way of viewing her surroundings. For example, she began to appreciate Breslau's lovely streets, buildings, and houses, which were entirely "according to our taste." She was also impressed by the beautiful gardens, which, along with the squares, were established for the benefit and enjoyment of the public; this predisposed and encouraged the people of Breslau to enjoy life and their city. She admired the large number of elegant carriages and the healthy horses, their fast pace made possible by excellent roads inside as well as outside the city. Characteristically, Rahel's attention focused on people, their social organization, and the extent to which institutions worked to their benefit. As a result, everything became noteworthy: garden parties, a Jewish wedding, convents as well as castles, the education and dress of women, the behavior of soldiers and officers, the Silesian inns, which almost always featured a forte-piano, performing and playing children, or a councillor of war whom she questioned at length about the economy and history of Silesia in order to escape a tedious table conversation. Moreover, Rahel, the lover of nature, was often so overwhelmed by the beauty of the landscape that she admitted to being unable to find words to describe it.

Of special interest, after Rahel's adverse reactions to Jewish religious practice and customs, are her comments on Catholicism. After visiting a convent and attending a service, she related in detail her essentially positive impressions: "If you see *nothing* but churches and convents here, you will have seen one of the greatest curiosities, at least we who know nothing of the sort and . . . believe little. . . . Therefore I am not at all bored here . . . the holy service is beautiful and pleasant, for it is an *eternal* music, paintings, beautiful buildings, fragrances, and pretty costumes. . . . in short, for people who don't amuse themselves *like we* do, there is nothing more amusing than the Catholic religion."[84] For Rahel, Catholicism was less a religion than an aesthetic experience, a theatrical and sensuous spectacle. She in fact was so intrigued that she asked to see all the monasteries and convents of the region and was particularly pleased when the Jesuits put on a Mozart mass for her.

Not surprisingly, the life of the nuns received Rahel's particular attention. It impressed her as quite "terrible," especially their lack of privacy and their spartan surroundings, from which even the abbess was not exempt. She noted that every order was different with regard to rules and customs. Some cared for the sick, some saw men but were not allowed to leave the convent's premises. Rahel was profoundly impressed by the "order, neatness, and cleanliness," something she had up to then always merely dreamed of but finally found there. She was further fascinated by the resourcefulness and capabilities of the nuns: "These women are gardeners, pharmacists, [they] let blood, bake bread, in short, [they] do everything; noticeable to me were their coarse manly hands, of which I saw not *one* exception, and even more their manly gate . . . many are not religious, but those who are, pray and sing only silently and amuse themselves." The difference in Rahel's response to the Jewish and Catholic religions is striking. While both systems and the accompanying ways of life were quite foreign to her, she expressed genuine interest in the latter but reacted with horror, even contempt, to the former. It is doubtful that she ever set foot in her uncle's synagogue or in her talks with him touched on Jewish religious practices, in spite of the fact that she had learned to revere and love him. Since religion and its rituals still carried meaning for him, he could have enlightened her about aspects of Jewishness that her father in his own drive for assimilation had neglected. The vehemence of her reactions to her Jewish origins points to many unresolved questions she must have harbored and perhaps also to a sudden realization about how recent and therefore precarious Jewish assimilation really was.

The printed letters constitute only a small part of this unusual family's written communication preserved at the Varnhagen Collection. A preliminary examination indicates that the correspondence promises to be especially informative with regard to three as yet unsettled questions: the siblings' relations to each other and to the mother, the family's financial situation, and their attitudes toward Jewishness, Jewish traditions, and contemporary political developments. Undoubtedly, Rahel was the most outstanding among the five siblings. But the letters give ample evidence that the others too were endowed with literary and musical talents and a superior intellect. Markus, who reluctantly devoted himself to the family business, for example, wrote plays that were performed by the family on festive occasions.

Several of his later letters also indicate considerable journalistic talent.[85] Louis, later known as Ludwig Robert, was musically gifted and achieved considerable success as a playwright, poet, librettist, and translator. Moritz was also talented and witty, as well as concerned about the intellectual welfare of the family. After visiting his younger sister, Rose, he expressed his disappointment with her development. After marrying into a traditional Jewish family in Holland, Rose had given up on reading and playing the piano. Instead, like her mother-in-law, she delighted in "servants' stories" and devoted all her time to her child. "In short," Moritz observed, "she has not remained a Levin."[86] Outsiders also remarked on the exceptional qualities of the Levin family, even when compared with the many other educated and outstanding Berlin Jews. Peter von Gualteri, for example, spoke of their possessing a certain *hauteur* (eminence). Not surprisingly, perhaps, the letters also display considerable friction within the family. It was a time of transition, with each sibling assimilating at a somewhat different pace and to a different degree. Ultimately, however, family pride and loyalty always won out over quarrels and differences.

Perhaps the most engaging of the family correspondences is that between Rahel and Ludwig Robert. Consisting of some three hundred letters written over the course of their lives, the epistles cover a great many topics—from literature, the theater, music, and the performance arts to philosophy, politics, and the meaning of Jewishness. The correspondence also bears testimony to the special emotional and intellectual affinity between these two siblings. Throughout his life Ludwig, or Louis, as he was called in the family, put himself in the care and trust of his older sister, as exemplified by the following declaration, written when he was nineteen: "since I am now far from you, from the only woman who loves me as a human being, i.e., who seeks to educate me through her purposeful will, I therefore now also have the courage to tell you all my opinions and thoughts of which you will surely lovingly correct whatever is wrong" (20 January 1797). These were the years when Rahel began to make a name for herself through her salon and her letters, while Ludwig Robert was in commercial training with his uncle in Breslau and, beginning in 1796, in Hamburg with a man named Zadig, who seems to have been a family friend. He remained in Hamburg until about 1800, at which time he resolved to forgo the comfortable and respectable life of a businessman for the uncertainties of a writer's career.

Rahel's letters during the 1790s are unfortunately lost, but Ludwig Robert's reveal the tone and manner of their written conversations. Louis assigned to Rahel the dual role of sister and friend, for which he coined the term *Schwester-Freund* [sister–(male) friend], accurately expressing the multiple and intertwined aspects of their relationship. At age nineteen he wrote asking for guidance: "My ideal of happiness . . . *that*'s what I am working on . . . and you must actively help me and give me your hand, for *you* are my friend, though unfortunately the *only one* I have" (21 August 1797). At age forty he addressed her as *Vater Freund und Schwester* [father, (male) friend, and sister] and confessed: "No one was ever quite so in harmony with me and so I have had many *good* friends, but never a friend" (11 October 1818).[87] Only rarely was he capable of responding with the kind of understanding and empathy that she had for him. On one such occasion he wrote: "I believe I have understood your letter and moreover, I believe we both have *one* principal feeling. How *much* I love you, how *very* happy I am that you are my sister, how *unhappy* all the people whom I meet on the street appear to me because they have *no such* sister, *no such* friend, that I don't need to tell you. And yet I say it, because I . . . passionately want to" (31 October 1797).[88]

Rahel accepted the role of providing the emotional support, encouragement, and confirmation her sensitive and insecure brother needed. She shared with him her knowledge of people and the world and served as the intellectual guide and critic of his poetic endeavours. Later she often became his anonymous literary collaborator. Her concern for him as a human being took the form of appeals to his better self. Over and over she counseled him to remain true to himself, to act according to his feelings (7 November 1818), for we "only err, when we act against ourselves" (10 November 1818). She also made use of her role as friend by reminding him: "You did *not* speak to yourself as a friend; *I* am the friend and I speak differently" (20 April 1814).

Rahel's educative role was particularly important during those early years in Hamburg when Ludwig Robert set out with great determination to become a human being according to the dictates of Enlightened Humanism and a gentleman in the manner of late eighteenth-century Gentile fashion. These twin goals and his intended commercial career constituted his main concerns during his time in Hamburg. Not surprisingly, this kind of ambition led almost immediately to questions and conflicts with regard to his Jewish origins.

In general, it seems to have been Ludwig Robert who brought up Jewish matters, perhaps because in Hamburg there was little social interaction between Jews and Gentiles, although well-to-do Jewish businessmen were accepted professionally. In Berlin, on the other hand, where Jews were successfully promoting a mixed society, it was much easier to subscribe to the illusion of an imminent happy integration of Jews into mainstream society. At one point, after apologizing for the ill humor that had governed his letter, Ludwig Robert exclaimed: "However, that you don't know why I was in this mood, I wouldn't have thought; you after all know best how a Jew feels in society and especially a Jew who is not taken for one, a common one" (14 February 1797). In Hamburg Ludwig Robert continuously faced the question of how to integrate his commercial activities with his humanistic concerns and creative endeavours. At first this seemed to cause him little difficulty, but as time went on he became increasingly doubtful. Although he conducted his business transactions successfully, he derived no pleasure from financial gains. Instead, he waited anxiously for the time when his training would be concluded so that he could devote himself entirely to literature. Since no writer at that time could live by his pen alone, it was primarily the family wealth that enabled Ludwig Robert to take this step. This did not, however, signify a life of ease and comfort. On the contrary, he had to make considerable sacrifices in order to live within his income. He resolved to forgo marriage and the social status commensurate with the economic standard he would have as a merchant. His letters, which resume in 1806, tell of financial difficulties, of the misery of living in an unheated room in Paris, and of his plan to abandon that city for a smaller German town, where he could live more cheaply. The decision to lead a free and independent life devoted to literature nonetheless reflects the opportunities that seemed to present themselves to gifted Jews at that time. It was thus in no small part an expression of optimism and confidence in a more egalitarian and progressive Germany.

Because Rahel and her brother pursued assimilation more energetically than did the other Levin siblings, their letters convey with particular poignancy the ambivalence of their quest. On the one hand, they sought emancipation from the confinement of traditional Jewish life. On the other, they knew that the Christian majority was, in many respects, unenlightened. They were part of a tiny minority of German Jews who chose to spend their lives as intellectuals outside the Jewish community, although they neither denied their Jewishness nor broke with their community. Although the majority of Jews pursuing traditional careers in business and finance were increasing their social ties with Gentiles, they led lives confined in the main to their own Jewish circle. Rahel, as salonnière, and Ludwig Robert, as author, were both free-lance intellectuals. As such, they, were much more dependent on the approval as well as support of their Gentile friends and acquaintances.

Rahel exchanged letters with her family, especially Ludwig Robert, throughout her life. Therefore, this lively written dialogue will be taken up subsequently in more detail.

The correspondences discussed above constituted the foundation of Rahel's extensive epistolary work, which in the course of her life would reach as many as three hundred persons. Some of the exchanges have been presented in greater detail than others in order to demonstrate the young Rahel's intellectual and stylistic versatility—a versatility that ultimately derived from her ability to recognize her partner's receptivity and sensibility, that is, the dialogical quality of her writing.

3

HOPES BETRAYED

THE END OF THE "FIRST SALON"

The social life Rahel had known and practiced ended with the military defeat of Prussia at the battles of Jena and Auerstedt and with Napoleon's victorious entry into Berlin in October 1806. Prussia's collapse signaled the end of that country's political ascendancy—at least for the time being. The costs were heavy: loss of territories in the eastern and western regions, trade embargoes, high taxation, and the expense of billeting French soldiers. The defeat, however, also made possible the implementation of long overdue reforms. These were taken on by some of the more forward-looking leaders, among them Baron von und zum Stein, Prince Hardenberg, and Baron Altenstein. The years 1807 to 1812 saw the modernization of the economy and the military and the abolishment of the most outdated feudal structures and practices. In the countryside the serfs were freed, and in the cities the power of the guilds was broken, which meant that the freedom to exercise any trade was now granted to everyone. At the same time, compulsory military service was introduced. The improvements also benefited the Jews. One by one, the myriad of special laws governing their exceptional status were repealed. Jews were now permitted to settle in the towns and the countryside, to take up any profession, to be appointed in the civil service as teachers, administrators, and officials at the communal, though not at the national, level. And finally, after more than two hundred years as more or less tolerated "aliens," the Prussian Jews were recognized as citizens in the Emancipation Edict of 1812.

But this was only one side of the picture. In contrast to the reforms in France, those in Prussia and other German states were not the result of pressures from the population at large; they were implemented by the Napoleonic occupation forces and by a small number of liberal, mostly aristocratic, German leaders. The new legislation in effect amounted to reforms from above and did not, therefore, affect the old hierarchies, nor did it succeed in paving the way toward more liberal attitudes. The bourgeoisie remained uninvolved in the political life, while the most retrograde factions of the aristocracy became all the more vociferous. Numerous open letters denouncing the reforms reached the king. One of the most notorious was by the arch-conservative Ludwig von der Marwitz, in which he railed against any curtailing of aristocratic privilege and warned of the coming of a "new-fangled Jewish state." (Ludwig was the brother of Alexander von der Marwitz, who, at the very same time, became a close friend of Rahel's.) The opposition against liberalization and reform was further supported by the younger intellectual and literary elite, many of whom came from the nobility as well. Although they had previously frequented the Jewish salons, they now avoided them. The cosmopolitan spirit governing these gatherings was suddenly equated with lack of patriotism. The younger generation of Romantics—the historian Adam Müller, the poets Achim von Arnim, Clemens Brentano, Heinrich von Kleist—congregated instead at the homes of prominent Gentiles, primarily members of the ruling bureaucracy. Among the sought-after assemblies were those of the Minister of State Stägemann, Countess Voss, and Prince Radziwill, all of whom had recently attended Rahel's assemblies. Additionally, in order to promote his Christian and Germanic type of patriotism and culture, Arnim founded a new literary club, the "Christian-German Table Society," which refused admittance to Frenchmen, philistines, Jews (including converted ones), and women. The exclusions make clear the direction of the society's new patriotism: from its anti-French stance, it followed that German society was on the verge of abandoning the eighteenth-century cosmopolitan world view; the jab against philistines and Jews revealed its elitist and therefore antidemocratic attitudes, while the exclusion of women was directed explicitly against popular Jewish sociability, dominated by women. Thus, despite the very real and positive changes in the civil status of Jews, their everyday experiences often changed for the worse. The new phenomenon of petty nationalism and chauvinism was aimed especially against those Jews who had been most thoroughly integrated into German society.

Not surprisingly, Rahel experienced primarily the negative developments. She found herself increasingly isolated, even abandoned. In January 1808 she reported to Brinckmann:

At my "tea table," as you call it, I sit alone with my dictionaries; tea is not being served, except every eight or ten days, when Schack, who has *not* deserted me, asks for it. Everything is different. Never was I so alone. Absolutely. Never so thoroughly and definitely bored. Imagine, bored! Because only cleverness, kindness, hopefulness can sustain one who has been so wronged, so devastated. But all is over. During the winter and the summer too, I knew a few Frenchmen: with them I conversed, and we discussed that which educated strangers, who love and practice literature . . . can discuss and dispute. They are all gone. My German friends, for how long already; as if they had died, as if they had dispersed! At this moment, I only see my second brother, who lives with me at my mother's and the man who is billeted with us. . . . I am as I was, Brinckmann; the blows have fortified the old [strengths] within me, and prevailed and made me truly new and more arable. I am still capable of joking, delight, and the highest suffering; only, there is nothing that can upset me completely, for I am *prostrate*.[1]

Although Berlin and vast areas of Europe were under French occupation, Rahel refused to adopt the anti-French attitudes that had become prevalent among her former guests. France remained for her a country to be admired and emulated for its established liberal institutions. She continued to improve her knowledge of the French language, which she called "European," in the hopes of joining Ludwig Robert in Paris. Cosmopolitanism and tolerance remained guiding principles for her.

Her fatherland, on the other hand, called forth complex and, at times, contradictory feelings, her letters expressing both deep loyalty and ambivalence. Thus, she wrote in December 1808: "Until now I have lived under the auspices, in the strictest sense, under the wings of Frederick the Second. Every enjoyment, external, that is, every good, every advantage, every acquaintance I can attribute to his influence: all this exploded over my head. I feel it especially! His spirit—and precisely because it is so unlike mine, I shall obey it blindly . . . —commands me to make a daring choice . . . I follow his signal and go to the next great man. Moreover, I cannot remain here; and there is war everywhere, except with Napoleon [in France]. That's how the matter is in German."[2] Rahel's positive appraisal of Frederick II is surprising in view of his self-serving and exploitative policies toward the Jews. She seemed to see only the king's tolerance in intellectual and religious matters, which did make possible two generations of Jewish assimilation in both social and economic terms. Her desire to go to France was, of course, not simply a matter of joining "the next great man" or "the victor Napoleon."[3] The reason was not disloyalty or opportunism but rather the need to escape demeaning conditions she and other Jews had confronted in Prussia since 1806. France promised relief from the humiliations experienced at home.

There are additional reasons for Rahel's surprising stance in favor of mighty rulers. Historically, Jews could expect little more than tolerance from the population at large, their fate having for centuries been directly dependent on the monarch's favors and goodwill. Jewish political acumen thus tended to express itself as loyalty toward the ruler. Furthermore, and here her thinking coincided with that of Goethe, Rahel's European orientation and sense of history made her see in Napoleon the representative of a necessary historical progression. And finally, as already noted, the new patriotism presented itself primarily in the form of chauvinism and narrow-minded nationalism, while under Napoleon, many German states were forced to introduce political, social, and economic reforms and to repeal their special laws against Jews and even grant them civil rights. For these reasons, Napoleon called forth ambivalent feelings among Jews generally.

In time Rahel's thinking did take on a more patriotic orientation. It was prompted by the hardships of the war and its aftermath, the first hints of the possibility of a unified Germany and, above all, Johann Gottlieb Fichte's "Addresses to the German Nation," which he delivered as public lectures in Berlin in the winter of 1807–8 and which Rahel attended. She had read his major early work, *Grundlage der gesamten Wissenschaftslehre* (1794, *Foundations of Science*), only a year after its initial publication, "with great gain," as she wrote to David Veit. Fichte was the philosopher she read, referred to, and quoted throughout her life and whom she put on a par with Goethe. Like Goethe, he legitimated her own thoughts and ideas, calling out to her: " 'You are not alone!' " Since she refrained from discussing Fichte's ideas in any detail, it is difficult to extrapolate from her early letters the precise nature of his appeal. A radical and independent thinker herself, she welcomed his political and religious ideas, ideas that Fichte's colleagues, students, and especially the clerics, viewed with alarm. She was also in full agreement with his rigorous moral demands.[4]

Rahel identified with Fichte's ideas in a fundamental way. Late in life, for example, she wrote in her diary: "To invent a [philosophical] system can mean nothing else but to investigate, name, [and] classify the possibilities of the human spirit, and to assign it the laws according to which it must act, including also all the ideas (or inspirations) it may have. This is what Fichte does."[5] The philosopher's ethical rigor, his trust in human reason and progress, the significance he assigned to the free self that is nevertheless conscious of its responsibilities, as well as his progressive social and political theory met with Rahel's full approval. She saw him as the enlightened educator of the German people and must have understood his "Addresses to the

German Nation" in this manner. Today it is impossible not to recognize in these speeches the seeds of Germany's later fateful hegemoniacal aspirations and sense of cultural superiority. At that time, however, they were admired as an expression of liberal and progressive thought. To Rahel, the philosopher's call for universal popular education and his notion of Germany's cultural mission must have appeared as entirely reasonable solutions. She could accept Fichte's kind of nationalism which did not disavow a European-oriented outlook because it drew on those German intellectual achievements that championed a cosmopolitan and humanistic world view.

In addition to the social ostracism Rahel suddenly faced after 1806, her situation was exacerbated by serious familial tensions and conflicts. Her mother, especially, found it increasingly difficult to understand and empathize with her daughter's quest for personal freedom and independence. In the summer of 1808 Chaie took an unusual and unprecedented step: she secretly and suddenly moved out, making the break explicit. Rahel was devastated. Unable to pay for the spacious quarters, she was forced to give up the home she had known since childhood and move to a smaller one. At thirty-seven, an age when women were considered old and not likely to get married, she was suddenly set adrift, socially and emotionally. Moreover, the war had adversely affected the Levins' business, so that everyone's living allowance had to be reduced. Desperate, Rahel vented her hurt in a lengthy and heartrending letter to her mother.[6] This highly unusual letter from a daughter to her mother calls to mind the parting letters of famous sons to their fathers, notably Ludwig Börne, Karl Marx, Sigmund Freud, Max Horkheimer, and above all, Franz Kafka.[7] Like them, Rahel attempted to make her mother aware of the injustices she suffered within the family, while she had proven herself as a loving and devoted daughter. The letter thus represents an accounting as well as a justification. However, as a daughter's letter to her mother, it was also very different, because a daughter, unlike a son, did not have the option of really breaking with the parent in order to strike out on her own. Categorically refuting parental authority and tradition in order to achieve or pursue one's own goals was possible only for sons. Similarly, the mother was not imbued with the kind of authority and power vested in the father. Chaie Levin may have been nominally the head of the family, but the actual affairs were in the hands of her eldest son, although he was younger than the eldest daughter. At the same time, Chaie Levin refused to perform the motherly role, namely, to extend love and empathy equally to all her children. It is to this motherly love that Rahel appeals most of all.

To safeguard myself against the quite possible event (that I don't know at all what I want is already revealed in all the answers I receive) that I am mad, you will kindly permit me to present to you my situation one last time. My age you know; my great inner distress will forever remain a mystery to you. Upon you I depend: therefore, only you could protect me and, through your loving treatment, guarantee a haven for my heart.

This is how Rahel begins the letter. She quickly passes on to the financial situation, claiming that the money allotted to her was not sufficient in her present circumstances, and then tries to assert her right to be treated fairly:

Good; all right! if I cost more than the interest from the capital which I would receive upon marriage, then I reply that I want to calculate the same for the others [the other siblings]. . . . That you granted me [my] freedom I cannot thank you for in spite of my greatest respect; if I had not had it I would have been outraged. And in return you cannot say that I used it to anyone's disadvantage, except to my own; each individual is his own person. And for this [I should like] to cite an example! Which of your 2 daughters was until now helpful to the family, eager to be useful, which one was called upon in need and asked for advice, [which one was] the friend to each one of you; and which one succeeded in rendering life pleasant to your children with sociable enjoyment, the married, protected, and praised one; or the unhappy one? Losses occurred; confusion, war and need; I lost my friends. Secretly, humiliated, I wanted to step aside: and waited for an opportunity, peace, and some clarity in your affairs, it did not come about: you moved out—gave notice secretly: like the Oppenheim company—before I had the means to get away. I am the only one who is inconvenienced by the bankruptcy. . . . No happiness can ever replace the summer I experienced . . .

The shock over being so openly, even publicly, abandoned and refuted by her mother speaks through Rahel's every word. Forced to justify not only her life but also her existence, she presents an assessment of the family's dynamics. At the same time, she is insistent that the life of sociability, which was now disapproved of by everybody, enriched that of the siblings as well.

In the second half of the letter, Rahel turns to describing and explaining more recent difficulties. She reproaches the mother for her callousness and lack of understanding, ending with the question: "Tell me, reasonable mother, where am I supposed to seek love? I should like to find it!" Her brothers, she claims, have failed her as well. She describes the specific manner of each one's indifference to her distress and their outright disrespect for her. In her difficulties, Rahel writes, she found it easier to turn to a foreigner, the

French civil servant, Henri Campan, for financial help.[8] And she concludes: "[My brothers] therefore, golden Mama! even if you wish it more than anything else, you cannot suggest as friends. . . . I no longer deceive myself: they are my brothers, my flesh and blood; that they will remain. But they still have to become my friends, through their behavior even more than through their deeds." Emphasizing once more her kindness, she concludes with the words: "Grant me to depend on you directly, *now* and <u>in the future</u>, as long as I remain unmarried; this is the only favor I still dare ask! As these are the last words about my miserably pitiful story." Signed: "Rahel."

Initially, the family had not objected to Rahel's social circle. On the contrary, as descriptions of the salon showed, they constituted an integral part of it. However, when Rahel failed to secure a husband, while a number of other young Jewish women had succeeded in marrying into the nobility, they became impatient and increasingly thought of their sister as a social and financial liability. Thus, at the very time when the newly established social ties proved to be most unreliable, the family failed her as well.

Her deep hurt is further revealed in a letter to the poet Friedrich de la Motte Fouqué: "With the opinion that I should be a queen (not a reigning one) or a mother, I experience that I am actually *nothing*. No daughter, no sister, no beloved, no woman, not even a citizen."[9] In time the situation improved at least externally. Rahel spent much time with her mother, who in turn lent her money from time to time. When the mother died the following year after a prolonged and difficult illness, Rahel admitted to a sense of great loss in spite of the many conflicts. She renewed her commitment to harmonious relations within the family. To her sister, Rose, far away in Holland, she wrote: "We here want to care for each other; and thus honor our mother."[10] It is of some significance that Rahel chose to remember her mother by keeping the items that most separated her from her: the head covering all married Jewish women were traditionally required to wear, the siddum or prayer book, and a needle box. She attributed the tensions and conflicts less to generational differences than to the unfortunate family dynamics and ultimately to her father's destructive influence.

THE LETTERS OF THE NAPOLEONIC ERA

Although Rahel led a much more curtailed and solitary existence after 1806, she nevertheless did not lose her talent for making new friends. Her epistolary exchanges, especially, expanded and intensified. Through writing she attempted to overcome her sense of insignificance and isolation. Among the new friends and correspondents were Rebecca Friedländer, a young woman from the same assimilated Jewish community as Rahel, the beautiful and unconventional Pauline Wiesel, the already mentioned nobleman, young Alexander von der Marwitz, and the equally young Karl August von Varnhagen, who was pursuing his medical studies at the University of Tübingen. Rahel also corresponded for some time with several of the Romantic poets, Clemens Brentano, Friedrich de la Motte Fouqué, and his wife, Karoline, who published mostly under the pseudonym Serena or as "author of the Roderich-novels."

Each of these written exchanges tells a story of its own, but they distinguish themselves in similar ways from Rahel's earlier letters. Gone are the youthful high spirits, the undiluted joy of life, the naive confidence and delight in the world and other people. Rahel, who always treated other persons according to her own lofty principles—as ends in themselves—experienced that they in turn failed again and again to extend regard and respect to her. Admittedly, she had accomplished a good deal. She was renowned among a select group in Berlin and beyond as a woman of great intellectual power and insight as well as tolerance and kindness. But she had been unable to achieve the seemingly simple, to attract a man who loved and respected her and who was also willing to make her his wife. This was no small failing at a time when women attained status only through marriage. For a Jewish woman of Rahel's ambitions, being single meant being further disadvantaged.

Thus, the tone of her letters grew more serious, even somber, while her language often evoked pathos but still lacked the smoothness she admired in others. As she remarked to Fouqué: "I know quite well that I am writing you things worth reading; but my words and yours! Everything of yours stands like drilled soldiers in beautiful uniforms; and mine, like hastily assembled rebels with cudgels!"[11] The letters of this period contain a great deal of practical wisdom, psychological insight, and understanding for others on the one hand and, on the other, repeated expressions of self-affirmation, which took the form of searching self-assessments or conscious self-praise. They also tended to burst suddenly into lamentations and protests over the indignities she had suffered. Rahel was now older and more experienced than her new correspondents, whose inner strife may have been similar but who did not possess her emotional and intellectual maturity or her analytical powers. Pauline Wiesel, self-assured and impervious to the dictates of society, was the one exception.

Rahel's letters had from the beginning contained a didactic streak that now became explicit. She viewed her fate as exemplary, in the sense that she was an individual who had cultivated within herself the highest sensibilities in order to experience life fully and yet was rendered deeply unhappy. She therefore made it her task to pass on to others the insights and strengths she had gained through her suffering. Along with emotional maturity, the letters of this period increasingly reflect the fruits of Rahel's intellectual pursuits. Her diminished or, perhaps more accurately, her unsatisfactory social life prompted her to seek refuge and intellectual stimulation in books. Belles lettres were still her primary love, but she also immersed herself in theoretical works on history, politics, and economics.

Also at this time, in addition to their dialogical qualities Rahel's letters began to take on other distinct formal characteristics. For example, she liked to situate a letter not only with the date and place but also with a report of the weather, the season or time of day, and her state of health or mood. As she explained many years later, this served to excuse her unmethodical way of writing. The weather constituted at least in part "the situation of the day" for her, and she intended the recipient to be aware of the frame of mind in which the epistle was written. This is what she meant by the letter being "a portrait of the moment in which it is written."[12]

Her insistence on dialogue and answers was now also more explicitly formulated. The admonitions "answer me!" or "I love answers" are repeatedly insisted upon during these years. Thus, she wrote: "But now a quarrel, my dear Fouqué! what is this, that you don't answer at all when you write. . . . I love an answer. . . . You must approve or find fault, or agree or oppose. You see, I am once again insisting on what is liveliest in letter writing."[13] The formal aspects of Rahel's letters were meant to facilitate the exchange of ideas and experiences, no matter how divergent or new or unusual they might be. And although she carefully distinguished between the spoken and the written word, she strained the written form to its limits by consciously approximating it to oral expression.

Rebecca Friedländer

Rahel's correspondence with Rebecca Friedländer occurred during the years 1805–11. It consists of some 350 letters, billets, and other brief communications, all of them by Rahel. After the two friends had grown apart, they returned the letters to each other, with Rebecca subsequently destroying her side of the correspondence. Just the same, Rahel's letters provide ample insight into how intensive a friendship theirs must have been, for the women wrote to each other on a regular basis, at times daily, in spite of the fact that they lived mostly in Berlin in close proximity and thus saw each other often.

Rebecca was an author of rather mediocre novels, which she published under the pseudonym Regine Frohberg. She came from the same background as Rahel but was twelve years her junior. She had been married at age eighteen to Moses Friedländer, a son of the prominent leader of the Berlin Jewish community, David Friedländer. The marriage ended in separation after only a few years. At the time of her friendship with Rahel she was entangled in love relationships as problematical as Rahel's had been. Two affairs, one with a Count Egloffstein and the other with a Frenchman named d'Houdetot, ended unhappily. Rahel stood by her as a loyal friend and generously gave whatever empathy and understanding she herself had not received. She termed her epistles "letters of consolation." They were nonetheless full of lamentations because she was of the opinion that someone else's "laments banish our own," and this renders us "helpful to the other person."[14] Mostly, however, she tried to cheer up her friend, reminding her how young she was and how great the world, that she would gain new strength, and suggesting that she read Goethe's *Wilhelm Meister* as one reads the Bible during times of misfortune.

Many of these letters will strike the modern reader as unduly self-absorbed. They lack the intellectual sparkle, the lively exchange of ideas, the *aperçus*, or a genuine meeting of the minds so characteristic of Rahel's other correspondences. They circle around a few themes: illness, moments of discouragement and despair and how to overcome them, and their relations to each other.

The considerable space given to health in the letters is not surprising. A preoccupation with one's health was a result, primarily, of attitudes toward medical treatment that were markedly different from our own. Consistent with Enlightenment thinking, more importance was assigned to the preservation of health than to the treatment and cure of illness. Additionally, the patient actively participated in and even took responsibility for his or her treatment, with the attending physician generally taking on the role of counselor. This explains the great popularity of the baths as well as the considerable space devoted to health problems and successful treatments in letters by both men and women.[15]

This active involvement in health matters is very evident in the letters. Moreover, both women were quite conscious of the psychosomatic origins of many of their symptoms and, as a result, wary of their doctors and their treatments. But Rahel, in contrast to her friend, made great efforts to resist giving in to despondency and illness. Repeatedly, she counseled Rebecca in this matter: "What you are saying is true, your spirit is sick. Evading the term, I have been telling you the same for a long time. . . . And the means to fortification . . . is precisely, to grasp a more general, spiritually more elevated interest. . . . Impress upon your memory the just hatred and disdain against illness and unhappiness, and they disappear! I too have tried it! we believe we can mollify fate and people if we evoke our deep unhappiness. . . . In vain! both have no heart."[16] Plagued by ill health since birth, Rahel became even more susceptible as she grew older and unhappier. She suffered from gout, rheumatism, colds, migraine headaches, spasms of the heart—conditions that tended to improve dramatically if the weather turned fine, if she could go for walks in the countryside or spend time in pleasant surroundings and with people who appealed to and stimulated her. This was not always easy. As a single woman she could venture out by herself only within the city or in a carriage, which she could not afford. Therefore, unless she was able to find company, she was banished to her rooms. Rebecca Friedländer seems to have been in a similar position. These letters then give insight into the restricted lives women, and single women especially, were constrained to lead.[17]

Although we do not know Rebecca Friedländer's letters, those of Rahel reveal only too clearly that she was the active and giving partner in this friendship. Rahel addresses her as "my dearest friend," "daughter," or simply "Dearest." Besides providing consolation and empathy, she tried hard to acquaint her friend with new and "nobler" ideas. In particular, she was intent on making her more honest with herself. To this end, Rahel bared her soul as she had never done before, hoping that the younger woman would learn from such candor and truthfulness. She repeatedly touched upon the topic of pretense, explaining why it had become so hateful to her: "until now I loved and hated . . . everything in other people that I understood and saw; and was satisfied *in a piecemeal fashion* with what I found to my liking in this person or that one. . . . I summoned all my strengths . . . and gave my *whole* heart. And am *ridiculed*. . . . Now I am tired: the *tiniest* pretense is too much for me; and honest is all I can only be."[18] Rahel's love of truth was well known among her friends. Moreover, it was a quality she herself was proud of and saw as an essential aspect of her personality. She was not merely talking about the everyday pretenses that governed women's behavior especially. She well understood the necessity of these. What she had in mind was the much more important pretended goodwill she had spontaneously extended to so many who subsequently slighted, ignored, or offended her.

The causes for her being repeatedly rejected can in many instances be found in Gentile opposition to Jewish efforts at assimilation. Often, however, anti-Jewish attitudes also combined with those against intellectually outstanding women. Jewish salonnières were particularly subject to this kind of animosity, as they distinguished themselves from bourgeois women through their sophistication and wit. Rahel, the exceptional woman par excellence, was only too aware of this multiple kind of prejudice. Her account of a visit by Count Egloffstein, who not only courted Rebecca Friedländer but frequented Jewish circles generally, is particularly revealing:

the whole pretty kettle of fish—this infamous word is the best here—came to the surface . . . his [Egloffstein's] understanding of the meaning of *genius*. A kind of monstrous creature as it actually doesn't exist. Trivial division between intellect and kindness—in short, I spare you the details, this only you must know, he thought *I* care nothing about kindness—only about— . . . intellect. It may—surprise you . . . that I am suddenly concerned about someone else's judgment! I will explain it to you. If it were an *impression* that I made, I would accept it! But it is a little system of pre-notions which Egl.[offstein] assumed about me before he ever heard a *single* word from me, and now that I met him openly, as I do with everyone . . . he does *not* hear me: and therefore knows less of me than *before* because he now can say to himself: "I know her!". . . . God! must I eternally clear away rubble which others leave me? How horrid it is to always have to legitimate yourself! that's why it is so *hateful* to be a Jewess!![19]

Prejudice or "the little system of pre-notions," as Rahel succinctly observes, against the Jew and against the woman, stands in the way of true communication. For Egloffstein, as for Gentz some years earlier, genius applied to men only. A woman of genius therefore lost her feminine qualities, such as kindness, and was transformed into a "monstrous creature." This is one of the rare instances where Jewishness and the difficulties associated with it are referred to in this epistolary exchange between two women aspiring to assimilation. For, although in this instance all of her difficulties seemed to crystallize in the fact that she was a "Jewess," Rahel was still reluctant to admit to herself the extent to which this stood in the way of acceptance. Mostly she took recourse in still vaguer formulations that did not attempt to identify the specific kind of prejudice involved. In 1807 she wrote to Rebecca: "Misunderstood, hated, I must always first legitimate myself."[20] A year later she took up the thought again: "*Here everything* turns into Rahel for me! that is, into the most abominable situation! *Never* do I appear as I am; I am passed on eternally from one to the next."[21] Her given name, Rahel, like the term *Jewess*, served as a repository for society's multiple and complex opposition to her aspirations as a Jewish woman of unusual intelligence and talents. As for

Rebecca Friedländer, she underwent baptism shortly after separating from her husband. Her intention was therefore to assimilate through marriage—a rather straightforward notion of assimilation. By contrast, Rahel thought of assimilation in terms of real acculturation, comprising personal emancipation, education, and a deep commitment to the ideas of the Enlightenment. This correspondence then was hardly conducive to exploring the painful subject of Jewishness.

Five years after she first devoted herself to this young woman, Rahel had to concede that her efforts at educating her were in vain. Rebecca Friedländer was incapable of rising to the level of honesty and human refinement Rahel expected of her. In September 1810 Rahel wrote a letter she declared to be "the best I've ever written to you," because it was ruthlessly honest. Conceding that she had never spoken like this, she nevertheless insisted that this letter had always been the subtext of all the preceding ones: "I have always carried it in my soul; only I flattered you because I did not want to hurt you." In the letter Rahel takes stock of her friend's progress as well as her failings: "Not that you haven't gained immeasurably since our acquaintance! The entire horizon of your concepts is illuminated, a whole jumble of old opinions, judgments, and desires has been removed; entire fields have been planted anew; your mind has become more active. You have cast your eye upon a new world and let go a ridiculous, deceptive one. Yet your being has not gained in coherence.—*And* how is it *possible* that you admire emotional *honesty* in someone else without immediately becoming so yourself?"[22] Four days later, obviously concerned about her friend's reaction to such straightforward talk, Rahel wrote another letter, once more explaining the meaning of her exposition and assuring her that she had been equally unsparing with Prince Louis Ferdinand, whom she had told as well: "What shall I say to you or rather, I have absolutely nothing to say if I cannot tell you the truth!"

There was no actual break between the two women. Rather, they drifted apart. Even Rebecca's novel *Schmerzen der Liebe* (1811, The pains of love) did not cause a definite rupture, although Rahel and her brother Moritz had read it in manuscript form and were outraged. The novel represented a gossipy roman à clef of Rahel's circle. Moritz found himself portrayed "unmistakably down to the smallest details, but so hideously and aggressively" and moreover recognized a letter of his "reprinted word for word." He asked Rahel to frighten Rebecca by telling her that he had "probably burned the manuscript out of anger."[23] Rahel's answer no longer exists, but she seemed to stand above such petty strife and, in one letter, even forgave her friend. The letters also contain several instances in which she encouraged the younger woman in her literary endeavors, and later letters, to Varnhagen, show that she tried to help her find publishers. Furthermore, among her papers there is an unfinished text in which she attempted to review the novel positively.

Pauline Wiesel

Rahel's friendship and correspondence with Pauline Wiesel was altogether different. The two women met in Rahel's salon early in the century; their close relationship, however, began after 1806, which was also the time when they started writing to each other. It was a bond that lasted until Rahel's death. Moreover, these letters represent a written dialogue from which misunderstandings are almost absent and in which each writer felt free to convey to the other her most radical thoughts and insights as well as her keenest hopes and aspirations. Although there were long periods when the women did not see or write to each other, this did not adversely affect their friendship. Their loyalty to each other as well as to their youthful ideals remained constant in spite of the very different lives they led. They gave expression to this constancy by reiterating over and over that they had not "changed" and that they would "never change."

Pauline Wiesel was a woman of extraordinary character, independence, and self-confidence. Born in 1779 as the daughter of a French émigré mother and the privy councillor César, who was in the services of Prince Henry of Prussia, she led her life according to her own wishes and thus achieved considerable freedom and notoriety. Not surprisingly, she was shunned by respectable society for much of her life. Later, literary historians also thought it prudent to pass over the two women's explosive correspondence, although a selection of their letters appeared in print in 1865.[24] Her dubious reputation notwithstanding, Pauline Wiesel became Rahel's most remarkable and important friend.

Although married since 1800 to Friedrich Ferdinand Wiesel, councillor of war, she became in 1804 the lover of Prince Louis Ferdinand, with whom she appeared openly at Rahel's salon. After the prince's death in battle in 1806, she left Berlin with her little daughter and roamed around Europe, living alternately with her mother or with a lover or husband or independently in Switzerland, Paris, Vienna, Italy, Southern Germany, and England. She returned to Berlin only once, in 1832, to visit her ailing friend Rahel. Throughout her adventurous life Pauline Wiesel never lost those qualities that had impressed Rahel from the beginning because they were so like her own: a thorough commitment to truthfulness and genuineness, a great love of nature, and an absolute lack of prejudice in the widest sense.

Pauline's strength and her disregard for the dictates of society were mirrored in her unconventional language. Her thoroughly idiosyncratic and inconsistent use of grammar and spelling, her intermingling of languages (German, French, and Berlin dialect), and her almost complete disregard for punctuation not only make for difficult reading but also multiple meanings. Regrettably, these characteristics cannot be rendered in translation. Rahel, whose own language and writing style were often similarly inventive, never attempted to correct her friend's letters and had no difficulty understanding their meaning. On the contrary, she recognized a close link between Pauline's unique personal qualities and her way of writing. In 1815 she wrote to Varnhagen: "Just now I reread Pauline's letter. It is worth *millions*. Such divine words (Götterworte), such a view, such truthfulness, such orthography."[25]

In an early letter Rahel boldly defined what she considered so unusual about each of them as well as their relationship:

Only once could nature permit two like us to live at the same time. In this age. Each day I behold you, and nature, and myself, more . . . there is only *one* difference between us, you *live* everything because you have courage and were lucky: I mostly *think*; because I had no luck and received no courage; not the kind that wrings luck from luck, that wrests it from its hand; I only learned to bear; but nature proceeded grandly with both of us. And we are created to live the truth in this world. And through different paths we reached the same point. We are *outside* society. For us there is no place, no position, no frivolous title! *All* the lies have one; the eternal truth, the proper way of living and feeling . . . *has none*! And therefore we are excluded from society, you because you offended it. (I congratulate you for it! At least you had something; many days of pleasure!) I, because I cannot sin and lie along with it. I know your entire story. Every insult which you inflicted on society, although justified within *yourself*, wounded you just the same. . . . You would have liked to be 'a home-loving wife, embracing and kissing your husband', as Goethe says in the Distichon; but it wasn't possible. And what to do with the terrible supply, with the entire contrivance of heart and life! Not all beings are sensitively self-destructive and sacrificing nuns. One should like to go to *war*, me too, in order to find nourishment for the claim with which nature sent us into this life. Just and omnipotent God . . . people go to war for much less than that! and are honored for it![26]

Theirs was a friendship sealed by an awareness of living at the margins of society, although the outsiderness was constituted differently in each case.

It was further cemented by a strong belief in themselves, their aspirations, and their insights. According to Rahel's formulation at the beginning of the passage quoted above, the world was divided in two halves. On one side, there was society with its conventions, lies, and pretensions; on the other, there were the two women, shown in a triad with nature—"you, and nature, and myself"—standing for truth and genuineness and therefore in opposition to society. The middle part elaborates on the differences between the two friends: while Rahel, for various reasons, was relegated to thinking, reasoning, and reflecting, Pauline's talents lay in taking practical steps toward realizing her needs and wishes, regardless of how unconventional they were. Rahel concludes the passage with a vehement and entirely modern protest against the limitations imposed on women.

The theme of sameness and difference appears in many variations. But contrary to what one might expect, only in the beginning did their considerable dissimilarities produce tensions or conflicts between them. In time, they emerged as the source of attraction and admiration for each other. In 1818 Rahel wrote: "and that which follows I *repeat*: Nature should have made *one* of the two of us. One such as you should have had my consideration, my prudence, my good sense! One such as I needed your high-spirits and your beauty. In all other respects we possess fully what can render a gifted human being happy: sense, senses, intelligence, humor, a sensitive heart, appreciation of art and nature—this means in our language, 'we love green things.'"[27] This private metaphor or *chiffre*, "green things," referred to anything free of societal constraints or pretense. It was associated with being or wishing to be outdoors, with children, with common and therefore more genuine people, or with each other.

Pauline Wiesel's personality and loyalty as well as her understanding of the differences between them are, in turn, reflected in a letter she wrote in 1808: "If you can sacrifice your personal happiness, your contentment, yes, even your personal convictions to the world, this is probably preferable to you—I don't understand it, [to be] so enlightened in one way and in another so backward. . . . You know what the two of us often said—if one has everything and no love in the heart, then one lives well, and this is now the case with me,—I pity you more than you imagine and am convinced that you are very wretched. But, dear Ralle [Pauline's nickname for Rahel], even with these contortions in your soul, you will not become calm—each gust of wind bends you low—and oppresses you. I considered you stronger, I admit it freely."[28]

Although this letter clearly contains a critical note, Pauline's admonitions

1. Rahel Levin Varnhagen.
Drawing by Wilhelm Hensel,
courtesy of the Leo Baeck
Institute, New York

2. Rahel and her brother
Marcus. Painting by Johann
Christoph Frisch, ca.1785,
courtesy of the Varnhagen
Collection (portrait no. 26),
Staatsbibliothek zu
Berlin-Preußischer Kulturbesitz

3. Rahel's father Levin
Marcus. Painting by Daniel
Chodowiecki, courtesy
of the Bildarchiv
Preußischer Kulturbesitz

4. Henriette Herz. Painting
by Anna Dorothea Therbusch,
courtesy of the Bildarchiv
Preußischer Kulturbesitz

5. Prince Louis Ferdinand.
Oil painting by Grassi, 1806,
courtesy of Matthes & Seitz
Verlag, Munich

6. Dorothea Mendelssohn-
Schlegel. Painting by Anton
Graff, ca.1800, courtesy of
Ullstein Bilderdienst.
© Ullstein

7. Wilhelm von Humboldt.
Drawing by P. E. Stroehling,
December 1814 in London,
courtesy of the Bildarchiv
Preußischer Kulturbesitz

8. Friedrich von Gentz.
Lithograph by Lieders, 1825,
courtesy of the Biblioteka
Jagiellonska, Cracow,
Poland

Carl Graf Finck von Finckenstein · Berlin 1796.

9. Karl Graf Finck von
Finckenstein. Pencil drawing,
probably by Johann Heinrich
Schröder, 1796, courtesy of the
Biblioteka Jagiellonska,
Cracow, Poland

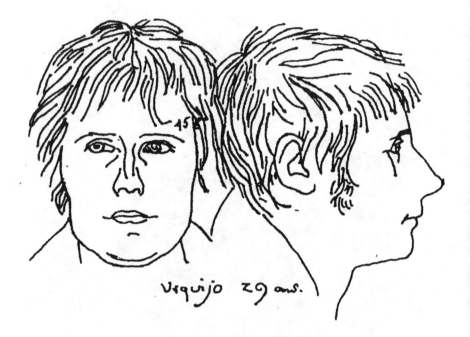

10. Raphael d'Urquijo.
Portrait after Gottfried
Schadow, "Polyclet or
on the dimensions of
men according to their
sex and age," 1834,
courtesy of Matthes &
Seitz Verlag, Munich

11. Karl August
Varnhagen von Ense.
Drawing by Wilhelm
Hensel, courtesy of the
Leo Baeck Institute,
New York

12. Alexander von der
Marwitz. Relief by
unknown artist, cour-
tesy of Matthes & Seitz
Verlag, Munich

13. Ludwig Robert.
Drawing by Wilhelm
Hensel, courtesy of the
Leo Baeck Institute,
New York

14. Regina Frohberg
(Rebecca Friedländer).
Contemporary painting, courtesy
of the Biblioteka Jagiellonska,
Cracow, Poland

15. Pauline Wiesel.
Contemporary painting,
artist unknown,
courtesy of AKG
London

16. Heinrich Heine.
Drawing by Wilhelm
Hensel, courtesy of the
Bildarchiv Preußischer
Kulturbesitz

im July 1809. gez. München ad viv

17. Bettine von Arnim.
Drawing by Ludwig
Emil Grimm, courtesy
of AKG London

are dictated primarily by a deep concern for her friend's unhappiness. She knew the trying circumstances Rahel found herself in during those years, both personal and social, and tried to entice her into leaving Berlin—efforts she continued over several years. At times she was quite blunt. In a letter dated 1811 she starts out with a declaration of love and regret that they must live apart. But then she cannot help but speak her mind: "listen, Ralle, If one really *Wants* Something seriously if one doesn't Easily permit the Thousand obstacles to interfere and Above all *ordinary* prejudice Then one can accomplish a whole lot—and you know how often I have—despite all your terrific intelligence—reproached you—for being insufficiently firm in your resolve for being still too attached to prejudice."[29] In a letter from Milan dated 1813 she again tried to persuade Rahel to resolve her untenable situation: "poor dear soul I cannot even say tear yourself from this whirlpool because it is a snail's life an ant's life Ralle. . . . you remain in a situation for years where I wouldn't stay for a month, I don't know who is stronger; you who endures it or I—who couldn't possibly endure it.[30]

Rahel in turn wished desperately to break free. She wrote to her other friends about letters from Pauline inviting her to join her in Switzerland or Paris and her firm resolve to carry out these plans. However, taking the decisive step seemed to present great difficulties for her, despite Pauline's continued coaxing. In the fall of 1810 Pauline wrote from Bern:

If we were together Dear Ralle How we would Experience this nature here. Ralle what plans do you have, are you still ill, don't you have a mind and possibility to come here, with me Ralle you cannot fare entirely badly, Remember our talks On the terrace of Charlottenburg. . . . Our projected inn . . . shall it no longer flourish, Again I spoke with someone who knows Christel Eigensatz[31] in Venice—She is still charming happy in her inn, shall we go to see her Rale, we would need little money there, the sea there is Beautiful. . . . Ralle where will you be this fall, the vintage is most lovely, if only you were here in the vineyards it is so pleasant now and the divine weather on top Everyone who has any sentiment is Invigorated by this weather Ralle Ralle our being apart is an outrage."[32]

At times Pauline's imagination seemed to know no bounds and her plans bordered on the fantastic. After her departure from Berlin, freedom became an end in itself. The very act of movement—rolling along in a carriage—signaled freedom to her. She took the tedious and often dangerous journeys by coach in stride. In contrast to Rahel's frail health, hers was unusually robust. Thus she wrote in 1815: "I travel easily, plainly of the knottiest health a woman could ever boast about—*never* was I ill in the time

I haven't seen you."[33] Rahel agreed, suggesting in turn: "You travel more easily; I need more money, more comfort. You come! ! ! !"[34]

For Pauline Wiesel freedom was always located outside respectable society: managing an inn, stealing oranges in Rome, appearing in Switzerland as *"beggars* . . . without begging, and in the evening dancing in the open air."[35] Passages in her letters reveal that there must have been times when she did in fact live among the outcasts. In 1816, for example, she wrote: "whoever has climbed as high as I [as the lover of Prince Louis Ferdinand] and again down *so* low as to live with *thieves* and murderers the whole winter on stolen beds, A hunchbacked shoemaker next to me who passed me the chamber pot every night and drank coffee with me in front of the bed—on credit—and with his credit—that person has experienced All, knows All."[36]

In contrast to Pauline's spirit of adventure, Rahel's inability to take action appears all the more trenchant: "*It's impossible.* Therefore I sit and watch my own life; so to speak. I am not living it: only quite inwardly."[37] However, Rahel was not deterred by fear and a lack of resolve alone. There were cogent reasons why she could not so easily follow in Pauline's path, and the letters give precise insight into her thinking:

You know, Pölle [Rahel's nickname for Pauline], I consider myself lacking in courage, and I have explained it to you thoroughly how nature proceeded with me. . . . However, that I have not long left my city and family, I failed to do not because I had less courage than you, and you did not do it, not *this*, because you *have* more courage than I. Outwardly—and perhaps halfway inwardly, too, my relations with my family are good. Our finances are joined and cannot, and could not, be divided and unraveled easily. My mother was ill for six months and died. Then I had to join forces with Moritz, so to speak. And a thousand affairs, orders, illness, and lack of money kept me here; also associations of sorts of which I had to await a yes or a no. I am not on bad terms with society, I still live in it. I am dissatisfied with it because I have neither social rank nor name, and also find no hearts which could substitute; but society is still seeking me out; and I it.[38]

Rahel the Jew, only recently escaped from the ghetto, was unwilling to turn her back on a society that was, even if tentatively and reluctantly, accepting her into its midst. Joining the rebellious Pauline would in effect have meant voluntarily excluding herself again. Although she was aware of society's faults and shortcomings, her social gatherings and her vast net of correspondences are proof of how much hope and energy she was willing to invest in it. Consequently, she wished for people like Pauline to rejoin: "With *you*, Pölle, I would love to live in society." Rahel, moreover, had a different notion of freedom. Her longing for "green things," for a natural innocent existence, always intensified during times of difficulties and was obviously indebted to the philosophy of J. J. Rousseau and other Romantics. As a Jew, however, she also knew that there could be no freedom for outcasts. In the eyes of society, Pauline was at times so compromised that she was close to being considered an outlaw. After her marriage to Karl August Varnhagen, Rahel became more mindful of social convention and expectations. She urged her friend to reintegrate herself up to a point by reconciling with her mother, in order that they could meet openly. "I would like to *get out*! [of society]. But one must be *free*! Do you understand! *Free*. You must be *free* to join, I must be free to *leave*."[39] Clearly, Rahel saw freedom not in opposition to society. Rather, she willingly accepted Rousseau's idea of the social contract—a mutual obligation between the individual and the group, even as she suffered under its strictures and constraints. For these reasons, she was unwilling to carry her rebelliousness as far as Pauline had, although she agreed with her in principle.

Agreement between the two women extended beyond social criticism and yearnings for freedom to include a rich variety of other topics. The letters contain reflections on men and women, literature,[40] theater and music, a great deal about Pauline's daughter, and, later, about Rahel's grandniece. Forever on the move, Pauline sent engaging and amusing letters about her adventures, while Rahel kept her friend informed about life in Berlin. They wrote to each other about the changing of the seasons, about technical advances, such as the newly paved streets in and around Berlin and improved or cheaper means of transportation, and about everyday matters, such as family feasts and other celebrations, fashion, or stories about servants. During the last years of the correspondence, as the spirit of reaction became all-pervasive, political themes intruded more directly: social abuses, famines, the cholera epidemic, and the aborted revolution of 1830. Throughout the correspondence the past, the era prior to 1806, is also evoked, not so much as an idealized time but as a time that had harbored the potential for human happiness and fulfillment. Pauline expressed it in her unique way: "*Where have those happy times gone when I was so unhappy!*"[41]

Unusual in these letters is the great tenderness expressed in them. Many contain not much more than assurances of enduring and never-changing love and friendship and hopes and plans for a reunion. Rahel once wrote: "My only Pauline: always and eternally! These words alone would suffice and be a letter for you."[42] The changes they underwent were external and did not affect their innermost convictions. Pauline, for example, wrote in

1815: "Dear, best Angel Ralle: you still love me, and I am still worth it, *if I was ever worth it*, for I have changed not at all, only the circumstances and surroundings. . . . I think and feel and see as truly as before."[43]

Their affection for each other is revealed in a beautiful and melancholy letter of Pauline's, written mostly in French, shortly after she had visited Rahel in Baden-Baden in 1826: "We take leave from each other, you to rejoin your friends, your relatives; I to find nothing but 'speechless witnesses.' I have come back sadder than I thought I could still be in this world. . . . How well, how kindly you wrote to me immediately. . . . I do know you, you have given me so many proofs of your love. . . . Just now I am still very sad over your departure; no matter . . . we have seen and spoken [to] each other!" And she concludes with the words: "Farewell, dear, Truthful friend of my sad Heart and my Suffering Soul, which nevertheless is conSoled a little since I have Seen you—laughing, Crying, eating, Sleeping—and always true—and always genuine, like Ralle on the Jägerbrücke."[44] Although Pauline experienced moments of sadness and resignation, she was free of self-pity or remorse. Karl August Varnhagen's contention, that Rahel was disappointed with Pauline after she visited her in Berlin in 1832, seems to have no basis. The two friends continued to correspond, and the very last letter Rahel wrote appears to have been addressed to Pauline. Pauline Wiesel died in 1848 in Saint-Germain en Laye near Paris, in her seventieth year.

Alexander von Marwitz

In certain respects, the remaining correspondence from this time (1806–15) can to a large extent be defined as educational projects in the manner of Rahel. Alexander von der Marwitz (1787–1814), Karl August Varnhagen (1785–1858), Clemens Brentano (1778–1842), and Friedrich de la Motte Fouqué (1777–1843) were young men who distinguished themselves not only by their considerable talents but also by their weaknesses. They belonged to a generation that suffered acutely under German backwardness and stagnation. The letters give insight into these difficulties, which, understandably, manifested themselves differently for the nobleman Marwitz, the bourgeois Varnhagen, or the well-to-do free-lance writers Brentano and Fouqué. In Rahel's letters they found understanding, empathy, and encouragement, as well as the emotional and intellectual range of an extraordinary woman's mind. Of the four correspondences, those with Marwitz and Varnhagen are the most substantial and shall be discussed in some detail, while those with Brentano and Fouqué are less encompassing and will therefore be referred to as the occasion arises.

Alexander von der Marwitz's symptomatic helplessness vis-à-vis life constitutes the essence of his correspondence with Rahel: "Oh, to find the unity in life where occupation and motivation become merged, where the inner world is activated by the outer and vice versa, this is infinitely difficult. The two domains grate and buffet within me, so that I often feel confused, almost always vacuous, bored, and insipid."[45] Marwitz, the sensitive, intelligent, and well-meaning young aristocrat, acutely conscious of the fact that his class had outlived its usefulness, immediately caught Rahel's interest. Valiantly, and ultimately unsuccessfully, he cast about for a way of life commensurate with the times, in the military and, tentatively, as a public servant. He wanted, as he put it, to prove to himself that he "possessed sufficient strength and inclination to animate the insignificant activities of a bourgeois life."[46] His capacity for self-reflection, for exalted moods, and his appreciation of nature and art mirrored Rahel's and endeared him to her. She encouraged his good qualities while ignoring the negative, notably, his diminished vitality coupled with his unwillingness to control an often violent temper. She had met him through Varnhagen in May of 1809 and remained devoted to him until his death in battle in 1814. The epistolary exchange comprises some fifty-eight letters (and notes) by Rahel and forty by Marwitz.

For Marwitz, as for so many others, Rahel's letters were of vital necessity. In 1811 he described the effect they had on him: "I am supposed to reassure you again and again with regard to your *volumes*, you write, dear Rahel. Hear then, how I receive them. I read them three to four times in a row, certain passages much more often, then I put them down with the sentiment of a miser who sees his treasure increased . . . and then I walk around my room for an hour and more and let the contents of your lines reverberate within me; in this mood I cannot answer. . . . This is the effect your letters have always had on me and always will."[47] His admiration and even love for her were genuine. He was quite convinced that she was "the greatest woman on earth."[48]

When Rahel and Marwitz began their correspondence, he was just twenty-two years old and, after a disappointing stint in the military, intent on expanding his knowledge of history, economics, and philosophy. Rahel encouraged these endeavours and helped him to apply himself in a more disciplined manner. Many of his letters contain a detailed account of his day and his reading. As usual, Rahel pretended ignorance, but a closer look reveals that frequently she was familiar with a work in question or was reading it along with him. Thus, she was an equal partner in this dialogue. Marwitz generally considered her opinions and insights superior to his.

The readings comprised primarily theoretical works, such as Adam Smith's *Inquiry into the Nature and Cause of the Wealth of Nations* (1776), Adam Müller's three-volume *Elemente der Staatskunst* (1810, Elements of statesmanship), Fichte's *Der geschlossene Handelsstaat* (1800, The closed commercial state), Honoré-Gabriel Mirabeau's *Lettres originales de Mirabeau, écrites du donjon de Vincennes, pendant les années 1777, 78, 79, et 80* (1792, Original letters of Mirabeau, written from the Donjon of Vincennes), and Friedrich Schlegel's *Course of Lectures on Modern History* (1811). Marwitz also studied matters that were of personal interest to him, such as the Hardenberg reforms of 1807–8 and the General Prussian Jurisdiction of 1794.

These inquiries into the seminal thoughts of the age carried different meanings for each correspondent. In Marwitz's case, they led to his passing an examination that would have ensured him a position and career in the Prussian administrative service had the war not cut short his life. On a personal level, the studies helped him achieve a world view commensurate with the times. He came to view the French Revolution as a historically necessary event and favored a constitutional form of government. Thus, he avoided succumbing to the reactionary views of his brother Ludwig, whose agitations against the Prussian reforms were so extreme that Chancellor Hardenberg had him arrested and jailed.[49] As a woman and a Jew, Rahel could of course never expect any practical gain or outward recognition from these readings. But they are an indication of the diligence and persistence with which a brilliant woman applied herself intellectually, as well as proof that she well deserved the esteem of gifted men.

Intellectual matters constituted not the only or even major topic of this correspondence. As noted earlier, Marwitz freely described his recurring ennui and feelings of disorientation and even disgust. Rahel, too, revealed her personal concerns, primarily her anguish over a life she increasingly came to see as a failure and her frustration over being rebuffed by the society she wanted to call her own. They communicated these moods and feelings to each other with a frankness that appears quite extraordinary from today's perspective. It was indeed a strange alliance between the young man from one of the most venerated noble families and the older Jewish woman with no tradition behind her. As Hannah Arendt perceptively observed, Rahel and Marwitz would never have come together "had it not been for the spiritual havoc the Enlightenment had wreaked upon this world."[50] It had made possible Rahel's entry into society and, to some extent, even into history, while calling into question Marwitz's place within it. As a result, feelings of alienation were common to both, although different in origin.

To both, the present and future offered itself as some form of bourgeois existence. In Rahel's case, of course, this was a step forward as well as an entirely logical and welcome development. For Marwitz, on the other hand, it meant giving up the nobleman's dreams of heroic achievement and worldly prominence, embracing instead the prospect of an inglorious position in a humdrum life.

Rahel deftly recognized and articulated for him the possibilities and limitations of the unfolding age as she understood them. In a long letter, written, for want of a properly prepared quill, with a piece of wood, she advised him: "You cannot escape your time."[51] Explaining that all are confined within their time, she defined "ours" as "that of an infinitely self-reflecting consciousness." This provided active, capable persons with few chances, especially if they also possessed human qualities—intelligence, imagination, and a strong but tender heart. The only heroism left to such doubly gifted individuals—and she counted Marwitz among these—in this "fragmented *new* world, where the Greeks, Romans, Barbarians, and Christians are finished, is the heroism of knowledge. Political heroes who must first destroy and conquer do not and must not have a great consciousness. . . . Battles alone can now remake the *whole* world." And she proposed a solution:

Huts, however, and quiet arrangements can be made; only, good people are too proud for this. Their deeds, their works must have a name; after Alexander, after Moses, after Christ, they are supposed to be named. There are more good people than ever; let them be good, let them live well; let them live close, as much as possible; and if this is considered a deed, then much is possible. . . . If one can save the world, his nation by dying: I urge him to, even if it were you. . . . Brooding about salvation and the times, ambitious experiments are the worst. To live, love, study, be diligent, marry, if possible, every small thing done well . . . this is living, too, and nobody forbids it. And from a large and ever larger association of well-meaning people nothing . . . should come? [It] should break up all barbarous institutions and absorb them. But this has no name and remains undone; or it happens unconsciously because it happens *perpetually*.

As Rahel saw it, history evolved not only in response to the deeds of what Hegel called world-historical figures but also and equally importantly as a result of the efforts of the multitudes in pursuit of their daily lives. Every individual, therefore, preferably in a vastly expanded free sociability, was obliged to contribute his or her share to a better society.

Following Rahel's advice, Marwitz pursued the "heroism of knowledge" for some time. Ultimately, however, he failed to commit himself to the new times. The aristocrat had little patience for the affairs of ordinary life, although he was hardly proud of it: "I cannot bear the touch of vulgarity; but (and this is the corrupt spot in me) I also cannot despise it where I ought to, and I cannot fend it off with prudence, but only with rage."[52] How deeply rooted in the past he was is indicated by his love for the family estate. Friedersdorf and its surroundings, which he described lovingly and in great detail to Rahel on several occasions, contained not only the history of his ancestors and their times, but also represented the "fixed point" for his own history.[53] Thus, when in 1813 heroism in the Wars of Liberation beckoned, he took the easier way out and joined.

As mentioned earlier, in addition to generously extended guidance and encouragement, Rahel's letters reveal a great deal about herself. To Marwitz she confided her anguish and frustrations over experienced slights and outright insults, conflicts with her family, and even difficulties in her relationship with Varnhagen. What motivated her? Was it just the need to communicate and to explain herself to one more person? Did she expect greater understanding and empathy from a Marwitz than from a Rebecca Friedländer? Or were these accounts and lamentations intentionally directed at the privileged and supposedly refined, to make them understand what it was like to be treated with disregard by people undistinguished by all else but class and to be excluded again and again by the very people who professed to be committed to the enlightened and humanistic ideas of the age?

In the wake of her disappointing experiences in love and society, every social situation appeared oppressive to Rahel; she seemed to find some respite only in nature, and her letters convey an increasing sense of alienation. Thus she related to Marwitz an experience on the elegant, tree-lined avenue, Unter den Linden, where the Berlin citizenry was fond of promenading:

Yesterday on Unter den Linden, I was swept by such a mood: strange, entirely strange, and shabby the linden, the street and houses appeared to me; people frightening; not one of them had a face, a physiognomy; the silliest, most superficial, most wooden, most distracted expression, silly, vain women; not coquettish, not inviting affection or drawing pleasure of any kind. The poverty of the city, where I can calculate what everyone has, consumes, wants or can do; the frightful, desolate unrelatedness [of people]. . . . I among them, *still* more unrelated, with a full empty heart, thwarted in attaining everything desirable, separated from the ultimate. In short, [it was] as if I stood before a temple of magic—for reality receded before my still soul . . . —a temple I can already *see* swaying; its collapse is certain and will strike me and everyone down. Not sure whether I was truly awake or dreaming I went on, telling myself, it is better that you go here. . . . But when behind whole families of ladies walked with us . . . and I as if among the dead . . . I resolved not to go there anymore.[54]

Marwitz responded with understanding: "I feel your walk Unter den Linden. Great, horrible, true."[55] Valiantly he tried to console her: "Must I remind you now of the noble, touching words which you wrote to me at the time of my great misery about the helplessness of every anxious soul? . . . How many half-consolations, and therefore utter vapidities, might I not say to you about the sublimity of your mind, the depth of your feelings, by virtue of which you annihilate your utterly *insubstantial* surroundings whenever you like, and enter into the splendors of true life. . . . May the God within you comfort you!" Another time she wrote to him:

My heart is *embers*; . . . I considered this only yesterday: it no longer loves on *its own account*; its soul only and spirit are alive; it is really dead. . . . See how sad I am! I weep, too: and never say most of what I feel. And yet I look at even this quite differently: and can regard it as a sort of happiness. I am so infinitely free within myself, as though I had no obligation to this earth. . . . I *still* feel as I did when I was fourteen years old. Then everything was for the others, for the grown-ups; that is the way I feel when I forget my horrible griefs, the fierce shame, and I really have no talent for dealing with these all the time, brooding upon them. . . . My nature was overflowing and proud, wild with joy when the earth received me.[56]

Again Marwitz responded with empathy and, especially, admiration: "Let Rahel's heart have sunk to embers; the human heart continues to beat in you, with a freer, loftier pulsation, turned away from all earthly things, and yet very close to them; the keen intelligence goes on thinking, taking in ever wider circles; from the green, fresh, living vale the tempest of fate has raised you up to the high mountains, where the view is infinite, man far but God near."[57] But this time Rahel responded with despair. She described how her needy heart absorbed proudly and with satisfaction everything he wrote in this letter until she reached the words that banished her from the green valley to the mountaintop. Reading this, her tears spilled over her face, into her lap and everywhere, for once again she felt herself excluded from human society. She did not quarrel with him, for she felt that he had spoken the truth:

That is unhappiness; if my friends are true, then they must say the dreadful words to me. Am I to be banished from the green, living, fresh vale and yet go on living? I!? who . . . *knows* the *God* to whom you refer me to only in Time, through the mind and the senses; and where there is nothing, I cannot think anything! He shows, he reveals himself to us in the earth, colors, forms, the heartbeat of joy and sorrow; he has *especially* to me opened up the consciousness of this knowledge; I worship the whole of nature as I know it. . . . I? am to be exiled without being dead? you have spoken, Friend. The best of friends can only name misfortune, not lessen [it] through consolation. You are right; name it; I shall do it, too; and again, because it is true, I will take it as it is and press it to my heart.[58]

Arendt takes this exchange as proof of Marwitz's breach of solidarity and of the "bankruptcy of [this] friendship."[59] It is true that Marwitz, like so many others, failed to live up to the kind of close and intense friendship that Rahel wished for. However, Rahel's answer contradicts Arendt's contention, for she accepted Marwitz's words as accurate and honest. Moreover, they continued to correspond with each other intimately for another year and a half. After Marwitz joined the war effort the letters became less frequent. But when he was wounded in 1813 he came to Prague, where Rahel had taken refuge, and put himself in her care. Marwitz's letter had such a devastating effect on Rahel because it pronounced what she admitted to no one but Pauline Wiesel—that she was both exceptional and an outsider. Pauline was the only friend who made common cause with Rahel, a step that Marwitz, by virtue of his youth and social station, could and would not take.

Even more revealing than the letters of this time are Rahel's dreams and dream sequences, the majority of which she noted down probably in the summer of 1812. Some she communicated directly to Marwitz; others she reworked and eventually included in her diary, specifically in diary D, entitled "The Dreams."[60] No other texts of Rahel's convey so starkly, even bluntly, albeit symbolically, what her letters intimate in so many variations, namely, how precarious and anomalous her place in society really was. All except one of the five "great dreams" concern her inferior status as a woman and a Jew. She was quite willing to share them with various people—Marwitz, Varnhagen, the Schleiermachers. It was obviously another form of self-presentation; only this time it wasn't she who spoke but rather the dream, and it carried its own kind of truth and objectivity. Not surprisingly, she considered the dreams highly significant, for she wrote them down with great care.

Rahel's first dream was one that recurred over a period of several years. She did not commit it to paper until she no longer dreamed it but then rendered the setting and happenings in great detail. In this dream, she always found herself in a splendid, inhabited palace, with a magnificent garden beginning right outside of the windows. . . . The rooms . . . were always illuminated, open, and filled with the movements of a large number of servants; I always saw a long vista of them opened before me, in the last of which was the actual assemblage of the most distinguished persons; however, I could not imagine a single one of these people, although I knew them all, belonged to them, and was supposed to join them. But this, in spite of the fact that the doors were open . . . I was never able to do. . . . whenever I was still six or eight rooms away from it, there appeared, in the room in which I was, an animal that I could not name, because its like did not exist in the world . . . half sheep, half goat.[61]

Rahel described this creature as her "acquaintance," a kind of pet that loved her *"tremendously"* and that she had to treat like a human being. It looked at her with more love than she ever remembered seeing in a human being's eye. The animal generally took Rahel by the hand, and they walked together through the rooms, although it kept her from joining the society, "tenderly, and as though it had an important reason." Rahel, in turn, responded to the animal in an erotic manner. She described its snout as "pinkish . . . like the purest, most delightful marble, the color of dawn — the paws likewise." It "wielded great power over" her; in fact, she did "not recall having felt during my whole waking life so powerful a stirring of the senses as the mere touching of hands which this animal gave me. But it was not this alone which defined my attachment; it was also an overflowing of the heart in sympathy; and that I alone knew that the animal could love and speak and had a human soul. But I was especially held by something secret, which consisted partly in that no one saw my animal or noticed it except myself, that it turned to no one else, that it seemed to be concealing a profound, highly significant secret." Only sometimes was she "startled by the thought: How can you give such caresses to an animal; after all, it is an animal!"

When the dream came back following a lengthy interval, the setting was the same, although this time there was "a kind of excitement" in the rooms. Rahel also did not see her animal, and it seemed to her that she had missed it for a long time already "without being especially concerned or troubled" about it. Because the commotion in the house disturbed her more "than the usual force," preventing her from reaching and entering the last room, she stepped out onto the terrace, where she suddenly saw her animal, "curled up, sleeping on its belly: it was quite black with bristly hair. My animal! My animal is back, I shout to the servants. . . . They pause in their activities, but do not come any closer. It is asleep, I say; and poke it with my toes in order to shake it up a bit: at that moment, however, it rolls over, falls apart, and lies flat, a mere skin; the rough side on the ground, dry and clean. 'It is a skin; so it was dead!' I exclaim. The dream vanishes; and never again have I dreamed of the black or the white animal." Rahel concluded her narration with a brief interpretation in which she identified the white animal as Finckenstein and the black one as Urquijo.

In this dream Finckenstein appears to have been truly loving and concerned for Rahel's well-being, notwithstanding his objections to her joining the society, while Urquijo didn't seem to have had much of an impact. In the end, although the white animal had exerted a strong if secret and somewhat forbidden fascination, both vanish without leaving any trace. The fact that they appear as animals, unnoticed by society, suggests that only Rahel recognized their individual worth, a recognition that permitted her to overlook their general lack of significance or mediocrity.

The first dream gives no hint of the emotional devastation either lover caused. This, however, was clearly not the case in the third dream, which is explicitly about Finckenstein. Here, Rahel found herself on top of the outermost rampart of a fort.

It was bright noon, and the weather on this day was characterized by those too bright shafts of sunlight which produce a kind of despair because there is nothing refreshing about them. . . . This weather affected me all the more because the whole region consisted of parched, grassless, sandstony earth which deteriorated into actual sand. . . . There was nothing to be seen on the accursed plain. . . . So I stood with my breast close to the edge of this old rampart . . . pressed by a whole mob behind me . . . . all dressed like Athenians. F[inckenstein][62] stood beside me, bareheaded, dressed like the rest, but in pink taffeta, without looking in the slightest degree ridiculous. I was to be thrown down from this rampart . . . deep down, among stones, chalky sand pits, rubble and broken-off fragments of the fortress. The mob was demanding it, and shouting to F[inckenstein], who was their king, to give his consent. He stood cruelly sullen, and looked down into the depths; the people shouted louder and more violently, insisting that he consent; pressed closer and closer to me; with their eyes on F[inckenstein], gripped my clothes; I tried to look into his eyes, and kept shouting: "You won't say yes, will you?" He stood unmoving, ashamed before the people for not yet having consented. The people were shouting too, and he—"Yes!" he said. They seized me, threw me over the wall; I fell from stone to stone, and as I was about to fall into the ultimate pit, I awoke.[63]

Rahel again concludes the narration of the dream with her own reflection: "And I suppose I knew in the depths of my soul what F[inckenstein]'s attitude toward me was. Moreover, the dream gave me the complete impression of the story's having been true; I was silent, but I had not been mistaken." Finckenstein sacrificed her, not out of malice but out of weakness. It was his indifference to her fate that gave society the license to cast her out in the dream and, in reality, to snub and insult her.

Another detailed but very different dream is concerned with Urquijo. Here the situation seems at first reversed: Rahel causes Urquijo's death. Rahel dreamed how, in front of family and acquaintances, after a grand dinner, Urquijo had vexed her so that she finally jumped up in anger, grabbed him, and asked, "why he did *not* think . . . that [she] wouldn't murder him on *the* spot." After Rahel shook Urquijo some more, he was seized by terrible convulsions (which Rahel knew him to have). Frightened, she tried to help him, while all the others, except for her brother Ludwig, turned away. After she had looked at him for a long time, Urquijo was suddenly seized by remorse. Bursting into fervent tears, he showered Rahel with kisses, which she returned, weeping as well. And, "through tears, sobs, embracings, and kisses," but so that all present could hear it, he said that she was right, that he loved her, that he was ashamed, that he had done wrong and was unhappy. His seizures nevertheless returned and everyone saw that he was dying. "And as a kind of murderess I stand amongst brothers and acquaintances, whose glances tell me everything. . . . Diplomats, the entire world is present, even Urquijo's girl. . . ." Still trying to help, Rahel lifted Urquijo, who has become frighteningly light, into her arms and carried him to a far corner of the house, to a room with a bed. Again, Ludwig was the only one to follow her. Urquijo "becomes worse and more rigid, and my fear is so great that I awaken." Now conscious, she told herself that she must forgive Urquijo everything. But she fell asleep again and the dream resumed: it was now morning and, after a deep sleep, she found out that Urquijo was dead. Rahel was unable to accept this news, however, because she was convinced that she would die with him. "And pacing up and down I constantly thought, so *this* is his and my end, *this* is how we die, this is our death, so you have killed him after all, for you are dying with him! This is how it had to be, it was like this *the whole time, too*, and everything resolved itself into a great contemplation of nature and an infinite feeling of love toward him. Then Feu [the servant] spoke of his death, I agonized, still pacing and suffering, as if I was to be excecuted . . . and thus I awoke from the agony."[64]

This was one of the dreams Rahel wrote down immediately and sent to Marwitz. Her comments are therefore addressed to him: "Now tell me: Do I still love him? Yes, the dream and my entire enchanted, supernatural heart tell me. . . . What do you think of my rage, my anger? Believe me, this is how I am. What on earth, however, keeps me from acting this way, I do not exactly know. . . . I don't find it disagreeable . . . that my heart still loves him, within it there is a different land, freedom, truth, unity, home!" It is perhaps this continuing love in a different reality that prevented Rahel from commenting on the other important meanings of the dream, Urquijo's behavior and the symbolic death of both lovers. Foremost is Urquijo's sudden and demonstrative show of remorse as a way of successfully manipulating the opinions of society in his favor. This results in Rahel's standing as his murderer although, according to the letters, it is very much the other way around. In the end, both must die, without, however, being united in death.

The fourth is perhaps the most disturbing of her dreams, for if the previous three were essentially about the cruelties and failures of the men she had loved, this one is explicitly about her suffering as a social outsider.

In this dream Rahel found herself on a wide bed, covered with a gray blanket. On the same bed, opposite her but also under the blanket though not touching her, lay Bettine Brentano (later, Bettine von Arnim) and to the right of her, the Mother of God, who seemed to have the face of "Schleiermacher's wife." Rahel could not see her very clearly because "over everything visible there seemed to lie an extremely fine, very thin gray cloud, which did not hinder seeing—only everything was seen as a kind of mist." The bed on which the three women lay was "close to the edge of the world," and they could look down on a "large strip of earth . . . on it microscopic human beings ran back and forth, performing the world's work." The core of the dream Rahel related as follows:

We were the maids of the earth and no longer living . . . our business on this bed . . . was to ask each other what we had suffered—a kind of confessional! "Do you know mortification?" we asked each other, for instance. And if we had ever felt this particular form of suffering in our lives, we said: "Yes that I know," with a loud cry of grief, and the particular form of suffering we were speaking of was rent from the heart, the pain multiplied a hundredfold: but then we were rid of it forever and felt wholly sound and light. The Mother of God was quiet all the while, only said Yes! to each question, and also wept. Bettina asked: "Do you know the suffering of love?" Whimpering and almost howling, I exclaimed, while the tears streamed and I held a handkerchief over my face, a long, long *Yes*! "Do you know mortification?" *Yes*! again yes. "Do you know enduring wrong, injustice?" *Yes*! "Do you know murdered youth?" *Yes*! I whimper again in a long-drawn-out tone, dissolving in tears. We were finished, our hearts pure, but mine was still filled with the heavy burden of earth; I sit up, look excitedly at the other women, and want my burden taken from me; in words spoken thickly, but with extreme distinctness, because I want to receive the answer Yes to this question too, I ask: "Do you know—disgrace?" Both shrink away from me as if in horror, though with still something like pity in their gesture; they glance rapidly at one another and try, in spite of the confined space, to move away from me. In a state bordering on madness I scream: "I have not *done* anything. It's nothing I have *done*. I have not *done* anything. I am innocent!" The women believe me; I see that by the rigid way they lie still, no longer unwillingly, but they no longer understand me. "Woe," I cry out, weeping as if my heart were threatening to melt away, "they do not understand me either. Never, then! *This* burden I must keep; I knew *that*. Forever! *Merciful* God! Woe!" Utterly beside myself, I hastened my awakening.[65]

Once again Rahel's comments support the truth of her dream: "And even awake the burden remains with me, for I really bear it, and if only there could possibly be persons who would wholly understand it, I too would be relieved." Disgrace, that is, Jewishness, was what separated her categorically from all others. More precisely, it separated her from those who made up the society she wanted to join, for she surely could find understanding among her Jewish friends. But they, who shared the same fate, could not relieve her of the burden of disgrace. That could be accomplished solely by those who had imposed it in the first place, in this case, Bettine Brentano and Schleiermacher's wife. As intelligent, sensitive, and enlightened women who shared many of Rahel's other sufferings, they possessed the potential to overcome their prejudice and extend understanding and empathy toward the woman who had been wronged. At least this was how the dream argued.

Except for the second dream, which will be discussed elsewhere, Rahel's dreams were invariably much more pessimistic and somber than her letters. In them anxieties surfaced with an acuteness and clarity that Rahel clearly fought against in her waking hours. The letters may be replete with lamentations, but in the dreams her situation appears desperate, even hopeless.

Karl August Varnhagen von Ense

The correspondence between Rahel and Karl August Varnhagen comprises six volumes, of which more than half date from the time before their marriage in 1814. By far the largest of all the epistolary exchanges, it started in 1808 and continued until shortly before Rahel's death in 1833.

Karl August Varnhagen was born in 1785 in Düsseldorf.[66] His father was a physician who passed his love for the French Revolution and liberal politics to the son. When Karl August was only a few years old, the father moved the family to Strasbourg in the hopes of securing an academic appointment at the famous university there. As revolutionary events engulfed the region, however, the university was closed and the father's chances ruined. The family was forced to separate. The mother and sister remained in Strasbourg, while Karl August accompanied the father in his search for a suitable position. Moving from town to town, he was left by himself for hours in various boarding houses and placed in schools only occasionally, depending mostly on his father's erratic instruction. Although the father believed in the egalitarian principles of the French Revolution, he did not permit his son to play with other children, fearing that contact with their local dialects might have a corrupting influence on his German. Thus, loneliness, a sense of isolation, and a lack of warmth became formative elements of Karl August's childhood. In 1796 the family was reunited in Hamburg, but three years later the father died unexpectedly, leaving the family without financial resources.

Karl August, fourteen years old, was placed in the Pepiniere, a Prussian cadet school in Berlin that trained medics for military service. He disliked the military discipline there but showed great interest in literature and philosophy classes. He left the school in 1803, without completing his course of study, to become a tutor with the family of a textile manufacturer named Cohen. This marked the beginning of his positive experiences with members of the urban Jewish middle class. The family treated the young man as one of their own, including him also in their social gatherings and other cultural activities. Only a year later, however, Cohen suffered bankruptcy and fled Berlin to escape his creditors. Varnhagen next found employment in Hamburg, this time with the affluent banking family, Hertz. Once again, the homeless young tutor experienced respect, generosity, and the comforts of family life. In 1806, with the financial support of the Hertz family, he left Hamburg and enrolled at the University of Halle. There he quickly became part of the inner circle of outstanding young academics, among them the philologist Friedrich August Wolf, the theologian Friedrich Schleiermacher, and the natural philosopher Henrik Steffens. His studies were interrupted when, during the second semester, the university was closed in the wake of the Prussian defeat by the Napoleonic armies.

After returning to Berlin, and still supported by the Hertz family, Varnhagen freely pursued his literary interests. Already as a pupil at the Pepiniere, he had edited, together with other young aspiring authors, an anthology, *Musenalmanach* (The almanach of the muses), referred to as the "Green Almanach" on account of its green binding. The first volume, published in

1803, featured contributions by Adelbert von Chamisso, a French émigré, still in the process of mastering the German poetic idiom, Friedrich de la Motte Fouqué, Ludwig Robert, Varnhagen's personal friend Wilhelm Neumann, and others. It continued to appear until 1807. Varnhagen's next project was an autobiographical novel, *Die Versuche und Hindernisse Karls* (1808, The trials and tribulations of Karl). It was to be a *Doppelroman*, with Varnhagen and Neumann each writing alternate chapters. In the end, in an effort to finish the work, Fouqué, Chamisso, and Bernardi were asked to contribute as well.

Varnhagen, who had met Rahel briefly in 1803 and again in 1807, was immediately and lastingly impressed by her personality and intelligence. In 1808 a closer acquaintance developed, which she discouraged at first. Although far less privileged, Varnhagen shared certain characteristics with Rahel's other young friend, Marwitz. He was similarly immature, impetuous, selfish, and talented, but without a goal. He was also said to be vain and somewhat petty. However, in contrast to Marwitz's always respectful behavior, Varnhagen's approach to Rahel was a passionate enthusiasm that puzzled and offended her at first. In time she recognized his good qualities and therefore set out on yet another educational project, guided by her unflinching trust in a gifted individual's potential for self-improvement or perfectibility. Only this time, she had found a pupil who was eminently willing and eager to learn from and be guided by her.

The correspondence of the first six years tells the story of this educational and maturation process as well as their unusual love. In Rahel the love grew gradually and never reached the heights of passion she had experienced with her first two lovers, Urquijo especially. Ultimately, however, it was a good and lasting love, one founded on mutual respect and trust. Rahel recognized that here was finally a man who both loved and appreciated her, who admired her deeply but guarded against placing her on a pedestal far above the rest of humanity, as Marwitz and so many others habitually did. He desired her, understood her, and wanted to live with her. In 1813 she described the relationship to Clemens Brentano, with whom she carried on a brief but intense correspondence, a correspondence that was doomed to failure for precisely the reasons that the relationship with Varnhagen succeeded: "There is only one man in the whole world who understands me: that I should be an individual. He does not want to use mere particulars of me . . . he loves me as I was created by nature and impeded by fate; he understands this fate; he wants to leave, grant, brighten the rest of this life for me, bear it toward Heaven; he wants to be everything to me, share all . . .

in exchange for the happiness to be my friend. This is the person whom people call my bridegroom."[67] Self-mockingly, the middle-aged woman then poses the question: "But how can I get into this silly condition of a bride?" only to become serious again: "I do not recognize as free and beautiful any relationship with another person which limits me, where I would have to tell lies, or which would want to deny the needs and possibilities of my nature."

How very much she appreciated Varnhagen's devotion and understanding is revealed in a letter accompanying her testament (written in 1816 during a prolonged illness from which she did not expect to recover but not found by Varnhagen until after her death). Calling him "my earthly angel," she expressed her deep gratitude: "As much as it was *possible*, possible for your temperament to understand one like mine, you did understand it; through a magnificent ingenious acceptance: with an insight which I cannot *comprehend* as it does not derive from any similarity of temperament."[68] Acceptance, or recognition, was one principle guiding the relationship between Rahel and Karl August. The other two were friendship and freedom. These three concepts can be traced like a golden thread throughout their epistolary exchange.

And yet, the relationship was unequal. Although Rahel often called him her "dear friend" or simply "Varnhagen," other forms of address are striking: "my dear child," "son," the diminutive forms "Varnhägken," "Gustchen," and even the feminine form "Guste." He, on the other hand, almost always addressed her as "my precious," "dear," or "beloved Rahel." That gender roles were reversed is indicated not only in the forms of address, but even more clearly in the use of metaphors. Rahel compared herself to a tree, ready to withstand the cold of winter, while Varnhagen was a "flower and free" or a "bird sitting securely on its branch." This lovely ideal, however, was immediately confronted by German social and political reality, patriarchal tradition, and the war. Consequently, the metaphors had to be revised. More accurate than the image of Rahel as a tall tree was that of the tree that had been uprooted and thrust back into the earth by its crown.[69] It dramatically and precisely conveyed the effects of her tenuous assimilation. Similarly, Varnhagen, even at the end of the war, was no longer a bird or flower, but rather "the plaything of foreign caprice."[70] Not surprisingly, these exterior constraints, long periods of separation, and constant insecurity led to periodic conflicts between them.

Some of the difficulties were of a personal nature. Varnhagen had yet to sever his ties with another young woman in Hamburg, a step he did not take until the spring of 1809. In addition, there were his desperate financial situation and his indecisiveness with regard to a career. For, although he went to Tübingen in the fall of 1808 to continue his medical studies, he was unable to muster real enthusiam for this occupation. At the same time, he realized that in spite of his love for literature, he was not sufficiently talented to justify taking up writing as a vocation. Only after the war did he find his special niche as a journalist and chronicler. Other possibilities that would make use of his abilities and interests were hard to come by. Circumstances were still such that, without title and wealth, it was almost impossible to succeed in a reasonably meaningful occupation. As Varnhagen bitterly remarked on several occasions, the world in its present state had no use for what he could offer it.[71] Only two choices were open to him. He could either find employment as a private tutor, or he could seek his fortune in the military. Thus, the war against Napoleon offered the bourgeois Varnhagen a way out as it did to the aristocrat Marwitz and, several years earlier, Prince Louis Ferdinand. The war promised adventure as well as the possibility of a later diplomatic career in recognition of services rendered.

In the summer of 1809 Varnhagen joined the Austrian army and was assigned to the regiment of Count Bentheim. Having spent his last money on a uniform and equipment, he arrived just in time for the Battle of Wagram, where he was seriously wounded and taken prisoner by the French. Held in French-occupied Vienna, he became somewhat of a celebrity as a fervent patriot because he continued to wear his Austrian uniform. In reality, he lacked the funds to buy civilian clothes. He was eventually exchanged for French prisoners and thus regained his freedom. He continued to be in the direst financial straits, despite having become Bentheim's private secretary and confidant. The count's affairs were in terrible disarray, and Varnhagen was sent periodically to Paris to entreat the elder Bentheim for money. A letter to Rahel dated 1 November 1810 reveals just how distressed Varnhagen was over his adversity. It was the only time he described these difficulties to her. Although he was deeply embarrassed, he felt compelled to write in some detail in order to defend himself against her reproaches. In the letter he admitted that on the surface it looked as if he was leading a life of ease and luxury; he traveled in elegant coaches, owned a few good sets of clothes (the bill for which the count most probably had not paid), and ate at the best tables. But in reality it was quite different. He was actually barely able to pay his lad, whom he didn't want to starve, or afford light and paper for writing a few letters; he ate with the count only once a day, for the rest he lived off bread and beer; he had been able to pay his tailor only recently, although the bill was from the previous year. Without prospects, he was therefore seriously considering joining the Turkish war, if only to find some means of surviving.[72] At times Varnhagen was even given to thoughts of suicide, although he admitted to these only after having refuted them.[73]

Rahel was not faring well either. Very unusual for her, she too mentioned suicide during these years. "If I shot myself, people would be surprised, as they were about Kleist," she wrote to Varnhagen.[74] Although her material circumstances were more secure, she too was forced to live on a reduced budget. This exacerbated her isolation and outsider status and also constrained her innermost needs for sociability and the enjoyment of nature. Like Varnhagen, she had to balance the demands for representation with her diminished resources. And although she would have willingly given up the elegant world because she felt that "without a certain affluence, without youth, cheerfulness, hope, title," one didn't belong or fit, family and friends continued to make claims on her. "If I was left alone and undisturbed I would accept that which I miss . . . and if I was permitted to say that I was poor . . . but the strain of performing and bothersome lying take their course, and I am not even allowed to lead the noble, quiet life itself."[75] Even in the summer, she was relegated to her "dusty" Berlin, and her status as a single woman without a task weighed heavily on her.

Small wonder that Varnhagen's life appeared enticing to her. In her view, he was free to indulge in adventure and travel, to consort with the elegant in Paris, and dine with Prince Metternich and other notables, all the while consoling her with love letters in which he promised to marry her "by the by." She saw her remaining youth pass, her fragile health vanish, and felt that this drawn out affair delivered her up to ridicule. And finally, there was the ever-present fear that this love too would not succeed. In 1808 she could still express her fears poetically: "Oh, if I could treat the future as it deserves to be treated, as if it did not exist at all!"[76] Over the course of the years her tone became shriller. If Varnhagen insisted that he couldn't make any plans for the two of them—"what kind of a plan is this which must include in its combinations Napoleon and the entire politics?"[77] —she admitted that she had lost the "grace . . . could no longer suffer, and be gracefully silent."[78]

The intensity with which the two lovers aired their conflicts was of course a result of the strains and constraints under which both lived. At the same time, the deliberations are testimony to the trust they had in each other, permitting them to write with complete candor. This trust is shown not only by their willingness to tell everything but also by their readiness to understand one another's situation and viewpoint. No topic was too insignificant or intimate; they wrote to each other of their strengths and weaknesses, their little successes and their repeated failures and disappointments, their moments of delight and enjoyment, their fears and insights, in short, the whole range of their feelings and opinions. These letters then, besides the manifold conflicts, also express the truly positive and unique aspects of their relationship.

Foremost among these is a very new understanding of gender equality. Rahel's strong personality and intelligence complemented Varnhagen's pliant disposition and open-mindedness; her original thinking rounded out his factual knowledge. In the course of these difficult years, the bond between them grew stronger as much because of their mutual respect and common interests, goals, and hopes as their longing to live together in harmony and love. "You have taught me to live in an atmosphere of love. . . . I know you completely and love you and count on you and your progress in every sense."[79] This is how she talked to him when circumstances permitted. And he, in response to yet another separation, would write: "What are you doing just now? you are not forgetting . . . your . . . grieving friend a little, are you? Oh no, I don't believe it, my Rahel! You are well disposed toward me, and I am precious to you. Your loving words ring forever in my breast. . . . Oh my Rahel, you are everything to me! the fulfillment of all of my life's desires! If only I was old, so that this idea that I should yet achieve and do something in this world wouldn't exist, my innermost destiny is after all only to be with you."[80]

In the spring of 1813, with the French troops appearing to be in retreat in Russia, Prussia seized the chance and declared war on Napoleon. Varnhagen immediately joined as captain under General Tettenborn, who was in the Russian service. The two men had become acquainted in Paris. At the same time, Marwitz became an officer in Field Marshall Blücher's army, another wing of the allied forces. Rahel, feeling unsafe in Berlin, fled via Breslau to Prague, where she remained until the end of the war. She found refuge at the home of the actress Auguste Brede, who was at that time the lover of Count Bentheim, Varnhagen's former commander.

Since Prague had become the center of the anti-Napoleonic forces, it attracted a flurry of diplomats, intellectuals, and artists. As a result, Rahel met many of her former acquaintances there: Friedrich Gentz, Wilhelm von Humboldt, Clemens Brentano, Ludwig Tieck, and others. She also made new acquaintances, including that of the young composer Carl Maria von Weber, who lived in the same house and whom she could hear playing music. Surrounded in Prague by a circle of interesting people, Rahel could surely have resumed her role as a hostess. Instead, her energies were pointed in quite a different direction. After the battle of Kulm, on 30 August 1813, the sick, the wounded, and the displaced began pouring into the city. The military hospitals were entirely incapable of meeting the needs of the soldiers. Bereft of shelter, care, and sustenance, the wounded lay unattended in the streets. As Rahel wrote to Varnhagen: "The government was not prepared for *so* many, one would have to believe they were prepared for none!"[81]

Seeing these terrible conditions, Rahel began to organize a rescue operation. She solicited money from her well-to-do friends and acquaintances who, in turn, appealed to their friends for contributions. Karoline von Humboldt, for example, sent more than a thousand *Gulden*, Bartholdy sent three hundred, and Lea Mendelssohn sent over a hundred. Rahel used the money to buy blankets, bandages, and medicine as well as clothes and food. She enlisted up to 150 women throughout the city to cook and distribute meals to the soldiers. She visited the wounded on a daily basis—friend and foe alike—notified their families, transmitted news about missed ones, and lent them money. In other words, Rahel, with the help of other women, accomplished what the government had neglected to do.

Among her papers is a notebook in which she painstakingly kept account of all the expenses and donations during these months, while her letters relate her many-sided activities. On 12 October, for example, she wrote to Varnhagen: "I am in touch with our office of commissioner and our staff-surgeon; I have a great number of *charpie*, bandages, rags, socks, shirts; I am having meals cooked in several quarters of the city; I personally see some thirty, fourty riflemen and soldiers a day; I discuss and check on everything, and make the *most* of the sum entrusted to me! . . . The correspondence. . . . The accounts, addresses, receipts, errands, consultations: in short, my undertaking is ramifying into a large enterprise."[82] In fact, the operation ran so well that in time even the authorities turned to her.

Rahel considered the opportunity to do good in the midst of widespread suffering and destruction a godsend: "I am ashamed that God sends me the chance to be able to help!" she wrote to Varnhagen, "and if I am ashamed that you are all battling each other, I console myself in turn . . . that I am active in helping and healing."[83] Rahel, who was generally timid and rather fainthearted and for this reason once ironically described herself as "the antipode of Jeanne d'Arc, the most fearful one," had taken on a practical and public project of great responsiblity that she accomplished most effectively. She showed herself to be admirably resourceful and enterprising, as well as courageous. Her health eventually broke down, but only after she had fulfilled her duty. For weeks afterward, she suffered from rheumatic palsy, which confined her to bed and inactivity. The opportunity, however, to be socially useful prompted her to think of other possibilities for women, an idea which she communicated to Varnhagen: "In my heart I carry a kind of plan, to call upon all European women that they will never participate in war and will all help those who suffer: then we could be *calm*, from *one* side at least, I mean, us women."[84] Her thoughts remain understandably vague since she hardly saw an opportunity for their practical implementation. But the idea that women should have a profession remained constant in her mind. In the nineties, she envisioned women in business, prompted, no doubt, by her family's background in commerce and banking; later, she considered women especially suited for overseeing orphanages or children's homes; and now, in light of her recent experiences, she saw possibilities for them in institutions of public welfare.

For Rahel, the significance of the rescue operation went beyond its humanitarian aspects and the personal satisfaction she derived from it. Being useful and needed strengthened her sense of national identity in a way that her rather rarefied sociable activities never could. As early as 1808 she had expressed this wish for inclusion to Varnhagen: "Just God, how easy and natural it is to love one's fatherland, if only it loves you back a little! You do it even without counterlove."[85] Her participation in the war effort provided her with an opportunity to demonstrate her loyalty and patriotism.

Besides the rescue operation, the political upheavals, the war, and the prospects for peace, Rahel's epistomological dialogue with Varnhagen reflects a great many other themes. The letters trace Varnhagen's beginnings as a publicist and writer of contemporary history. They also trace their intense love of literature and the writings of Goethe especially. In 1812 Rahel appeared in print for the first time—anonymously, as was to be the case throughout her life. It was Varnhagen's idea to publish the exchanges about Goethe's works contained in their letters in the renowned journal *Morgenblatt für gebildete Stände* (Morning paper for the educated classes). Under the title "Über Goethe: Bruchstücke aus Briefen" (On Goethe: Excerpts from letters), the fragments appeared in four consecutive issues. Rahel was represented by the initial G and Varnhagen with E. Goethe, whose permission had been secured beforehand, praised the publication and especially the opinions expressed by G.[86] The author, Caroline von Wolzogen, who knew Goethe well, provided a more personal account. She informed Rahel that Goethe was infinitely pleased by the publication, that he needed such expressions of appreciation since he was so often misunderstood.[87] Although the excerpts appeared anonymously, it was not difficult to trace their origins. Goethe, however, retained his aloofness and Rahel her anonymity. In contrast to Bettine von Arnim, Rahel remained discreet. She met Goethe only four times in her life, in Carlsbad in 1794, in Frankfort on the Main in 1815, and in Weimar in 1825 and 1829.

Nonetheless, as the discussion of Rahel's correspondence with David Veit showed, Goethe's works represented a pivotal experience in her life. She read them with biblical devotion, intuitively grasping the meaning of his prose and poetry for her own life and aspirations as a woman and a Jew. The letters and diaries of the very young Rahel already revealed her keen insights, then still tinged with youthful enthusiasm. Over ten years later her pronouncements revealed greater maturity while her admiration had deepened. Goethe, as she confided to Varnhagen, "accompanied" her and "stood by" her. He was her "friend," the "most artistic German," and "great historian." At the same time, she stressed as she had done before that she was equal to him: "I shared his wealth, he was always my most unique, most certain friend, my guarantor . . . of whom I knew the kinds of hell he was acquainted with!—in short, with him I came of age, and after a thousand separations I always found him again, he never failed me; and I, because I am no poet, shall never express what he meant to me!"[88] The reader will recall that her favorite works were those of the Classical period—*Iphigenia*, *Hermann and Dorothea*, *Faust*, and especially *Torquato Tasso* and the *Wilhelm Meister* novels. In the latter three works she also found her notion of what constitutes a tragic fate confirmed.

In Tasso's, the Renaissance poet's, predicament, she recognized her own. Goethe depicted in this drama the fate of the highly sensitive, exceptional, and artistic individual condemned to live in a prosaic world, inimical to his innermost needs. "Completely against his nature, [Tasso] must in the end rely on the one who appears the most abominable to him; defeated in the battle over his heart's happiness he must let it go; and finally, in order to seize that which is reasonable, he must contort his soul in the most unnatural way; he must expend his heart in harsh foreign regions, a heart born to strive toward his self-chosen heavens. Such death (Todschlag) means eternal suffering: it cannot be fought, changed, it remains eternally tragic."[89] The life of Torquato Tasso (1544–95) had fascinated Goethe since childhood, when he immersed himself in the poet's biography. Later, rendered wiser by his own experiences at the court of Weimar and his love for Charlotte von Stein, he imbued the figure's plight with the depth and passion that so captivated Rahel. Goethe himself pointed out the autobiographical element by characterizing the drama as the symbolic portrayal of the "disproportion between talent and life." Tasso, the poet and genius, must bow to reality. Too unwordly, he cannot prevail against his opponent and enemy, Antonio, politician and man of experience. He also proves unworthy of the loving empathy offered by Princess Leonore. Rahel's above-quoted words concerning Tasso's tragedy are but variations of ones she uttered about herself. She too, the brilliant woman, the perpetually offended Jew, the progressive-minded German, could only break forth with a "contortion," as a "paradox," as a "truth which can as yet find no place to present itself."[90]

From her readings of *Tasso* and other works, notably Diderot's *Jacques le Fataliste*, and in close association with her personal experiences, Rahel developed her notion of what constitutes a truly tragic fate. It placed her somewhere between Aristotle's "objective" and Shakespeare's "subjective" tragedy, particularly as she emphasized the psychological effects of tragedy upon the individual concerned. It also situated her between Enlightenment optimism and the later Romantic and even post-Romantic acknowledgment of the tragic side of human existence. She defined the concept to Varnhagen as follows: "Tragic is that which we absolutely cannot comprehend, to which we must submit; tragic is that which no cleverness, no wisdom can either destroy or avoid; where our innermost nature drives, pulls, coaxes, inevitably leads and holds us; when this destroys us, and we are faced with the question: Why? why me, why am *I* made for this? and all our intelligence and strength merely serve to grasp, to feel the destruction or to let us be detracted from it."[91]

In contrast to the Greek tragic characters, who meet their fate and grow beyond, thereby reaffirming the contested values even as they are being destroyed, Rahel's tragic individual is able only to submit and to go on living. In her scheme, there is no contest of values in the larger sense. The tragic fate happens to an individual whose innermost needs are being denied and whose sufferings are not perceived to have universal meaning. And, unlike the Shakespearean tragic heroes whose undoing is occasioned by their own character or temperament, Rahel's tragic figures are neither guilty nor self-destructive in that sense. Something within them draws them to their fate, but the forces of doom lie outside them and beyond their control. Furthermore, tragedy, in Rahel's view, happened not only as a paradigm or symbolic representation of our human predicament in myth or on the stage. It was real and could strike anyone capable of feeling and suffering deeply and therefore tragically. Tragedy, for her, arose from the irreconcilable conflict between an individual's will and the existing world. The expression and manifestation of this will, however, constituted a precondition of the individual's existence. Many passages in her letters, notably the outcries against her fate as a woman and Jew with their poignant image of being condemned to "immobility," express this: "my life is a slow bleeding to death. By keeping still I can delay it. Every movement in an attempt to staunch it—new death; and immobility is possible for me only in death itself."[92] Rahel's deep empathy with the figure of Tasso suggests that she experienced her own fate as ultimately tragic because she saw herself as an individual whose unique talents were thwarted by a retrograde world. And finally, the tragic fate, for Rahel, did not entail death and manifest destruction. The devastation was spiritual and emotional and therefore invisible. Outwardly, she remained almost unchanged, agreeable, open to joking and delight as well as suffering, but inside she was seized by a sadness that would never go away or, as she expressed to Brinckmann, "only there is nothing that can upset me completely, for I am *prostrate*."[93] For Rahel, as for Goethe's Tasso, the truly tragic entailed the continuation of life in its outer form.

Earlier, it was pointed out that Rahel's reading of Goethe's masterpiece, the Bildungsroman *Wilhelm Meister's Apprenticeship*, did not concentrate on its primary idea of *Bildung* (self-improvement and education) because she had long made that concept the guiding force of her life. Instead, she esteemed the novel for its social criticism, namely, as a reflection of the times and the portrayal of what even then was called the German *misère*. The term served to characterize conditions in a fragmented land and a society ineffectually struggling between its feudal remnants and capitalist beginnings. In her words, the novel was a "plant, grown around the nucleus of a text which occurs in the book and goes like this: 'Oh, how strange it is that man is denied not only so much that is impossible but also much that is possible!'. . . . And then the other thing, that people are deprived of every strip of land, river and everything. With one magic stroke, Goethe portrayed through this book the whole prose of our infamous, little lives, and he presented it decently enough . . . to the theater, to art, and also to swindel he had to refer the citizen who felt his misery and did not want to kill himself like Werther. . . ."[94] Her comments refer to two interrelated points. One concerned Wilhelm Meister's original desire to promote man's good, noble, and great qualities via the stage. This was an idea that had dominated the German theater since the early Enlightenment. The stage, furthermore, served as a forum for the dissemination of new social ideas in the German lands, where an adequate public sphere in the form of newspapers, political debates, and other public venues was missing. In Goethe's initial version, entitled *Wilhelm Meisters theatralische Sendung* (*Wilhelm Meister's Theatrical*

Calling), the protagonist's quest centered on realizing his ideals for a better society on the stage. In the later and final version, the theater represents only one episode at the beginning of the work. In the end, Wilhelm Meister's attention is turned to reality, that is, to a socially useful life, wherein he resolves to become a surgeon.

The other point addresses the limitations even gifted individuals have to come to terms with owing to Germany's social and political backwardness. Rahel realized early on that no amount of *Bildung* would overcome the lack of progressive social institutions. Retrograde outer circumstances impeded not only her own modest aspirations but also those of talented and even privileged men like Varnhagen and Alexander von der Marwitz. It was this aspect of the novel that caught her attention. In spite of Goethe's social and political conservatism, his imaginative works, with their underlying conception of man as a free and educated individual, nonetheless revealed the inadequacies and dissolution of the old forms of life and pointed to the necessity of fresh ones.

Tasso and the *Wilhelm Meister* novels are related in that both works concerned themselves with the strictures a stagnant society imposes on creative individuals. For this reason, they held a special appeal for Rahel.

Rahel's youthful correspondence with David Veit showed the intense interest with which she responded to Goethe's female characters as well as his portrayals of the affairs of the heart. In her letters to Varnhagen it is the mature woman who finds solace and insight from the poet's work. Her reflections about *Wilhelm Meisters Lehrjahre* close with the words: "Then there remains the question of love; and beyond that the most concise observation . . . people don't come together; prejudice, once they have met, separates them . . . in the meantime, however, people do move about, and this is what Goethe shows us in his book as in a mirror."[95] She ascribed to Goethe's wisdom and sense of realism the fact that he let those female characters perish for whom love encompassed the entire life. "Marianne, Aurelie, and Mignon, who love, could not live: no institution exists for them yet."[96] Not that she disapproved of great passion; she herself had been only too willing to follow her heart, for fulfillment and suffering in love meant the affirmation of one's individuality. But experience had taught her that such relationships, unless sanctioned by society, were doomed.

Rahel's appreciation of the realist in Goethe at the same time elucidates her position vis-à-vis representatives of the Romantic movement. She was personally acquainted with most of them, including Ludwig Tieck, Friedrich Schleiermacher, Johann Gottlieb Fichte, Friedrich de la Motte Fouqué,

Achim von Arnim, Heinrich von Kleist, the brothers Friedrich and August Wilhelm Schlegel, Clemens Brentano, and his sister, Bettine von Arnim. She felt great affection for the latter two especially, in spite of their periodic anti-Jewish invectives. She was born into this generation and shared with it not only the claims to personal freedom and individuality but also much of the malaise of the times, the sense of not fitting in. In her letters to the Romantics, however, fundamental differences emerge. Again and again she refers them to reality, to the actual present, and to their fellow men in an effort to curb their flights of fancy, their otherworldliness, and their backward-looking tendencies. In her case, the characteristic romantic inner strife or *Zerrissenheit* was constituted differently. Rather than having its source in an often vague existential malaise, it derived primarily from her status as a social outsider.[97] The growing estrangement between her and the Romantics, so painful to Rahel, was thus caused as much by deeply diverging attitudes toward life and society as by the Romantics' ideological reorientation at the beginning of the nineteenth century. The latter included their embrace of Catholicism, Germanic patriotism and chauvinism, and the glorification of the Middle Ages. Rahel remained irrevocably convinced of the dialectic between the individual or particular and the general. In her view, Goethe was a master at portraying this interaction in all its complexity. This explains her preference for his mature works, in which he succeeded in leading his characters to a state of harmony through the realization of humanistic and enlightened ideals, while intimately connecting them to reality.

Rahel's deep agreement with Goethe in regard to life, art, history, and society led her, at various times, to equate herself with the poet and other creative minds. As early as 1805, in a letter to her friend David Veit, she proclaimed: "I am as unique as the greatest manifestation of this earth. The greatest artist, philosopher, poet is not above me. We are of the same element, the same rank, and we belong together. And he who wants to exclude one, is only excluding himself. I, however, was assigned *life*; and I remained as a germ until my century, and I am *totally* buried from outside, therefore I say it myself."[98] This is indeed a surprisingly daring statement, deemed presumptuous by many ever since it was published. And yet, a closer examination reveals it to be once again quite accurate. Like her contemporary, Friedrich Schleiermacher, Rahel is here considering sociability as a creative activity on a par with the other arts, such as literature, music, painting, dance, acting, and so on. Moreover, although Rahel equated herself with the greatest, she was far from competing with them directly.

She did not aspire to produce great written works, rather her expertise was one which no one had yet laid claim to—life or, more precisely, sociable life. Rahel's self-praise is therefore more accurately a self-definition from a historical perspective. She alone knew what talents lay buried within her but could not come to fruition as no "institution" existed for them. And she alone recognized the radical possibilities lying dormant in the art of sociability.

The second of Rahel's five remarkable dreams, only recently come to light, confirms her above self-definition.[99] It represents her most comprehensive attempt at an aesthetic self-definition, for in the dream, art and life come face to face. In contrast to the other four, where Rahel is an outsider, even an outcast, due to her status as a woman and a Jew, in this dream she appears privileged and ultimately in control. The very fact that she dreamed this dream seemed a privilege to her.

In the dream, Rahel finds herself in a large Gothic hall, in which "all the works of art of all time" were collected, as well as the sculptures, busts, and portraits of all the artists. The artists themselves were around her, talking and judging their works: "a kind of last judgment of art!" She describes the scene in great detail:

I saw men of every . . . age, from about 17 years on; . . . facial expressions [and color] from all nations which art, the power of imagination, and reality had ever shown me; whole worlds of the imagination streamed from my brain which I never thought were contained therein. All the national dress which I ever saw in such books where they are collected, in the theaters, or in the world, were there in actuality. Men with and without beards; with long ones and moustaches, with moustaches without long beards; and again the other way around. Men with helmets, without helmets, with curly hair; with caps, and turbans of every kind; with coats, with jackets, with tight, with very flowing clothes. . . . The most beautiful little boots, sandals, and strange shoes they wore . . . they often also went barefoot. . . . The sculptors, however, had bare arms, as the women now have; that's how you recognized them. Many of the men carried their tools in their hands. The noise was almost supernatural, because they all spoke and judged their works. The crowd prevented them and me from coming close to the works of art, and most remained quite far. For me, however, the artists were the works of art, and I was busy observing them with infinite care, and my dream lasted a very long time.

The room too receives a great deal of attention. It is a great festive hall that resembled a church, with a mysterious source of light: "But I also had to look at the hall a lot, and I could not understand the light, it was very friendly in its decoration, above, with its pointed arches; and the many colors of the many people and pictures, the colors of the room even above, the very light yellowish-reddish light, all of this seemed to produce a bustle before the eyes . . . but the impression remained large and joyful." At one point Rahel is carried and dragged

between coats, clothes, backs, and arms into a smaller room, into which everyone was converging and shouting: "The ideal! the ideal!" Then all of a sudden, the artists respectfully drew back. "The ideal," many say quietly, hissing softly; and amazement palpitates through the room where we are: I, however, see in the middle a young man of about 20 years, in ordinary clothes, without a hat, . . . holding his hands in front of him, forcefully casting down his eyes, who is fairly pretty, has red cheeks and, although he seems to be embarrassed, is trying to suppress his laughter. The others do not see this; but I call, it is a person, he lives; he cannot refrain from laughing: upon which the artists all again call: the ideal! It is the ideal! I go closer, try to look this man in the eyes, which he keeps covered, but he smiles more; I put my hand on his shoulder and say, I see that you are alive, you can't refrain from laughing; whereupon he raises his head, puts his arms around me, and we both begin to waltz in the happiest way. With great pleasure and quite without inhibition. Happily; the artists watch a little astonished, they step back . . . and my dream as well, for here it ended.

Even in the freedom of her dream, Rahel's ideal consisted of a vision oriented toward life, joy, and harmonious human interaction rather than an objectified, autonomous work of art. She did not negate the ideal but brought it in even closer proximity to nature than, for example, her realist Goethe, by refusing to relegate it to a separate category removed from every-day life. Thus, life and art appear inextricably linked: the artists are the works of art, and the ideal is symbolized by the dancing couple rather than the motionless and somewhat reluctant model on a pedestal. Although alluded to variously also in her letters, Rahel's conception of art finds its fullest expression in this dream. It reveals her intellectual sovereignty vis-à-vis her revered Goethe as well as the Romantics. The art of sociability, represented in the dream by the dancing couple, appears not as the subterfuge of a talented woman restricted by virtue of being female but as open and equal in significance to any artist's oeuvre. It also represents more than the wishful realization of Rahel's inherent and unique sociable talent. Its significance in the dream must be seen as springing from the outsider's longing for a tolerant and just society. The realization of such a society merited devoting one's life to it. In the dream, therefore, it appears as an essential, joyful, and urgent human activity and responsibility.

The second dream confirms and elaborates on Rahel's self-definition as quoted above. The difference from her other dreams is striking. There, Rahel remains an outsider or is cruelly cast out. Here for the first time, she appears not as a victim but moves naturally among the chosen in a kind of sanctuary. The only woman and nonartist in the gathering, she holds her own and even confronts the artists from throughout the world and across the ages by insisting that the ideal lives and belongs to reality. She is proven right in that the young man abandons his assigned pose by simply and happily engaging in the waltz with her. Because Rahel's sphere was life or social life, she envisioned the aesthetic ideal as a process. In the dream, it is symbolized by the activity of dancing. Social dance serves as a metaphor for Rahel's conception of an ideal state. "Dancing," she wrote elsewhere, "is the most beautiful art form! the art, where we ourselves become the material (Kunststoff), where we present ourselves as free, happy, beautiful, healthy, complete; this also includes, agile, modest, naive, innocent, wholly in accordance with our nature, liberated from misery, constraints, struggles, limitations, and weakness."[100]

Rahel's aesthetic notion differs fundamentally from the established one represented by the other artists. They are determined to objectify the young man by elevating him to the category of a model to be imitated, thereby also excluding him from human society. Rahel's ideal, on the other hand, is not represented as an object but as a state involving movement and mutuality instead of exclusion and specialization. Her image of the waltzing pair takes into account the spiritual and sensual nature of human beings as well as their desire for freedom and equality. Although all dancing carried a special meaning for Rahel, the choice of the dance here is important. For, in contrast to the earlier courtly dances, which faithfully followed the dancing master's choreography and kept the dancers' bodies apart, the waltz permits the closely embracing couple to circle freely through the room. Originating in the country dance, the waltz became popular during the French Revolution and thus carried an egalitarian message of its own. Because Rahel conceived of art as an activity rather than a product, her ideal envisions a continuing and ever newly forming process. Moreover, artists and viewers, or nonartists, are not separated; all are included and considered fully responsible for art's further development.

The dancing couple serves as a fitting image for Rahel's conception of sociability. Like social dancing, sociability requires no outstanding talent but can and should be practiced by anyone because everyone is entangled in human interaction. For the duration of the dream, Rahel's aesthetic vision holds its own against the established aesthetic norm. Sociability, Rahel's "oeuvre," appears on a par with the artist's oeuvre. The dream is an accurate illustration of her audacious self-definition. However, this forward-looking vision could be realized only in a dream or in conversation—spoken or written—and, later, in the *Buch des Andenkens*, which she helped to conceive.[101]

4

MADAME VARNHAGEN VON ENSE

On 27 September 1814 Rahel and Karl August Varnhagen were quietly married in Berlin at the home of her youngest brother, Moritz. Just four days prior to their wedding, Rahel was baptized and given the new names Friederike Antonie Robert Tornow. Formal conversion was then a condition of the church for any union between a Christian and a Jew. Rahel had used the name Robert since the nineties while traveling, the same name her brother Ludwig used as his pen name.[1] In 1812 the entire family adopted the name Robert Tornow legally and for official purposes. Since Varnhagen had discovered an ancestral title of nobility a few years earlier (which he adopted with a view to furthering his career), Rahel's married name became Friederike Antonie Varnhagen von Ense. In spite of this radical outward change of identity, she continued to be Rahel for her old friends and acquaintances. Referring to the letter *R* with which she often signed her letters, she pronounced: "The stroke *R* remains my coat of arms."[2] For most of her new friends she became Friederike Varnhagen von Ense.

At first surprised that this marriage was actually taking place, the family soon expressed great satisfaction and joy. Not only had Varnhagen's personality and behavior improved greatly since they first knew him, he was now an officer and had fairly certain prospects for a career in the diplomatic service. The new esteem with which family, friends, and acquaintances treated Rahel on her return to Berlin from Prague was an indication not only of the regard Varnhagen was now enjoying but also of Rahel's improved status as a woman about to be married.[3] It greatly pleased her and rendered her confident and tender. Nonetheless, mixed marriages were unusual, and both the baptism and the marriage required a good many formalities. Rahel settled these with dispatch because Varnhagen had to leave town and because the conversion needed to be kept secret.[4] Pastor Stägemann performed both ceremonies, deeply honored to be the one selected to receive this outstanding woman into the Christian faith. He did his best to move matters along, even passing over certain irregularities. As Rahel related to Varnhagen: "He received me as if *Spinoza* wanted to be baptized: so crushed was he with honor."[5] Rahel's own thoughts and feelings about taking this formal step are unknown.

Just as the union between Gentile and Jew was unusual, the marriage between the older woman and the much younger man was out of the ordinary. The Romantics had begun the trend of marrying older women with outstanding personalities and intellectual and artistic talents. For example, Caroline Böhmer-Schlegel-Schelling was twelve years older than her husband, the philosopher Friedrich Wilhelm Schelling. Dorothea Mendelssohn-Veit-Schlegel married Friedrich Schlegel, nine years her junior. Sophie Mereau-Brentano was eight years older than Clemens Brentano. Although these men subscribed to the emerging ideology of gender and even helped shape it, they were also fascinated by the intellectual brilliance and self-assurance of these unusual women. This new theory, while proposing separate and quite unequal spheres for men and women, also endorsed the cultivation of female individuality. It was thus that these exceptional women could emerge. Not surprisingly, the men expected their gifted wives to serve as muses and helpmates in their creative endeavors. Caroline and Dorothea both dutifully and selflessly translated and edited literary and scholarly texts and even wrote entire articles on their own, work that quietly became submerged in their husbands' oeuvre. Only Sophie Mereau-Brentano struggled to establish herself as a writer. Varnhagen alone among these younger husbands seems to have been capable of accepting his wife's intellectual superiority. He dedicated a good part of his life to furthering her fame.

Marriage did not end the transient life Rahel had been leading since her flight from Napoleon's armies in 1813. The couple was to spend the next five years in Vienna and then, variously, in Frankfort on the Main, Karlsruhe, and Mannheim. Only days after the marriage, Varnhagen left Berlin for Vienna in order to present himself, at the suggestion of Chancellor Hardenberg, as a candidate for the Prussian Civil Service at the Congress of Vienna. There he was given the position of something akin to press secretary. His task was to stand in the corridors and intercept the public, dispensing the official information concerning the proceedings, to which he had no immediate access. He had hoped to write an eyewitness history of the congress, but he soon found out that this was neither expected of him nor feasible, as he was unable, under these circumstances, to obtain the facts necessary for arriving at a historian's insights. The most important task he was given concerned the defense of Prussian interests in the State of Saxony, which it succeeded in annexing. To this end Varnhagen wrote *Deutsche Ansicht der Vereinigung Sachsens mit Preußen* (A German view on uniting Saxony with Prussia).[6]

Rahel followed her husband after overcoming a bout of illness. In Vienna she found many of her old friends and acquaintances. Friedrich Gentz, as Prince Metternich's "right hand," was now at the apex of his political career. Wilhelm von Humboldt, also very eminent, had been sent to the congress as Prussia's second deputy. Rahel also saw the Countess Josephine Pachta, whom she had accompanied to Paris in 1800. Other long-standing friends included the witty, charming, and now quite old Prince de Ligne as well as Friedrich and Dorothea Schlegel. But she did not belong to the inner circle; neither Varnhagen nor she was important enough to be invited to the balls and parties that formed so essential a part of the congress's political happenings. To be sure, through Varnhagen she had occasion to meet Chancellor Hardenberg and others of his progressive circle. Moreover, she attended the festivities at the Arnsteins' palace, where large numbers of guests were invited to concerts, balls, and dinners. Baroness Fanny von Arnstein, daughter of the well-to-do Berlin merchant Daniel Itzig and married in 1776 to Baron Nathan von Arnstein, first financier in Vienna, was one of the most sophisticated women in Vienna.[7] During the congress she relished the company of friends from Berlin, and above all, that of her women friends from her younger days. Rahel and Dorothea Schlegel were warmly received, as well as Henriette Herz, when she came for a visit. The Baroness Fanny von Arnstein, then in her fifties, was renowned for her elegant, even regal, demeanor. But she had not lost the characteristic wit of the Berlin Jews, and when these brilliant women were together, this wit sparkled freely, to each others' and everyone's delight.

Rahel may have had little contact with the actual political movers of the congress, but she grasped quite well what was being accomplished, or rather, what failed to be accomplished. Being excluded from most of the social activities, she was less distracted and less partisan and thus able to concentrate on what was essential. She therefore quite agreed with Prince de Ligne's famous dictum: "Le congrès danse bien, mais il ne marche pas" [The congress dances well but it does not work]. Foremost among her concerns were a reliable peace agreement and progress toward a constitutional government. Her letters to the family in Berlin indicate her critical view of the reaction developing under Prince Metternich, which was to dominate Europe until the Revolution of 1848. Already during the summer in Teplitz she had been horrified by manifestations of Prussian self-conceit over the military victory and a new narrow kind of patriotic fervor among the guests. In Vienna she saw the nobility desperately trying to conserve its power and privileges. She recognized that the "heads [of state] were merely manipulating empty forms" and that they "wished to stop the world in its course like a wheel and lead it back to the old position, where it pleased them."[8] She also saw more and more clearly the disadvantages of German particularism: "Here, where you can see all of Germany together, you can see so well how very apart it is. This is not a *bonmot!*"[9] A common language was insufficient to make a nation, she argued; a nation required living under the same government and the same laws, as the example of France showed. When in the spring of 1815 Napoleon escaped from his banishment on the island of Elba and returned to Paris, she feared most of all a renewed outbreak of war.

Napoleon's return precipitated the hurried conclusion of the congress and its seemingly never-ending amusements in June 1815. Varnhagen, then part of Chancellor Hardenberg's retinue, returned to Berlin but soon afterward traveled to Paris as the chancellor's press chief, where he remained until November. Unsure of future developments, Rahel stayed in Vienna for the time being. She spent part of the summer with Fanny von Arnstein at her summer residence in Baden, an elegant spa near Vienna. In August she traveled as far as Frankfort on the Main, where Varnhagen hoped to meet her. The political dealings in Paris, however, dragged on. The Holy Alliance between England, Russia, Austria, and Prussia was not concluded until 26 September 1815. With this agreement the monarchs succeeded in restoring the political balance of Europe to a prerevolutionary state, firmly resolving to suppress any and all liberalizing tendencies and efforts. Varnhagen and others who hoped for a more forward-looking outcome observed these developments with alarm.

Varnhagen was further distressed at Rahel's refusal to continue her journey in order to join him in Paris. The reasons for her equivocation were complex. As always, her health was far from stable, rendering her fearful of a risky journey through a defeated country that she believed to be in turmoil and still essentially in a state of war. She was reluctant to find herself once again in a situation she had every reason to dislike, as in Vienna among "political factions, soldiers, troops, and congresses! Among people who take me for an enemy."[10] She was also afraid that she would make the arduous journey for nothing if the peace accord was concluded and everyone left Paris. And finally, she had arrived in a part of Germany that pleased her immensely. Frankfort was a Free Imperial City, and she marveled at its beauty and the absence of poverty as well as the industriousness, order, and friendliness she encountered there, contrasting it to "*our* land [Prussia]" with its "curtailment, coarseness, leanness."[11] Frankfort was, moreover, the city of Goethe's childhood and youth; it and its environs figured very prominently in his autobiography *Dichtung und Wahrheit* (1811–22, *Poetry and Truth*), the early installments of which Rahel was reading with great delight at the time. On her excursions through the city and the countryside she retraced his steps as she knew them from his writings.

Goethe was actually in Frankfort, and Rahel was half hoping and half fearing an encounter with the revered writer. Their paths crossed twice, briefly. Once, while walking in the countryside, she recognized him riding in a carriage. The second time, he paid her an unexpected visit, during which she felt extremely awkward because she was not dressed and, in order not to make him wait, met him, as she was, in a black quilted housecoat. The conversation never went beyond polite formalities, and Rahel in her nervousness spoke far too much. She nevertheless felt honored, writing to Varnhagen: "Goethe was here this morning at a quarter to ten . . . this is my patent of nobility." After he left she dressed very carefully in honor of the event and went out visiting.[12]

In time Rahel came to see the limitations of Frankfort and its status as a free city. She likened it to a family living in great comfort and happiness. In such a family, however, neither great achievements nor substantial progress were likely to occur. "So much is clear to me," she wrote after a few weeks' stay, "the free Imperial cities will not last much longer, even if the princes preserve them as a humane gift to themselves; they [the cities] were, in my opinion, artificial and natural islands of a free Earthly Kingdom which looked up from and strove out of that churning and raging sea of the world of conquering aristocrats. . . ."[13] She set her hopes on the Bundestag, the federal diet, scheduled to meet in the near future in Frankfort, where the liberals hoped to make progress toward German unification and a constitutional government. This was the direction envisioned by the reform-minded, including Varnhagen and Rahel.

Meanwhile, in Paris Varnhagen was as busy and industrious as always. He embarked on a vast network of correspondence, published political essays and portraits of historical personalities, and made the rounds among diplomats and politicians, often dining with the chancellor, then again being kept at bay. He reported for various newspapers on the developments in Paris, something he greatly enjoyed, owing to his passion for contemporary or subjective history. Often after approving Varnhagen's articles Hardenberg sent them on to be published in the Berlin newspapers. Through this work,

Varnhagen hoped to prove himself a worthy and insightful candidate for the diplomatic service.

As the affairs in Paris drew to a close, Varnhagen insisted on more explicit discussions about a future position. He would have liked most of all to return to Berlin to publish a paper of his own, but nothing came of it. Instead, Hardenberg appointed him Prussian attaché at the court of the Grand Duchy of Baden in Karlsruhe. This exceeded Varnhagen's wildest expectations and was a clear indication of the trust Hardenberg placed in him. The post entailed independence, respect, and a generous salary of three thousand *Reichsthaler*. Moreover, in Baden Varnhagen expected to be able to promote his liberal ideas. The little principality had only recently been consolidated by Napoleon out of disparate geographic elements. Its centralized and rationalized government was designed after the French model, sweeping away the vested interests of various groups, particularly the remnants of the feudal aristocracy. Constitutional reform was next on the agenda, and Varnhagen, as Prussian emissary, hoped to influence this process, intending to make Baden a model state for a future Germany.[14] He was sure that Karlsruhe would appeal to Rahel as well; it offered, as he wrote to her: "a garden residency, a theater, a French princess,[15] Switzerland, Stuttgart, Frankfort, Strasbourg in the vicinity, Baden-Baden [the spa] within a few miles."[16] Confident that she would rejoice with him at this happy turn of events, for he indeed appeared to be headed for a remarkable career, he signed the letter: "Forever yours truly, Chargé d'Affairs and Minister Varnhagen." The appointment was not formalized until March, however, and the move to Karlsruhe did not take place until July of the following year. The letters also reveal that Varnhagen was not formally presented at court until the very end of September.[17]

In reality, Karlsruhe had little to offer the demanding Rahel. Although lovely, it was in many ways backward as well as pretentious. As she put it in her inimitable way: "Karlsruhe is a beautiful irksome place: the cause of this irksomeness lies in its pretensions to be big . . . and the limitations and stagnation due to its being small."[18] She was without her family and a circle of friends and acquaintances and the easy social life she was accustomed to. The latter she had had in Vienna and even, to some extent, in Frankfort. In the little Grand Duchy of Baden, however, social gatherings were large, formal, and dressy affairs. Open houses that permitted casual visiting, so conducive to easy and free social interaction and so popular in Berlin, were entirely unknown. And once again Rahel was without an occupation or task, such as the rescue operation in Prague. Furthermore, as the wife of the emissary of the powerful state of Prussia, she was subjected to new demands and constraints. At the same time, due to her Jewish origins, powerful conservatives kept her from being accepted at court and in other social settings. The same factions, and foremost among these, Prime Minister Hacke, also delayed Varnhagen's presentation at court. The new demands for diplomacy, patience, and forbearance were trying for Rahel, who felt less and less inclined to put up with social pretense, class and confessional prejudice, and other forms of petty narrow-mindedness.

In time and for Varnhagen's sake, she adjusted and made the best of the situation. She was grateful for pleasant living quarters, although she could not really call them home. The meals still had to be sent for from a nearby inn, and there was no china or silverware. However, the rooms were attractive, looking out over the rooftops, gardens, and fields across to the forest. It was a view after Rahel's heart, and one she had never enjoyed in her "dusty" gray Berlin. There was a sofa in every room and lots of books. On the other hand, among the more unpleasant aspects, and an indication of the backwardness of the population as well as the power of the privileged, was a servant "who *still* did not comprehend the existence of napkins, knives, forks, tea trays, and clean hands" and whom Varnhagen scolded and beat so hard that Rahel trembled in fear whenever he was called.[19]

On the whole, Rahel's life as the wife of the Prussian envoy became more varied and eventful, and she took the role very seriously, for, in spite of being slighted or rebuffed by some, she succeeded in gathering a social circle. In time, family and friends found their way to Karlsruhe or its vicinity, so that Rahel no longer felt so isolated. She enjoyed visits from her brothers Markus and Moritz and their families in Berlin. Ludwig Robert was living in nearby Mannheim, which made possible more frequent and intimate contact with her favorite brother. Pauline Wiesel visited, as did the actress Auguste Brede. The couple also undertook several journeys. They regularly stayed with Varnhagen's former commander, General von Tettenborn, and his family in their exquisite homes in Mannheim and Baden. Tettenborn, now a very wealthy man as a result of the booty from his Hamburg campaign, had accepted a commission in Baden's army, which meant that he too had a stake in the future of Baden. Their common interest in the fate of the little principality deepened the ties of friendship between the two men. The Varnhagens also traveled to the Frankfort fair and the spas of Baden and Heidelberg.

The most ambitious journey occurred in the fall of 1817, when Varnhagen, Rahel, and Dore, the second of Rahel's devoted servants,[20] journeyed along the Rhine to Brussels. Here Rahel was reunited with her sister, Rose, whom she had not seen since 1803. Rose's husband, Carel Asser, a councillor at the Ministry of Justice, was in Brussels to assist in the drafting of a new statute book. Although from a traditional Jewish community in Holland, he was a highly educated and enlightened man whom Rahel had always been very fond of. A similar empathy arose spontaneously between Varnhagen and Asser. The two men had much to talk and agree about, and this not only was personally but also professionally and politically beneficial. During the Period of Restoration, personal links between forward-looking men were important. Through Asser, Varnhagen could establish connections with other like-minded men and thus further his career and the cause of liberalism.[21]

Rahel, who in her youth had yearned to see the world, was now not entirely thrilled to travel. She suffered more than ever from poor health. Her old ailments, rheumatism, gout, chest pains, migraine headaches, and severe colds, had not abated. On the contrary, they increasingly impeded her from participating freely in what life offered. She now rarely enjoyed a sense of well-being, even when she was free from any specific malady. In the spring of 1816 she was so ill that she secretly wrote her will.[22] The new life had come too late. "I am too old, too smart, too lazy, too wretched, too poor, etc., etc.!! to still find pleasure in drifting into a strange place," she admitted to Pauline Wiesel, the friend who traveled with such ease.[23] She now wished to live in some comfort among a small group of truly like-minded friends. At the same time, Rahel apparently retained her youthful looks. Except for her graying hair, she looked considerably younger than her age, as she informed her brother Moritz. She followed these observations with a characteristically wry comment that also betrayed a complete lack of vanity: "Actually, I would like to present myself as old as I am: this I cannot do because I look so very much younger and would have to always explain; at least often; and then because I have a young husband who loves me so very much. There is nothing more comical. The inverted crown upon my fate, for which I am *also grateful.*"[24]

THE CORRESPONDENCE OF THE YEARS 1815 – 1820

Her maladies notwithstanding, Rahel took an active interest in her husband's affairs during these years, making every effort to be of use to him in building his career. In the months following the signing of the Second Paris

Peace Treaty, in November 1815, there was much clamoring and vying for appointments and positions as the new old order was being established in practical terms. Through her many connections, Rahel could often gather useful information.

At the same time, she continued to carry on an extensive and ever-expanding correspondence. In addition to relatives and old friends, she exchanged letters with Varnhagen's friends as well as with new ones the couple had come to know and appreciate during their stay in Vienna. As a diplomatic wife, she also wrote many "business" letters to persons of importance on behalf of people who were mere acquaintances or even strangers. In the spring of 1817 she wrote: "I have between twenty and thirty correspondents who all *want* something from me."[25] The letters she and Varnhagen exchanged during the four years of his employment as a diplomat alone take up two volumes. The correspondence with her brothers and their families was, for reasons that will become clear, also very brisk at this time, as was that with her sister. Among the most interesting new correspondents were the actress Auguste Brede, with whom she had shared those fateful years in Prague, the Count Astolphe de Custine and his mother, the Countess Delphine de Custine, whom the Varnhagens had met in Vienna, Ignaz Troxler, the editor of the periodical, *Schweizerisches Museum* (Swiss museum), who published excerpts from Rahel's letters, and Konrad Engelbert Oelsner, a diplomat, true democrat, and great admirer of Madame Varnhagen. The latter two were both originally friends of Varnhagen's.

The letters Rahel wrote during these four years as wife of the Prussian envoy reflect her increased participation and interest in political life. Contemporary events and developments began to intrude in her life in a way that she could not ignore. Her ardent involvement in the practical aspects of Varnhagen's career and in the larger questions about Germany's future constitutes a new and distinguishing focus in her writing, while her old fascination for literature, the theater, and human affairs receded somewhat to the background. Since Rahel's new concerns were of considerable public and intellectual interest, they pervade the letters of other luminaries of the time. Together, this correspondence forms a corpus of diverse opinions and insights into contemporary events. In Rahel's letters the new concerns reach across her individual correspondences. Therefore, a thematic discussion, rather than a consideration of individual exchanges, is most appropriate. Besides politics at all levels, the significant topics of this period included the newly evolving Jewish question, marriage, and literature and the theater.

Politics and Its Relation to Jewish Aspirations

Rahel's efforts on behalf of her husband's career are revealed particularly well during the fall of 1816, when the couple was separated for several weeks, Varnhagen staying with Tettenborn in Mannheim and Rahel in Frankfort, where she visited several old friends. They exchanged letters almost daily, writing long passages in which they assured each other of their love and devotion and reporting on political happenings. Since preparations for the Bundestag were now earnestly under way, the city was teeming with notable persons. Rahel, as a result of her many personal relations and friendships, quickly became part of the social rounds. She was asked to the gatherings of the Countess Pappenheim, a daughter of Chancellor Hardenberg, the Countess Delphine de Custine and her son Astolphe, and Caroline von Humboldt. She was in frequent contact with another old acquaintance from Berlin, the Prussian diplomat Friedrich von Otterstedt, who was now chargé d'affairs at the Bundestag, and his wife. She visited often with the Schlegels, or the von Schlegels, as they now also called themselves, and Dorothea, especially, always seemed to have news. Friedrich had been named a councillor of the Austrian delegation to the Bundestag and, although he greatly overestimated the significance of his position, was privy to all kinds of information. Then there was Konrad Engelbert Oelsner, who had been chargé d'affairs of Frankfort in Paris during Napoleon's reign and later served as Prussian envoy to the Bundestag. Oelsner was active as an author and journalist and a close friend of the Varnhagens until his death in 1828. The list of names of important diplomatic and political figures mentioned by Rahel in her letters could be extended by many more.

In Mannheim Varnhagen met with other personalities, all of whom pursued the liberal cause, among them Adolf von Philipsborn, an officer and attaché at the court of Karlsruhe, Justus von Gruner, president of the police of Berlin and, later, Prussian ambassador in Switzerland, and Neidhardt Count von Gneisenau, a former chief of staff in Blücher's army during the Wars of Liberation.

Considering the list of names, it is striking to what extent the political affairs were still in the hands of the nobility, with bourgeois representatives being almost entirely absent. Although bourgeois delegations, including Jewish ones, were received at the Bundestag, the political course of the German lands was still determined by the titled nobility. Rahel, the former Jew, was a notable exception in these circles. However, these men and women represented, with few exceptions, the more forward-looking segment of German society; they had supported or at least sympathized with the French Revolution and, as German patriots, staked their lives against Napoleonic hegemony. They now expected to continue the reforms initiated in 1807 by Stein, Hardenberg, and Altenstein. Varnhagen and Rahel were part of this group of liberals or, perhaps more accurately, liberal conservatives. Varnhagen enjoyed the respect due a promising young diplomat and was furthermore appreciated for his intelligence and his commitment to progressive ideas, while Rahel was esteemed, as always, for her rare qualities of mind and heart. At the same time there were many, especially among the old aristocracy, who considered the Varnhagens upstarts and far too radical and who attempted to block Varnhagen's career.

In her letters to Varnhagen, Rahel dutifully conveyed what appeared to her to be pertinent information. Much of it is treated only briefly or referred to obliquely on account of the sharpened censorship, and therefore difficult to assess. Varnhagen, however, was grateful to obtain her *faits* or facts as well as her thoughts and reflections, assuring her that her letters were expected with greater impatience than the newspapers.[26] He called her a "fine statesman," and Tettenborn, for whom these reports were intended as well, recognized her as his "ambassadorial secretary" or "commissioner."[27]

One of the most closely observed persons was Wilhelm von Humboldt, then probably the most prominent representative of the liberal camp after Chancellor Hardenberg. At that time, however, although not readily apparent and least of all to Humboldt himself, his political star was in decline. His considerable differences with Hardenberg prompted the latter to keep him away from Berlin. After languishing in an unrewarding position in London, Humboldt was sent to Frankfort as one of the founders of the Bundestag as well as a member of the commission charged with settling territorial questions. Having to devote himself to the rivalries among various petty princes could hardly be satisfying to someone deeply committed to constitutional reform. As a result of these disappointments, Humboldt was often moody and made himself rather unpopular.[28] Nonetheless, he was a person to be reckoned with. There was always the chance that he might succeed in replacing his rival, Hardenberg. In Paris Varnhagen had already carefully related to Rahel Humboldt's behavior toward him. In Frankfort it became apparent that the ambivalent feelings that characterized the relationship between Humboldt and Rahel in their younger years persisted into middle age.

Moreover, Caroline von Humboldt's friendship toward Rahel seemed to have cooled considerably. To her surprise, Rahel was suddenly once again addressed with the formal *Sie*, rather than with the familiar *Du*, a custom which was then not very widespread even among close friends, but which Caroline had insisted upon some seventeen years earlier. At that time Caroline had confessed to Rahel: "No individual ever gave me the sense of understanding everything as you have. Therefore I can and will not abandon the hope that someday I shall live with you. It seems to me that we are [destined] for each other."[29] By now, however, eighteenth-century cosmopolitanism had given way to a new era of Germanic nationalism, to which Caroline quickly succumbed. She therefore must have found it necessary to reestablish what she considered a proper distance from her longtime Jewish friend.

From Frankfort Rahel reported to Varnhagen the manner in which she was treated by Caroline von Humboldt, whether and to what gatherings she was invited, as well as which invitations she accepted. The presence or absence, the disposition, and behavior of Wilhelm von Humboldt were also carefully noted, as were the opinions circulating about him. In spite of the tensions, the Humboldts and Rahel saw each other frequently, especially the two women, and every so often the letters betray that their old and mutual affection and admiration had not completely disappeared. Rahel evidently handled the delicate situation with considerable skill, insisting, on the one hand, on her right as Madame Varnhagen von Ense to be admitted to these affairs and, on the other, avoiding outright humiliation by not being overly anxious about being included. "You see, I go there quite cavalierly when it suits me: why should *they* alone treat me according to their pleasure and irregularly,"[30] she related to Varnhagen. Moreover, her capacity to be offended seems to have reached its limits, as a remark to Ernestine Goldstücker, one of her Jewish friends in Berlin, reveals. Obviously alluding to Caroline von Humboldt's behavior, she wrote: "and then I've discovered changed friends. This discovery, however, found no offense within me, I had borne it *already*, and my heart refuses to accept any more. I came to realize this with amused, almost proud, joy."[31] Fortunately for Rahel, both the Countesses Custine and Pappenheim were free of such petty conceits. They openly showed their affection and admiration for Rahel, leaving no doubt about the sincerity of their feelings.[32]

At this time even very prominent Jews could be insulted with impunity. In some ways Rahel fared better than one of the Rothschild bankers, as the following incident shows. According to Rahel's account, Rothschild had been approached with a request for a loan by a Count Flemming, who was suddenly dispatched to his diplomatic post in Brazil. Rothschild refused, explaining that he was not acquainted with the count, adding that he would gladly oblige if Mr. von Humboldt confirmed the appointment. Flemming angrily replied that naturally Rothschild could not know him, as he, Flemming, was not in the habit of dining with Jews.[33] As the reactionary influences spread, incidents of this kind became more widespread after a period of quiescence.

It is difficult to assess the extent to which Varnhagen and Rahel were aware of the Humboldts' true feelings. Rahel at times expressed considerable cynicism with regard to both Gentz and Humboldt, a cynicism that originated in Prague, where both had treated her disrespectfully at the very time she was devoting all her energy to the care of wounded soldiers. Late in 1813 she wrote to Varnhagen with Gentz in mind: "Where a friend is not a friend, not a human being, he should only be used."[34] Now, in Frankfort, although she still deplored the idea of using disloyal friends for her own purposes, she repeated it with regard to the Humboldts.[35] The intelligent and sensitive Humboldt, of course, was aware of Rahel's tactics and vexed in turn.[36] The Varnhagens' nickname for Humboldt, "Mephistopheles," similarly suggests that they did not regard him as entirely benevolent. At the same time, however, Rahel was capable of being quite objective and fair in her assessment of this arrogant man, as the following report to Varnhagen indicates: "Yesterday . . . I dined at the Humboldts . . . where Humboldt has donned a new skin of true graciousness. Yesterday it reached its height. . . . He controlled the conversation all alone . . . and mildly; did not permit any awkwardness or stupidity to come up: he uses the same tone with the staff, the guests, and the children . . . he is now of the most profound, carefree sincerity . . . and this gives his behavior and his conversation a truly mild and happy gracefulness. . . . It seems to me, he has more sense than ever. Or do I have more? The two of us are also very tender, very gentle, very mild, very true, and very far, far forward in our utterances to each other. That evening I found him again at the Countess Custine: the same."[37]

The letters Caroline and Wilhelm exchanged with each other during that same period, however, contain no such generosity and leave no doubt that they categorically disapproved of Varnhagen's marriage to a Jew. In August 1813, when Rahel approached her with a request for money in support of the wounded soldiers, Caroline was delighted to hear from her. Still using the familiar "Du," she wrote: "I was so unspeakably happy to see your handwriting again, to find you so in particular words that the long time period in which we did not see each other disappeared . . . from your letter I can feel that we have not changed so much that we have become incomprehensible to each other."[38] At about the same time, on the other hand, Humboldt bluntly expressed his lack of tolerance: "The little Levi . . . irritated me a great deal," he wrote to his wife from Prague, where he had seen Rahel. He continued: "Only, what is to be done with the Jewish miss? To be sure, Gentz still assures me that she is the most brilliant woman on earth. It is necessary at times to forgo brilliance. Therefore, I remain pitiless."[39] While Humboldt had earlier disliked Rahel for her supposedly "monstrous" intelligence and her disregard of social hierarchies, his later animosity was due to her marriage to a Gentile and the accompanying rise in social status. In both instances, his pride of class is clearly evident. As a liberal he was not averse to social contacts with Jews. In fact, in his youthful years he sought out the company of Jews in Berlin. His association with the men representing the Berlin Enlightenment, among them Moses Mendelssohn, shaped his thinking in decisive ways. His intimate friendship with Henriette Herz, who taught him Hebrew, and his frequent appearances at Rahel's early salon have been mentioned earlier.

But there were clearly limits to Jewish integration into German society, as the following statement reveals: "I am told that [Varnhagen] has now married the little Levy. Thus, she can one day become an ambassador's wife and her excellency. There is nothing that the Jew will not attain."[40] The same thought is expressed again more vehemently after Varnhagen was appointed to the court of Karlsruhe: "I have long said that the little Levy would become her excellency. . . . The good chancellor [Hardenberg] made the choice, without telling me and Jordan a word. I have . . . spoken against it. I wouldn't have anything against Varnhagen's so-called Jacobinism, if it were real. . . . But the lady, the tribe Levy, the Ark of the Covenant! What effect is this supposed to have on the Grand Duke, and just what gain is there in his being appointed there, to overcome such disadvantages?"[41] Caroline was in complete agreement with him: "Varnhagen's nomination to Karlsruhe came indeed as a surprise to me. He is being promoted quickly. I cannot approve of it, and although his wife is surely better than he, she is nevertheless a real hindrance for a post of this kind. . . . I cannot so unconditionally endorse [Hardenberg's] liberalism toward the Jews. It makes us look ridiculous in other countries and therefore harms us in many other respects."[42] In many ways she was more militantly anti-Jewish than her husband, whom she accused of having too much sympathy for the Jews: "You pride yourself of never abandoning the Jews. It is the only fault of yours that I know."[43] Caroline was referring to her husband's endorsement of the Edict of Emancipation of 1812. Humboldt was in favor of granting Jews citizenship outright and unconditionally, as the French had done in

1792, when they set out to realize their democratic ideals. He opposed the other option, gradual legal emancipation, as recommended by the Prussian administration, which argued that Jews must first prove themselves worthy of citizenship.[44]

Humboldt's answer to Caroline's reproach is as complex as it is revealing. It acknowledges, without condemning, Caroline's hatred of Jews and contrasts it with that of the younger generation of "new Christians," represented by their daughter Adelheid. For the *new Christians*, a term then coming into use, Christianity was no longer confined to religious dogma and practice; it was now symbolically and conceptually intertwined with national ideology.[45] Explicitly anti-Jewish, the new Christianity's representatives went so far as to demand the repeal of Jewish rights and partially succeeded in these efforts. Finally, the letter sheds light on Humboldt's own contradictory attitudes toward Jews: "I also resign myself completely to the fact that I am the loser in regard to the old creed [Judaism], it's impossible to prevail against it. Actually I only like the Jews *en masse, en detail* [individually] I avoid them."[46] Humboldt favored Jewish emancipation in principle. Having a ghettoized underclass did not agree with his liberal world view. This did not mean, however, that he was willing to accept Jews as his equals, as indicated by his outrage at even one diplomatic wife of Jewish origin. In his diatribes Humboldt refused to acknowledge Rahel by any of her given names. She was now neither Rahel, nor Mademoiselle Levin, and certainly not Madame Varnhagen, but merely "the little Levy," "the tribe of Levy," "the Ark of the Covenant." By reducing one who had long left the tradition to a mere category, that of Jewishness, he refuted what he knew to be Rahel's distinguishing features, her individuality and human worth.

The Humboldts were not alone among liberals in harboring such contradictory feelings and views. Brinckmann, another regular guest and friend of Rahel's and other Jewish women, also felt free to express anti-Jewish sentiments in letters to Gentile friends.[47] Nor is this the only record of explicit objections to Rahel's incursions into mainstream society. Earlier, when Rahel intended to marry Karl von Finckenstein, the opposition came not merely from his family. There were other voices, notably, that of the architect Hans Christian Genelli, whom Ludwig Tieck identified as the one who "alienated [the weak Finckenstein] from Rahel by explaining to him the inappropriateness and her unworthiness."[48] This is how Ludwig Tieck presented the matter many years later in a long letter to Varnhagen. In the same missive, Tieck admitted that he had not always shared Rahel's opinions but insisted that he had always been her friend. Therefore he was even now, "forty years later, outraged at how Genelli had, in the presence of the servants, leveled a barrage of disparagement, slander, and defamation about *Rahel*." Tieck, however, in reliving this shocking experience, conveniently forgot that he too had maligned Rahel in rather similar terms only a few months earlier in a letter to Gustav von Brinckmann. There, he denied Rahel any aesthetic sensibility and reproached her for the "unprincipled capriciousness of her being and thinking." He further observed that "it was an artful pleasure of hers to destroy the best purposely, only to bewail its loss in desperation." The epistle ends with the words: "And was she ever able to forget the Jewess? In the end, Jewish literature and the dissolute Heine, this messiah of the Jews, in a certain sense triumph over Göthe after all."[49] Tieck, Humboldt, Gentz, and so many others were unwilling to recognize their own contradictory attitudes. Instead, they assigned any and all blame to Rahel and Jews generally. And, although they considered themselves enlightened and progressive, they were not interested in combatting the continued prejudice against Jews, but in maintaining boundaries. These Rahel had overstepped twice—initially, when a marriage with Finckenstein seemed imminent, and again some fifteen years later, when she actually became the wife of the promising young diplomat Varnhagen von Ense. Even if she lacked any direct knowledge of these sentiments, Rahel must have been aware of them, which may explain the sudden and seemingly unmotivated outbursts and lamentations in her early letters about her "erroneous" birth, her lack of social standing, her Jewishness. In 1816, however, she reacted rather philosophically, as we have seen. The intolerance and narrow-mindedness of Germany's leading politicians, intellectuals, and artists, whose world view was originally shaped by Enlightenment thinking, are a telling indication of the difficulties even a few of the most assimilated Jews faced if they strove for full integration into German society. The liberals' indifference to or even abandonment of these ideals, moreover, explains how the most retrograde elements in society could acquire the prominence that increasingly led to public vilification of and actual violence against Jews in the years following the Vienna Congress. And finally, the failure of these early liberals to commit themselves to a truly democratic way of thinking foreshadows the much more encompassing failure of German liberalism later in the nineteenth and into the twentieth century, up to the catastrophe of 1933.

During these years Jewish matters became a frequent topic also between Rahel and Ludwig Robert, who faced the new Judeophobia very publicly. Robert had achieved prominence as a playwright, librettist, and translator of French plays for the German stage. In particular, his tragedy *Die Macht der Verhältnisse* (The power of social class), written in 1811, was performed successfully on many stages, although not without controversy and anti-Jewish attacks. In Berlin, its performance had been prevented for some years. When, in November 1815, it was finally shown, it had to compete with the hugely popular anti-Jewish farce *Unser Verkehr* (*Our Crowd*), by Karl Borromäus Alexander Sessa.[50]

Because the central conflict in *Macht der Verhältnisse* derived from aristocratic conceit and pride of class, many suspected that the play was inspired by an incident a few years earlier between a Gentile and a Jew, specifically, the famous Arnim-Itzig affair. According to Varnhagen, Moritz Itzig had challenged Achim von Arnim to a duel because the latter had insulted his aunt, Sarah Levy, by appearing uninvited and inappropriately dressed at one of her soirées. Arnim refused, stating that he could not accept a challenge from a Jew. Itzig, "justly indignant" (in Varnhagen's words), replied that he who failed so ignobly in the use of the sword would be beaten with a stick. Shortly thereafter Itzig attacked Arnim. The affair was brought before the Prussian Supreme Court, which sentenced Itzig lightly for this attack.[51] In the letter to his sister, Ludwig Robert vehemently denied that the play had any connection to that particular incident. He insisted that he had conceived of the plot long before the incident, and that in any case one could not make "a tragedy out of such a dirty affair."[52] He assured Rahel that when he first heard of the scandal at a social gathering, the play had already been written, for he went home to fetch it and, upon his return, read it to all those present, who were deeply moved. Robert then launched into a full-scale indictment of Achim von Arnim's behavior in this matter, which he based on a reading of documents secretly made available to him. He was particularly incensed at what he considered Arnim's condescending manner toward Itzig, which, in effect, amounted to a refusal to acknowledge Itzig as a man and citizen. This is surely what prompted him to conclude his account with a comparison of Jewish versus aristocratic patriotism and courage. With biting irony, he wrote: "And this Jew Itzig participated in the war and fell [in the battle of] Lützen as a volunteer rifleman, and the nobleman Arnim cravenly remained at home."[53]

Anti-Jewish hatred seemed to provoke very different reactions in the two siblings. While Rahel had become rather resigned, the free-lance writer Ludwig Robert protested vehemently, if only to his sister. For, although he threatened to make public the documents of the affair, he failed to do so. Varnhagen finally wrote the account, which, however, was not published until 1875.

Four years later, another play of Robert's, the "arch-romantic" comedy *Cassius und Phantasus oder Der Paradiesvogel* (1825, Cassius and Phantasus or the bird of paradise), occasioned a discussion among the entire family. Rahel was by then again residing in Berlin, as were Markus and Moritz, both of whom were leading very comfortable and quiet lives. Ludwig Robert, as he was wont to do, sent the play to the siblings for comment. At the same time, he inquired whether they thought the play might be suitable for the Berlin stage. In this drama Robert made one of the characters a comical Jew who functions as a deus ex machina, with the intention of parodying the many maliciously conceived comical Jews then populating the German stage (including the ridiculous Jewish figure in Sessa's *Our Crowd*). He did this by mocking the existing Jewish stereotypes that presented the Jew as either base and groveling or overly noble. Robert's character typically has no name, being identified simply as the "Jew," while the traditionally alleged Jewish obsequiousness and resourcefulness appear to have no limits. In fact, the Jew's resourcefulness has taken the form of magical powers capable of restoring fortunes and kingdoms. The character is also made to speak in a language which then passed for Yiddish on the German stage. Ultimately, however, Robert's Jew is not only a noble figure, functioning all along as a guardian spirit, he is also the protagonist and moral force, who, after imparting some needed lessons, generously sets things right. At the same time, we are never quite sure whether he really is a Jew or simply the personification of a Jew. Among his last words are the following, no longer spoken in jargon: "I am a fantastic abomination, innocently condemned to be the guardian spirit. My most difficult and last punishment, however, was to be a cursed Jew. Fortunately, I was delivered . . . and can now get my romantic peace."[54] His voice then rising to a high pathos, he pronounces the moral of the play: "Fate is the individual's destiny, and the individual's destiny is—not to know anything definite about destiny."[55]

This comedy seems to be an attempt at undermining preconceived notions about Jews, but the polemics appear quite tame and even confused, so that we may ask what prompted the family members to counsel against trying to place the play in Berlin. The protagonist appears to the other characters in various guises—as a Jew, a Turk, a heathen, a genie, or "nothing at all." Even at the end, he cannot be pinned down to a definite set of qualities or identity. At most, the audience can say that his effect has been benevolent. It was Rahel who conveyed both her views and those of the others in a very long and rambling letter. Significantly, her arguments were political rather than literary, although she also criticized the work on aesthetic grounds, including the use of mock Yiddish. The political climate and the mood against the Jews evidently were such that the family feared that a comedy of this kind might provoke further anti-Jewish sentiments. As Rahel pointed out: "a surprising number of passages, and especially biting ones . . . could be turned against the author by ill-meaning people: and here you can simply assume them to be ill-meaning. Especially if the *riches* is called to mind by the eternal J:[ew]."[56]

From his reply, it is clear that Ludwig Robert was hurt in his pride as an author. He understood the family's prudence but refused to be intimidated: "Is this supposed to mean that someone could attack the baptized Jew? to this I answer: I shall meet him as a Christian! It is no longer the case that I feel the word Jew in a review about me as the greatest insult, to be avoided like the devil. On the contrary, let one person try it, and I shall publish a thundering word against the philosophical unChristian hatred of the Jews with the signature L. Robert, baptized in Fr[ankfort] the 30th March, etc., known previously as the Jew Lipman Lewin!"(February 1821).[57] Ludwig Robert's outrage contrasts refreshingly with his siblings' timidity and moderation, but we must bear in mind that he confined his protestations to his letters, never publishing either his "thundering word" or an account of the Arnim-Itzig incident.

The Hep Hep Riots of 1819

Rahel and her brothers in Berlin may have been especially cautious about a possible performance of Ludwig Robert's comedy in the wake of the most frightening manifestation of Judeophobia consistent with pogroms of earlier times. The Hep Hep riots, so called because Jews were taunted with the cry "Hep! Hep!,"[58] broke out in the city of Wurzburg, Bavaria, on 2 August 1819, and from there spread to some thirty other German cities over a period of two months. They consisted of threats to and outright attacks on Jewish life and property and were most severe in Wurzburg, Frankfort, and Hamburg, where Jewish citizenship was not yet a fact but still a matter of heated deliberations.

Wherever possible, Jews had taken advantage of the new freedoms of residence, occupation, and business granted to them after the Napoleonic conquest and the Emancipation Edict of 1812. As a result, the condition of the more well-to-do had improved greatly, although the great majority remained much worse off than the Christian population. The improved status of Jews was especially striking when compared to only fifty years earlier, when they were confined in the main to their community, emerging only to conduct their business. Now, they were settling in towns, such as Wurzburg, from where they had been banished for almost two centuries. In Berlin they acquired houses in the most elegant parts of the city. Elsewhere they sometimes became the owners of the impoverished nobility's country estates. They also contributed in important ways to German artistic and intellectual life and generally were a more visible presence in German society. Jews also advanced as the feudal agrarian economy gave way to industrial capitalism. In trade and business Jews now competed directly and success-fully with Christian merchants, owing to their international connections, while those in banking and manufacturing were, for historic reasons, in the vanguard. Since the economic changes propelling Jews forward also led to the impoverishment of entire regions and even to periodic famines, Jews were seen to be the cause of these co-occurring developments.

The same period saw the publication of a great many books and pam-phlets, almost all of which further stirred up anti-Jewish sentiments by warning against the "Jewish menace." Two of the most incendiary texts were Friedrich Rühs's "Über die Ansprüche der Juden an das deutsche Bürgertum" (1816, On the claims of the Jews for German citizenship) and Jakob Friedrich Fries's "Über die Gefährdung des Wohlstandes und Charak-ters der Deutschen durch die Juden" (1816, On the endangerment of the well-being and character of the Germans by the Jews). Rühs, professor of history in Berlin, and Fries, professor of philosophy in Heidelberg, both argued against Jewish citizenship owing to the alien nature of the religion and the lack of morality. While Rühs foresaw the eventual conversion to Christianity of all Jews, thus making possible their absorption into German society, Fries was less optimistic. He showed impatience with the persistent Jewish refusal to convert and therefore recommended withdrawal of their civic rights and state protection. He even advocated their expulsion.[59] Fries's brochure was so inflammatory that the government of Baden confiscated it. Although Rühs's and Fries's publications were the most notorious, there were many others that similarly warned of the increasing power of the Jews and their alleged role in the impoverishment of the Christian population. Jews were blamed for every conceivable ill, including spiraling prices, unemployment among artisans, the pursuit of luxuries, the decline in morality, and the increase in children's asylums. Most of these books and pamphlets also advocated repealing Jewish civil rights and citizenship.[60]

Common to all these publications was the warning against impending violence. Popular indignation, they cautioned, might lead to an uprising against the Jews. These intellectuals, then, instead of rationally discussing the questions pertaining to the rights and civil status of Jews, reinforced old prejudicial notions, using the misery of the general population to further stir up anti-Jewish sentiments. They not only failed to educate the masses but, by raising the prospect and possibility of violence, helped prepare the ground for the actual outbreak of the riots.

Jewish reactions to the Hep Hep riots were extremely muted. Contemporary accounts and even private communications barely mention them.[61] It was as if the Jews had been shocked into silence by these events. At the same time, emancipation continued on its course, albeit more slowly. In Prussia, for example, Jews were gradually being eased out of the civil service again.[62] On the whole, however, enough progress was being made to permit most Jews, long accustomed to periodic setbacks, to consider the riots a regrettable aberration.

This was not the case with Rahel and Ludwig Robert. The letters they exchanged during this time are exceptional not only because they address the problem forthrightly but also because they reveal a precise insight into the causes of the hostilities. It was Ludwig Robert who initiated the discussion with a report and eye-witness account about the events in Karlsruhe, where he was living at the time. Robert starts out by observing that, in his view, the gravity of the anti-Jewish hostilities was being underestimated. He points out how in Heidelberg "four houses were completely plundered, the beds slit open and the like." He praises the students there who, under the leadership of some professors, "reestablished calm, seized some of the guilty and guarded them themselves" (until the police arrived). About his own Karlsruhe, he relates the following: "Yesterday finally it started here too. Help was quickly at hand and, except for the well-known call [Hep Hep] . . . nothing happened." He then gives a step-by-step description of what he observed as he walked through the town and talked to various people, trying to sense the mood—the behavior of the patrols, the city commander's handling of the matter, and the attitude of the people watching from their open windows, commenting, finally, on the visible absence of indignation on the part of any responsible person: "Not one of the men or women . . . would raise a voice in warning . . . to the many children standing in front of the doors. Giggling, laughter, and the children talking with childish interest, that's all one could hear. Even less visible were the clergymen, here where the teachers of the religion of love should rightfully be present." Others, he relates, made rather light of the matter, saying that the people were in the streets mostly out of curiosity, owing to posters announcing that on the twenty-seventh the Jews would be killed. They

were unwilling to believe that the disturbances were still going on and that
Ludwig Robert had himself been accidentally struck lightly by a rock. He
further relates that, though the mood toward the Jews was generally not
bad and that everyone was full of praise for Cusel (presumably Jakob Kusel,
a member of the Council of the Baden Jewish Community), a notice had
nevertheless been posted at his house. Similarly, Professor Meyer Marx,
also Jewish, was insulted by an officer of the guard. He concludes: "How
corrupt people are and how little sense they have for justice and the law,
not to mention love of one's fellow man, can be seen in the fact that no
indignation is expressed over all these incidents, not even in the official
papers. — There is something else which puzzles me. How do the common
people come by the word Hep? the origin of which they cannot know. In
Wurzburg apparently, it was the *educated* rabble which began the affair."[63]
Before concluding the letter, he went out once more to see for himself. He
reported that everything was "quiet, as usual. Shabbos, a few dressed up
Jews on the street. Hilbert with 20 men is in charge of keeping order. . . .
The citizens are dissatisfied that Brückner promptly closed the pubs. They
threatened to pull him from his horse. The Grand duke is outraged and
thinks and so on. If the slightest thing happens, I'll write. I shall be careful
and not put myself in danger."

From Baden, Rahel answered with a characteristic outcry: "I am *bound-
lessly* unhappy; in a way I have never yet been. On account of the Jews."
Like her brother, she speaks of *the* Jews rather than *us* Jews, thereby establishing a distance between herself and the victims. She was well aware, of
course, that assimilation and baptism would not offer protection from such
hostilities — on the contrary — as she makes clear when speaking of the Berlin
Jews: "there it was to be feared most of all: there the Jews have served; half
of them are baptized and married to Christians."

The main body of the letter consists of an unusually perceptive and, in light
of twentieth-century history, even prophetic analysis of relations between
Gentiles and Jews. In her view, Jews served a specific purpose in present-
day Germany, that of a scapegoat, as she states at the beginning of the
letter: "They want to *keep* them, but only for the purpose of mistreating and
despising them; to abuse them as *Judenmauschel* [Jewish rabble]; to reduce
them to the little, needy peddler (Schacher); for kicking and throwing them
down the stairs." This way of thinking made her freeze up in dread:

I know my country! *Unfortunately*. A cursed Cassandra! for 3 years I have been
saying: the Jews will be attacked. . . . *This* is the German courage of rebellion. And

why? Because it is the most proper, good-natured, peace-loving, slavish (Obrigkeits-ehrendste) people, what it ought to demand, *it does not know*: only its educated members could teach it: but among these, there are many uncultured ones with crude hearts; where there is also room for envy toward those *Jews*—whom one was, thanks to religious excesses, permitted to hate, despise, and persecute as inferior beings. A few wise German rulers and much time . . . put an end to this license. The new hypocritical love for the Christian religion (may God forgive me my sin!) for the Middle Ages, with their art, literature, and terror, incite the people to the *only* terror they *can* still be provoked into, because they remember having been permitted it as of old! the pogrom. The insinuations which for years have been in the newspapers. The professors Fr[ies] and Rü[hs], and others, whatever their names. Arn[im] Brent[ano], our crowd; and even more highly positioned persons full of prejudice.[64]

Rahel was not taken by surprise. She had seen the signs for some time and knew how to read them. She was familiar with the inflammatory polemics of intellectuals like Fries, Rühs, and so many others. She carefully distinguished between the old Christian hatred of the Jews and that of the newer kind, which merged Christianity and Germanness and led to the modern calumny against Jews as "inferior beings." And although the past several years had roused her patriotic feelings too, she never abandoned her cosmopolitan outlook. She had long disapproved of the Romantics' backward orientation and glorification of the Middle Ages. But never before had she faced the fact that it was her circle, "our crowd," that proved particularly susceptible to such retrograde influences. Among the "more highly positioned persons full of prejudice," she could have named many more, including Wilhelm von Humboldt. It remains unclear whether she used the term "our crowd" as a deliberate allusion to the Sessa farce (which she knew). Most importantly, Rahel recognized that the roots of the disturbances lay in the political, social, and economic backwardness of her country, in the resurrection of vicious prejudices by the so-called educated elite, in the resentment against a few successful Jews amid the widespread economic misery, and, finally, in the German people's inability to formulate their demands, which she also attributed to a failure in leadership.[65] At the same time, she remained fully confident that the people, if guided properly, would abstain from such base actions: "in the little Bavarian village, where the synagogue was attacked, the Old Testament torn, etc.: a clergyman should have stepped forth and explained what the Old Testament *is*, and what *all* religion means: I *know* the people would have realized their sacrilege and stopped immediately." Both siblings wrote as Christians, but to them, Christianity was truly a religion of love, not to be used in the service of bigotry and hate.

Among their contemporaries, Rahel and Ludwig Robert were unusual in recognizing that the widespread and covertly sanctioned attacks against the Jews constituted more than a temporary aberration. They discerned in these outrages the symptoms of the deeper ills of the age, which repudiated the eighteenth-century commitment to tolerance and human progress. Even more significantly, they considered Jewish assimilation and emancipation as essential outcomes of Enlightenment thinking. Thus, writing about his elder brother, Markus, whose reaction to the attacks he found shockingly superficial, Ludwig Robert observed: "*He* surely was not as enraged, anxious, and tearful about the row over the Jews as . . . we were—He sees in it neither the present nor the time being born out of pain that is unfolding, and he knows nothing of the unhappy ruin nor the . . . consolation of the belief in the world's eternal perfectibility."[66]

The riots against the Jews, along with the suppression of the liberal cause, could not, however, shake Rahel's and Ludwig Robert's faith in the "world's eternal perfectibility," that most fundamental Enlightenment concept. The notion pervades the letters of this time. Early in 1816, for example, Rahel communicated her views on the state of Europe and history in a long letter to Ludwig Robert. She described eloquently how subdued and ruined the people were throughout Europe. Only men whose aspirations were altogether common, coarse, and devoid of any higher purpose could hope to benefit and succeed. The present state of confusion, however, indicated to her a time of "fermentation" and thus allowed for the affirmation of historical progress: "Therefore I truly and really think that mortal life is no rigid, lifeless repetition but progressive change and development, like everything: for our discernment and through our discernment, and I call our age really new and am expecting great and new things, in a word, miracles of invention, of emotional strength, revelation, and development."[67]

About the same time, Ludwig Robert expressed very similar views. In the first of many long philosophical letters to his sister, he wrote: "I know . . . that the world, even if *slowly*, moves . . . *forward*; and I am, in my *innermost* soul, calm and serene—But the air of this my fatherland oppresses me, because my hopes were great and because I now clearly see a . . . relapse . . ." (27 January 1816).[68] By 1820 his historical and political understanding had sharpened. He now accused the church of spreading intolerance in Germany and throughout Europe and pleaded for the separation of church and state.[69] As a "relapse," as a time of "fermentation" for great and necessary changes—this is how Rahel and her brother were able to interpret the reactionary events of the new era, thanks to their optimistic, enlightened world view, and in spite of the fact that they grasped the larger meaning of these retrograde developments.

There were others, of course, who also regretted the reactionary spirit of the times. A few even recognized the gravity of the anti-Jewish polemics. Like Rahel and her brother, they saw in the turning against the Jews a general abandonment of an enlightened, humanistic world view. Konrad Engelbert Oelsner, for example, wrote to Varnhagen from Frankfort in the fall of 1816 elaborating on his impressions of Germany as he encountered it in Frankfort, its surroundings, and among the Bundestag delegates. In his view, very little progress had been made in the previous twenty-five years. He found the same old conceits firmly in place, "pride of birth and . . . wealth, social ambition, sectarian thinking, hatred of Jews, and other kinds of prejudice."[70] Barely a month later, obviously prompted by the flood of anti-Jewish publications, he again addressed the problem of Judeophobia: "The hatred of the Jews which suddenly arose throughout Germany and will end in actual persecution, brings us ever closer to the fine Middle Ages with which the sensibility [i.e. the intelligentsia] of our age is so tenderly in love. We may yet see Jews, witches, and freethinkers roasted on the same spit. What a lovely light this sheds on our civilization."[71] Unfortunately, Oelsner was content to communicate his insights in letters to like-minded friends. Although a committed defender of liberal and democratic ideas, he participated in contemporary events as a spectator and would have been loath to engage in polemical discussions with professors Fries, Rühs, and the like.

Marriage and Women's Lot and Possibilities

Although Rahel was deeply grateful to be finally a married woman, the new state did not prove an easy one for her. The couple was often separated for extended periods, and she seemed to welcome this. All through the summer and fall of 1815 she had resisted Varnhagen's entreaties to join him in Paris. A year later she again had to console and appease him, when he expressed unhappiness about living alone in Mannheim while she was on an extended visit in Frankfort. "Enjoy everything, dear friend," she wrote from Frankfort, "and imagine my taking part in it: I am doing the same here. . . . How strange that even in the most sublime affairs of the heart, we must step back . . . to see them clearly . . . : thus, I recognize from here anew and completely the situation into which my relationship with you has placed me.

It is probably so with everyone; but you know me: my nameless striving for freedom! Every closeness . . . at least *seems* confining; and therefore I must sometimes consider my situation from afar, in order to press it again, along with you, to my heart!"[72]

Rahel periodically had to escape the constraints of married life. Moreover, the old ambivalence toward marriage persisted. She willingly underwent marriage for the sake of social convention. But [she felt then and now] that, as an institution, marriage had outlived its usefulness, existing merely as a remnant of an earlier era. Rahel was well aware that the fault lay not with Varnhagen but with the circumstances. She appreciated his generosity, his regard for her needs, and his truly unselfish love and devotion. Just the same, she struggled with her role as a wife and, particularly, as the wife of an official obliged to keep up appearances.

Since she could and would not burden Varnhagen with her difficulties, she often poured out her heart to others. In a letter to Rose she exclaimed: "Freedom, freedom! especially in a closed state such as marriage. Ah—a!—the old Rahel! Ah!—"[73] To Pauline, on the other hand, Rahel wrote that she was completely free with Varnhagen, otherwise she could not have married him, and that he thought about marriage like she did.[74]

Interestingly, it was the young Count de Custine who received the most detailed account of what she found so intolerable in her new life. In explaining why she hadn't written, she described the unending obligations, interruptions, and visits she had to contend with in Karlsruhe as the wife of an aspiring diplomat. At the same time, she asserted that she was leading "the most doleful, forsaken, unsocial, unfriendly life: without diversion, charm, excitement, stimulation of any kind; without any occupation and activity, lonely and alone; but in uninterrupted commotion! So that I am becoming quite stupid and unable to write. Now you understand it after all! I am no longer of any account. That is, whatever could emanate from me finds no bearing; all that touches me, does not relate to me. All relates only to Varnhagen; and this to his duty, his position; I have none and am also not free."[75] Rahel, who had for so long impressed the eminent of the age with her personality, intelligence, and social skills, suddenly found herself ignored and passed over, defined solely by her status as a wife. Understandably, she objected to being treated as a mere appendage to her husband and his position, for, as a single woman, she had indeed turned her hostess's role into something akin to a profession, from which she could derive satisfaction and acknowledgment, and, at times, even the feeling that through the spoken and written word she was of some consequence.

Periodically, she dared imagine herself in a regular occupation, where she could apply the talents that lay unused within her. Thus, she wrote to Varnhagen in 1815:

God! what fortune, what bliss, if destiny places you where you can apply the gifts given to you by nature. That is completed happiness. If I stood high in society, where it is necessary to oversee, to choose, and to act resolutely! I would do it well, forcefully and gently. I know it. I feel it, I prove it often. I have no ambition whatsoever. That is for sure. Because as soon as I can only suspect that another knows something, does it better, I would happily see him do it; and with pleasure and delight, wherever and whatever it may be. I haven't the slightest envy for talents that I do not possess. But to let mine wither is hard; and to see that done badly which I could do well, is bitter fruit (Höllenspeise).[76]

Knowing how competent and resourceful she proved in organizing the rescue operation in Prague, her claim is certainly justified.

Short of having a real occupation, however, women needed diversion and stimulation, Rahel reasoned. Thus, she counseled her sister, Rose, to permit herself some amusement by seeking out "places where objects, words, and people touch you, revitalize blood, life, nerves, and thoughts. We women are doubly in need of this."[77] She argued with considerable sarcasm that men's occupations were, in their eyes at least, affairs that flattered their ambition. They provided the possibility for advancement and human interaction, whereas women's lives related solely and entirely to their husbands' position. She emphatically refuted the idea that women's minds were constituted differently from men's and that they therefore could find contentment through their husbands and sons. "This claim derives from the assumption that a woman's soul knows nothing higher than the demands and claims of her husband . . . or the talents and wishes of her children: this would render *any* marriage, as such, the highest achievable human state. But this is not so." Women, of course, did love and care for their families and generally made them their highest and most urgent concern, but this could not fulfill them or give them strength and fortitude for an entire life. "This is the reason for so much frivolity seen in women . . . : they have . . . no space for their own feet, they must put them only where the man has just stood and wants to stand; and they see with their eyes the entire fascinating world like one who has been bewitched like a tree with its roots in the ground: every attempt, every wish, to undo this unnatural state is called frivolity or even considered culpable behavior."

During the three weeks spent with Rose, Rahel not only reestablished a sisterly bond but also gained insight into the limited and subservient life Rose was leading. In her frequent letters, she implored Rose to free herself from her wifely and motherly obligations ("Your son is big, your household small"[78]) and visit her in Karlsruhe. She suggested books for her to read and described in detail her own life with a view to motivating Rose into becoming more active. These sisterly concerns meshed with Rahel's intense and long-standing interest in the lot and possibilities of women and increasingly led her to surprisingly modern insights of a general nature.

The Old Loves—Friendship, Literature, and the Theater

To Rahel's great relief, political matters and events did not intrude into every epistolary exchange. With some friends she could still engage in the spontaneous, free, and far-ranging kinds of dialogue that suited her eternally active imagination so well. She could write letters in which "the soul shall take a stroll, where it will not pursue a purposeful and especially not a premeditated journey along the rutted, dusty highway. We shall walk upon fresh, little, abstract paths that we ourselves did not yet know: and even there, we shall follow the play of the clouds, we shall enjoy the enchantment of the light and even go after the darkness, if it beckons!"[79] This is how Rahel corresponded with Astolphe de Custine. He responded with similarly imaginative letters, observing, for example, that a letter must be a surprise as much for the one who is writing it as for the recipient and that, therefore, a missive with a given topic loses all charm.[80] Like Rahel, he saw epistolary writing as a creative act:

There are two kinds of letters; those which give the portrait, the description of life, and others which are their complement, that is, those in which the distressed heart searches for a way to make up for experienced vexations . . . ; and not even always for vexations, since there are situations which are agreeable in themselves and yet call forth the desire for other things; as there are musical chords which prompt our ear to demand others. It is for this purpose that letters seem to me especially good, they turn out to be not a portrait of life but real action, a life within life . . . they are something in themselves, and they often appear in outright contradiction to our occupations and situation. But there are very few people one can write to like this; you understand everything, and by this you spoil me, for in order to educate myself, I should always listen to people like you and speak only with animals.[81]

Custine was a remarkable young nobleman, ideally suited to explore with Rahel the human psyche, philosophical and moral questions, or the turns of history. He combined unusual intuitive powers with a keen intellect. He had benefited from a superior education and the broadening effects of many years of travel. Personal adversity, moreover, had rendered him highly sensitive to moral values and ethical questions, censorious of hypocrisy and pretense, and even capable of rising above the prejudices and conventions of the time.[82]

Astolphe de Custine (1790–1857) came from a liberal noble family. His grandfather was the famous general of the French revolutionary army who, in 1792, conquered Frankfort on the Main and Mainz, but shortly afterward paid for a pro-monarchist remark with his head. Astolphe's father, who spoke out in defense of the general, was guillotined as well, and his mother only barely escaped a similar fate. Astolphe devoted himself to travel, the study of languages and literature, and religious literature especially. His ambition was to become a writer and to this end, he tried himself at almost every literary genre—poems, dramas, novels, and novellas. Although these were not failures, real success eluded him. He made a name for himself only later in life as a writer of travel books, especially with his four-volume work on Russia, *Russie en 1839* (1843).[83] It is unclear to what extent he carried on his father's and his grandfather's political liberalism. In his book on Russia, he stated that he traveled to that country as a monarchist in search of arguments against representative government but returned instead a partisan of constitutions.

His regard and admiration for Rahel were genuine and deep. He confided in her with long, introspective, and romantically moody letters, and she responded as usual with empathy, understanding, and lovingly given advice and emotional support. At other times he wrote amusing travelogues or lengthy essays on what he observed to be characteristic differences between the French and the Germans. A beautiful concert could prompt him to devote many pages to the event and the emotions it awakened in him. Custine wrote in French, Rahel mostly in German. They rarely began their letters with a formal address. But within the body of the letter she called him "my dear Astolf" or, somewhat ironically, "my dear count," while she was his "chère amie." Although she had met him after her marriage, she signed with her old name, Rahel, or the letter *R* and he with Astolphe.[84] Late in life, Rahel summed up what she considered so good about their relationship: the fact that they had no relationship at all but agreed with each other as human beings, no matter that she was old and he young, that she was a woman and he a man, that she was German and he French.[85] In other words, they were able to transcend all social differences and categories, including the fact that he was an aristocrat and devout Catholic and she a Jew converted to Protestantism.

In spite of his privileged social position, Custine was somewhat of a misfit in society. The traumatic events of his early childhood, the absence of a stable father figure, and the overpowering love of his beautiful and lonely mother, for whom this only son became the object of all her affection and devotion, combined to produce an insecure and emotionally troubled man. In the years 1816 to 1819, when the correspondence was at its most intense, Custine was not yet suffering from the notoriety of later years nor had he experienced the tragic deaths in rapid succession of his young wife, small son, and beloved mother. The notoriety pertained to his homosexuality, a further indication of his social marginality. It is unclear whether or to what extent Rahel was aware of his homosexual leanings.[86] It would, in any case, hardly have affected her attitude toward the young man. Rahel seems to have been completely nonjudgmental in matters of sexuality. Friederike Liman, for example, who was involved later in life in two lesbian relationships, remained the intimate and dear friend she had been since they were children. Custine's letters contain passages that can be read as allusions to his homosexuality, mainly in the form of descriptions of nature, which served as reflections of his inner state.[87] In April 1817, for example, he wrote to her of his great disappointment over the belated arrival of spring, which he described as "a winter without hope. Not a ray of light in the sky, no life on earth, not a presentiment of abundance, nothing. It appears that nature ceased its eternal conversation, and . . . we are still here listening." He preceded this lament with an even more personal observation about how he felt separated from the external world and was "naturally outside nature. . . . All that I sow on this earth lacks sun and dew and is finally carried off by a hurricane."

About the same time, Custine told her about having broken off a proposed match. Since the letter is lost, we do not know how he described the affair. We only have Rahel's answer, which tells of her relief that he didn't marry:

In short, I am content with everything. Except if you marry. You will no longer be the same if you put yourself under this moral yoke. You yourself condemn yourself again and again by remaining in it for morality's sake. Your freedom, your happiness is gone: and then you are *immoral* because you ruin yourself and are nothing to the others. You may still find the goddess of your heart and your eyes. . . . Don't *attempt* another marriage. Don't go like a *fils de famille*: and don't make a name destined to go under happier than *yourself! !* But my words are superfluous chatter, why should you not resist them if you are resisting your best inner self?[88]

A year later, pressured by his mother, Custine was again close to marrying. He describes the traumatic events—for the girl, for the girl's mother, and for himself, in a very detailed letter. Once again Rahel was overjoyed that he had extricated himself at the last moment. *"What* happiness that you are not married! ! ! ! ! ! . . . . —I knew you *weren't in love*: I knew you under the spell of a coterie. . . . What a blessing your letter today, dearest Astolf! I keep the friend; *he* is saved. Saved through his own strength; the strength of truthfulness within him. And therefore fortified for all times."[89] Each time, Rahel opposed the marriage because she knew that Custine was following not his heart but societal pressures. And she feared that by compromising his own principles he would ruin the best qualities within him.

The correspondence reveals Custine to be a deeply religious man. He greatly admired the writings of the German mystics Johannes Tauler (ca. 1300–51) and Angelus Silesius (1624–77), the latter having just been rescued from oblivion by Friedrich Schlegel. Among the French mystics he appreciated especially Louis-Claude Marquis de Saint-Martin (1743–1804), whom he discovered through the Varnhagens. Rahel, in turn, had for some time immersed herself in the writings of these very same authors as well as those of Jakob Böhme (1575–1624) and Jeanne-Marie de la Motte-Guyon (1648–1717). In 1833, and again in 1834, Varnhagen published excerpts from the writings of Angelus Silesius and Saint-Martin along with the markings and comments Rahel had added in the margins while reading them. An enlarged edition followed in 1849. The small volume is testimony to Rahel's intense preoccupation with these two religious thinkers.[90] It is a side of Rahel that is not well known and, like all religious feeling, difficult to explain fully. What drew Rahel, rational, sociable, worldly, sensuous, and not at all given to asceticism, to these texts? No doubt, her interest emanated to a large extent from the same need for spiritual solace and guidance that drove so many of the Romantics into the lap of the Catholic church during this time of turmoil and uncertainty. But, instead of submitting to ecclesiastical authority, Rahel turned to those thinkers and poets whose intense religiosity led to a direct and often spontaneous relation with the Divine, unaided and often in opposition to the church and its hierarchy of worldly deputies.

The mutual regard for the mystics and a very personal form of religious experience forged a special bond between Rahel and Custine. There was also much that separated them, as a long letter of Rahel's on praying makes clear.[91] Prompted by a missive from Custine in which he confided his deepest inner beliefs to her, she used a text by the Swiss theologian Johann Kaspar Lavater to convey her own convictions. Rahel copied several long passages of Lavater's that she liked. But she also argued in detail against those she didn't agree with, because she knew that they would appeal to Custine. These concerned above all Lavater's way of separating praying from thinking because, in his view, the good prayer emanated from either a state of rapture or anguish. "Quite differently," argued Rahel, "to think of God is to pray. Holy, pious, earnest, upright resolutions are praying." She maintained that it was "childish . . . to speak of God in any other way than as the embodiment of reason and goodness." Reason and goodness were the highest goods given to man by God, Rahel continued. Through reason and goodness and empathy we are able to know each other and relate to each other. She did not rule out rapture and despair but placed them at the extreme ends of the scale of human activity, calling them a "thoughtless élan." She also allowed for the possibility of spiritual revelation and miracles.

In addition to their explorations into mystical literature and religious devotion (as well as the "fresh, little, abstract paths" along which they told each other of their moods, philosophical insights, and experiences), Rahel and Custine exchanged their views on contemporary literature, notably Goethe and Custine's compatriot, Germaine de Staël, prompted by her much talked about last work, *Considérations sur les principaux évènement de la révolution française* (1818, *Considerations on the Principal Events of the French Revolution*), and her death the previous year.

Rahel often talked with Custine about Goethe. But although his knowledge of German was exceptional and his interest in the poet genuine, his understanding of the poet did not agree with Rahel's. Custine met Goethe in 1816 and described his impressions in a very long letter to Rahel.[92] The missive consists of one great encolmium, while taking exception to the poet's lack of commitment to the Christian faith. Custine, the devout Catholic, joined others in reproaching Goethe for his "heathendom." Probably for this reason, Rahel returned the letter, explaining that she did not wish to have among her possessions a "libel against the great man."[93]

Rahel and Madame de Staël became acquainted with each other in 1804, when the latter attended Rahel's "open house" while visiting Berlin. At that time, the much younger and less experienced Rahel succeeded in impressing the famous visitor with her intelligence and kindness. Now, clearly touched by her recent death, Rahel frequently reflected on this writer's strengths and weaknesses. She told Custine that she loved Madame de Staël and probably more so than the people who admired her uncritically and believed all the contradictory things by and about her.[94] At the same time, she was quite explicit in her criticism of this brilliant woman and her fame especially.

She protested against the sanctimonious acclaim she was receiving: "I wish she was still alive and could smell *this* incense." Rahel thought that people granted her too much spirit. In her view, de Staël did indeed have spirit but lacked thoroughness. There was too much in her works that was disparate, that remained unintegrated and therefore lacked "genius." De Staël lacked "self-knowledge," which for Rahel constituted "the keystone of artistic greatness."

About her latest work, Rahel wrote: "Madame de Staël on the French Revolution! This European book, because all of Europe is reading it, is not as good as its effect will be; she says everything, repeats everything and herself on every page, often in the form of antitheses, thus not merely spoonfeeding but inculcating with knives that which has not yet become part of Europe's flesh and blood."[95] Quite obviously, Rahel appreciated the book's significance. Not only had de Staël authored the first full-length treatise on the French Revolution, but the work also represented a strong endorsement of the Revolution's democratic goals. At the same time, Rahel insisted on treating its author not merely as a gifted woman writer but as any writer of note who therefore deserved a critical assessment. De Staël, she stated, had plenty of intelligence but her soul was inattentive (keine horchende Seele). It was "never quiet within her, never, as if she was thinking for herself, but always as if she was already telling it to the multitude. . . . However, in her book, she stirs up those things . . . which must indeed by discussed." Rahel also felt that de Staël did not possess the characteristic French sensitivity for the language. Words "don't serve her willingly like they do with good authors. . . . I see the words in rebellion all around her, like flying spirits, when she is sitting at her writing table before a blank sheet of paper; it never becomes music." In her letters and her conversation during those years, Rahel turned her attention again and again to what she considered this outstanding woman's accomplishments and shortcomings.

Following four years of lively correspondence, Rahel and Custine seem to have lost contact for almost a decade. Only two letters by Custine interrupted this long silence, one brief and undated and another from 1825, in which he informs Rahel that he had lost both his wife and his son and that, moreover, witnessing the terrible suffering and death of these two people had also destroyed his mother's health.[96] There seems to have been no other communication during this tragic period of Custine's life. The reasons for this long silence are unknown. The few letters exchanged in 1829 and 1830 indicate no rupture. They express the old feelings of friendship and trust and familiarity. Sometime in 1829, Rahel and Custine must have met again, for he writes that for him the encounter constituted a major "event in his life," and he timidly inquires whether it had made a similar impression on her.[97] Both are making plans for a longer reunion. Rahel tells him of her life, of her latest publication in Fouqué's journal, *Berlinische Blätter für deutsche Frauen* (Berlin papers for German women), and of her discovery of *Les Orientales*, by Victor Hugo. One letter also contains a detailed but well-meaning critique of Custine's autobiographical novella *Aloys*. After that she once again lost track of her young friend. Four years after Rahel's death, Custine expressed his deep-felt admiration for her by writing a lengthy eulogy for the *Revue de Paris*.[98]

Another epistolary dialogue very much to Rahel's liking was the one she conducted with the actress Auguste Brede. In the foreground stood the discussion of Rahel's other great love besides literature, the theater. In their letters the two women deliberated a multitude of subjects relating to the stage—the quality of plays and operas, the merits of actors, singers, dancers, and directors, performance techniques, costumes, scenery, as well as more fundamental questions regarding the purpose and merits of the theater.

Their close friendship dated from the time when Rahel, fearing the ravages of the Napoleonic wars, found refuge in Prague at the home of the actress. Auguste Brede, highly intelligent, gifted, and beautiful, had a special talent for appreciating Rahel's unusual insights and wit. Born in Berlin in 1784, she acted in Stettin, Leipzig, and Dresden before coming to the German theater in Prague. After the war, she found employment at the court theater in Stuttgart, where she celebrated her greatest success.

Of this lively and sizable correspondence only a small number of letters by Rahel has been published to date and none by the actress.[99] The friendship as well as the letters they exchanged, however, were unique, the bond between the two women being personal, social, and professional. Not only had they shared a home for nearly two years in Prague through war, uncertainty, and hardship, but each had cared for the other during a prolonged and serious illness. Auguste Brede had also lent a helping hand in caring for the wounded soldiers. Moreover, both women shared a rather marginal social status, which they experienced and expressed above all as a sense of being "without a homeland" (ohne Heimat). Auguste Brede's itinerant life as an actress, dependent on various liaisons with well-to-do men to augment her meager earnings on the stage, placed her outside respectable society. Rahel, as a Jew who had freed herself from the constraints of her community and, to some extent, her family, leading the life of an independent intellectual woman, was similarly uprooted and only tenuously connected to mainstream society.

Both women were also single at that time. And finally and perhaps most importantly, they were united in their common love for the theater.

Rahel was not alone in regarding the theater as an institution of utmost significance for the welfare and progress of society. In Germany, where the myriad of borders, censorship, and various, more or less retrograde, political orders severely impeded the dissemination of ideas, many considered the theater the one institution that took the place of an otherwise absent public forum. Open to all classes, it allowed for the presentation of new ideas and the enjoyment of art. As Rahel put it: "A city without a theater . . . is like a person with his eyes shut: a place without a breath of fresh air. . . . In our time and our cities [the theater] is the one general [institution], where the circle of joy, of intellect, of participation, and the gathering . . . of all classes is drawn together."[100] The stage provided the lens through which the audience could partake in the evolution of social and ethical thought.

Rahel's notion of the theater concurred with Schiller's idea of the stage as a moral institution in the widest sense: a morality in support of change toward greater social and political justice. The theater was also seen as a venue for forging a national consciousness. Establishing a national theater was a major concern of Goethe's and Schiller's earlier in the century, and one which they discussed at length in their letters to each other. It was also foremost on Rahel's mind, as her remarks to Ludwig Tieck, whose theater reviews she greatly valued, indicate. Tieck had been active as a reformer of the German stage with his translations of Shakespeare and other great European dramatists and as a dramaturge in Dresden until his turn to conservatism in the 1840s. Urging him to continue to publish his critical assessments of a theater that had, in both their views, recently embarked on a wrong course, she wrote: "My best Tieck! . . . have everything you promise printed soon! Hurry. It is no small matter what kind of a theater a nation has, if [this nation] is ready for one. . . . It is as much the proof of what a nation wants as the guide to what it is supposed to want."[101]

Rahel was similarly demanding of her actress friend. After one of Auguste's stage successes, she urged her on: "Don't tire and help wherever you can. With word and deed! You have greater responsibilities: for you have greater means; you are beautiful, and you have a talent, and a *position.*" With these gifts, the artist was expected to fulfill a mission: "Out with the truth! Get the truth out of the dark crevices!"[102]

Auguste Brede, in turn, was deeply committed to her art. Intent on becoming an excellent actress, she was at the same time surprised when fame actually came. In 1814 she was invited to give a guest performance in

Frankfort, and she described the anticipation that greeted her in a letter to Rahel: "Just think, my dear, to my greatest surprise I have quite a reputation as an actress, the whole city is full of it, that I am here, and they all look at me as if I were a strange bird—and everyone asks when I am appearing—this is good and not good."[103] More importantly, Auguste Brede seems to have considered her profession in similar, if not quite so explicitly political, terms as Rahel, as a calling in the service of art and progress. Thus, she felt most fulfilled and achieved her greatest success in those roles that promoted the cause of liberalism. In December 1819 she wrote to Rahel in her modest and matter-of-fact manner: "I am very diligent, I study a great deal—as it is my fortune that in the new tragedies wonderfully appropriate roles have been written for me."[104] The parts Brede referred to were the female leads in Ludwig Uhland's historical dramas *Ernst Herzog von Schwaben* (Ernest Duke of Swabia) and *Ludwig der Baier* (Ludwig of Bavaria), both of which had their world premiere in Stuttgart in 1819. Uhland (1787–1862), a personal friend of Varnhagen's, took an active part in the struggle for a constitutional government. He worked as a lawyer and for many years held various government appointments, including a professorship at the University of Tübingen; he renounced the latter position in 1833, when the government put pressure on the oppositional professors. Today, Uhland's reputation rests primarily on his lasting achievements as a lyrical poet and his theoretical writings on medieval literature, Germanic legends, and folklore. His dramas, although well received at the time because they espoused the cause of liberalism, have been forgotten.

Rahel responded to her friend's triumph by putting her on a par with two other great actresses. One was the late French actress Claire-Joseph Léris (1723–1803), known as Clairon, who had achieved fame in the dramas of Voltaire. The other was Brede's contemporary, Sophie Schröder, who was acclaimed in Vienna as Sappho in Franz Grillparzer's tragedy of the same name: "That I live to see such honor coming to you! Clairon raises Voltaire's scales; Schröder carries Grillparzer on her wings and Auguste Uhland on hers to Parnassus! This pleases my soul for a hundred reasons!"[105] Following this initial accolade, she urged Auguste to take care of her health and her voice and then went on to the larger meaning of her success: "You must be so very pleased to have established yourself in Stuttgart and to be so effective; it is difficult to pull the German cart along; its wheels are not yet aligned symmetrically on both sides; and many take this for an excuse when they should be helping: those from whom help comes at this time must . . . be wheelwright, smith, coachman, or the extra team of horses."

In other words, promoting the national cause required unusual devotion and ingenuity. Although Auguste relished roles and plays with which she could identify, she could pursue such lofty goals only when the circumstances permitted. Given the dearth of interesting roles, her primary concern was to obtain parts that would further her reputation. For a brief time, she hoped to succeed grandly, to "perhaps *yet* be named among the best."[106] In the 1820s, however, this proved to be increasingly difficult. The correspondence reveals that for many years Brede was unable to secure an appropriate engagement.

Ever solicitous about her friend's career, Rahel counseled her about artistic matters and assisted her financially. She also stood by her with personal advice. In 1815, when Brede was reluctant to accept a possible position in Berlin without Bentheim's, her lover's, approval, Rahel wrote: "Dear Auguste, only a few of the most pressing words because I am so tired and irritated. Don't permit Bent: [Count Bentheim] to confuse you *again*, no matter how much you love him! I know this attraction, this charm, this feeling, but you must have a *sort* [be provided for]. *He* cannot give you one as long as he lives and lives in *this fashion*. . . . And even if you live in the same place, you still have [to contend with] the vexations and boredom because the life he leads is completely different from yours: and yet you are not free."[107] Rahel was speaking from experience. She knew only too well what being separated from a lover meant. At the same time, her relationship with Finckenstein had taught her how much suffering derived from a liaison across class lines. She therefore tried to strengthen Auguste's sense of independence and pride in her art by appealing to her responsibility as an artist. At one point she even urged her to go against the current trend of specializing in one kind of role (such as tragedian, comedian, or ingénue) and look for a position where she could prove her varied talents. In her view, such narrow specialization was detrimental to the actors as well as to the theater.[108] Brede agreed with Rahel and followed this advice for a time, but without success. She then went with the fashion and applied for a role in her old specialty. This, however, proved equally difficult, as evidenced by the correspondence right up to Rahel's death. Only in 1836 did August Brede succeed in obtaining adequate employment, at the Burgtheater in Vienna.

In the correspondence, Rahel once again appears to have been the source of comfort, advice, help, and deeper insights. She never neglected to write to her friend on holidays, especially around Christmastime, when Auguste often felt abandoned and adrift. Auguste lovingly acknowledged the beneficial effect of her friend's letters, assuring her that she felt more courageous and optimistic whenever she communicated with Rahel.[109] Another time she wrote: "Dear Rahel! Your letter has cheered me. And if I could enjoy your company for two weeks, I would be completely content."[110] Rahel, too, benefited from this friendship. In her dialogue with the actress she was able to hone her tools as a theater critic. Her very first letter to Brede, who was away performing in Frankfort, closed with the question: "Shall I write a theater review?"[111] Another time, she requested the return of a long and detailed letter about the theater in Berlin, claiming that she needed it for a review she was about to publish. Although this particular letter was never printed, Rahel published excerpts from others either anonymously or in the name of her brother Ludwig Robert. Having been an aficionado of the theater all her life, she obviously could speak knowledgeably about such matters. The close relationship with her actress friend, however, must have provided her with valuable additional insights, including those aspects usually hidden from the audience.

On 22 July 1819 Varnhagen's promising diplomatic career came to a sudden end when he was recalled from his post in Karlsruhe. No reasons were given, except that the king had decided to eliminate the post. In actuality, it was the government of Baden who requested the removal of this all-too-liberal envoy, who not only supported constitutional government but whose sympathies were quite clearly on the side of the increasingly radical political opposition.[112] Varnhagen, who had recently paid a visit to Berlin, had been warned by Minister Stägemann. At the same time, he must also have become aware that his staunchest advocate, Hardenberg, would be unable to provide the necessary support, since he was himself struggling to survive as one of the last defenders of liberalism. Rahel, in Baden for a cure at the time, reacted calmly. She too had repeatedly warned her husband not to be so brash. Now she counseled him to remain calm, to undertake nothing and wait for instructions.[113] These arrived soon enough: he was to go to America as a Prussian envoy. Varnhagen declined, considering the appointment as a form of banishment. On the advice of Stägemann, he went instead to Berlin to plead his case. Thus, the Varnhagens returned to Berlin following a seven-year absence.

Meanwhile, in August of that same year, Metternich was meeting in Carlsbad with his ministers. Precipitated by the assassination of the popular playwright August von Kotzebue by the student militants, he issued the Carlsbad Decrees. These became the nucleus for the suppression of all liberal, democratic, and nationalist endeavors throughout the German lands.

The measures increased the already severe censorship laws (especially for the press), forbade all student associations, and called for the dismissal of professors suspected of revolutionary sympathies. The Reaction was indeed taking hold, and Varnhagen saw himself, not unjustly, as one of its first casualties.

5

RETURN TO BERLIN:

THE SALON VARNHAGEN

Rahel's feelings toward Berlin had always been fraught with ambivalence. Berlin was her birthplace and the locale of her intensely experienced and unhappy childhood. In Berlin she also made her initially successful strides toward assimilation and integration into Gentile society; these, of course, led her to recognize just how difficult and even impossible the realization of her dream would be. Not surprisingly, her return to Berlin after a seven-year hiatus proved difficult, as it was in no way accompanied by a sense of coming home. The Prussian capital was as forbidding and unwelcoming as ever. All the negative and retrograde aspects, against which Rahel had railed as a young woman, were now entrenched and officially condoned. At every step she was reminded of her outsider status. Rahel's letters document her impressions and reactions with varying degrees of disappointment and outrage.

To Pauline Wiesel she described it bluntly as "a *curse*" that had been visited on her and that she must endure. "*Nothing* pleases me here. . . . May no one have to return to his place of origin where he hasn't been for a long time! . . . My greatest main torment here is: that whatever remains of my previous life has become so old, so worn, so stunted, so ugly. Nothing but infamous ghosts . . . such old, withered, petrified, ossified *masses*, in the old and yet so devastated rooms, are *furies from the past* which unshield our eyes *by force* with their torches, angrily show us, illuminate, what we do not want to see."[1] To Auguste Brede she confided that it was not gratifying to return to one's homeland after a lengthy absence, because she really didn't belong. She "met nothing but obsolete figures, antiquated views, worn-out opinions, twisted knowledge (verparktes Wissen), and . . . obstinate pride." She experienced "meanness from people of high outward and inward standing" who had been "intimate friends."[2] Her sister, Rose, received a letter some eight months afterward that described the experience in very similar terms.[3] Only with Brinckmann did Rahel manage to find a more moderate and even nostalgic tone: "Berlin . . . does not enchant me. . . . Death, aided by the war, has taken its toll among our friends, whom you portray to me along with our whole way of life: at every corner . . . where *our kind* used to live, there are *strangers*. . . . The whole constellation of beauty, grace, coquetry, liking, love affairs, wit, elegance, cordiality, urge to develop ideas, true earnestness, uninhibited calling on each other and visiting, good-humored jest, is dissipated. The ground floors are all shops, the gatherings *dinés* or formal *assemblées*, all discussions almost . . . a pale confusion of ideas."[4]

These accounts represent variations on a few themes: the old feeling of being a stranger in her homeland, exacerbated by the uncertain situation the Varnhagens found themselves in, as well as the familiar indignities, which Rahel experienced almost immediately; the keen disappointment at the lack of progress that she deduced from the widespread embrace of retrograde ideas among old acquaintances, the generally depressed atmosphere, and the different, much more ostentatious kind of sociability. Returning after a long absence also meant a confrontation with the past. At every step she was reminded of the years of her youth when her optimistic belief in human progress seemed natural and justified.

Additionally, Rahel couldn't help but see the contrast to the southern states of Germany, where, until the Carlsbad Decrees, the liberals had been able to work actively for a constitutional government in several lands. A constitutional monarchy was established in Wurtemberg, and, as seen earlier, in Baden the democratic opposition was so active that Varnhagen, as one of its strongest supporters, had to be dismissed. In Frankfort the Bundestag, although ineffective and burdened by bureaucratic constraints, served at least as a symbol of progress. In Berlin, on the other hand, the reactionary forces were firmly entrenched, and the king had no intention of giving up his despotic rule. Rahel, the progressive thinker as well as the outsider, felt doubly estranged. The notion of homeland was for her intimately bound up with the larger sociopolitical context.

For Varnhagen, too, returning was difficult. Coming to terms with the abrupt change in his life proved an arduous task, as his hopes for a brilliant career had been raised and suddenly dashed. He was often deeply depressed. For many years his situation remained undecided. Initially, he was put "on disposition" until a suitable position could be found for him. But this proved difficult. He had refused the post offered him in the United States, and Metternich opposed his being appointed anywhere else in Germany. Thus, he waited, often deprived of his salary for months. Finally, in 1824, he was officially retired at half his pay and, in 1825, given the title Geheimer Legationsrat, or privy councillor. He served in this capacity for many years, writing dispatches and reports for the foreign office.[5] In the main, however, he devoted himself to writing and publishing.

THE SECOND SALON

Continuity and Change

In time both Rahel and Varnhagen adjusted to their new life. Until 1827 they made their home in a furnished apartment on Französische Straße. It became the first locale of Rahel's "second salon," to which Varnhagen contributed in significant ways. For, although the famous Berlin sociability had changed, it certainly had not disappeared. There were still "open houses" that easily competed with the tedious social life among the highborn. Women and Jews still played an important role. Jewish women continued to impress with their intellectual and artistic sophistication and refinement, their wit and kindness, as well as their active promotion of egalitarian social relations. But the favored centers of sociability now included Christian just as often as Jewish homes. Among the most renowned were those of Friedrich Stägemann, councillor of state, Karl von Savigny, minister of justice, and Jacob Herz Beer, the well-to-do and cultivated merchant and father of the composer Giacomo Meyerbeer and the playwright Michael Beer. Very much sought after were the Sunday musicales at the distinguished home of the Mendelssohn-Bartholdy family, where both Felix and Fanny performed. The author Amalie von Helvig, a niece of Goethe's great love, Charlotte von Stein, received guests at her home, and so did Bettine von Arnim. As the list indicates, the representative "open houses" were now led by the highly positioned, well-to-do, and established—Gentile and Jewish. Upstarts like the young Rahel, Henriette Herz, or Dorothea Mendelssohn-Veit-Schlegel could not have had the impact they did a quarter of a century earlier.

Rahel, although she continued to infuse her society with the old unconventional, open-minded, and tolerant spirit, also adapted to the times. Whereas earlier she had insisted on simply serving tea and also discouraged readings or other artistic presentations or entertainment, thereby making conversation the sole focus of her gatherings, she now often treated her guests to elegant dinners and musical offerings. She delighted in describing these evenings, and especially the meals, to her friends and family, developing quite a competitive spirit and pride as a hostess. She informed Pauline Wiesel, for example, about a dinner she gave for the Mendelssohn family, occasioned by the marriage of Fanny to Wilhelm Hensel in 1829: "Leah's daughter married the painter Hensel Saturday a week ago. All are happy. Yesterday I gave a soirée for them. The family, six persons, and ten more. Macaroni, anchovy salad; venison and duck, bread pudding, *baisers*, pears, grapes, nuts, apple compote, red bilberries; raspberry and hazelnut ice cream. Everything prepared to perfection."[6]

At the same time, Rahel took great care in preserving those aspects that rendered her first open house so distinctive, by treating her visitors in accordance with her humanistic and egalitarian principles. Each one was still seen as a unique manifestation of the rich fabric of human nature. She thus justified her contention that the second salon was a continuation of her first, the "attic room — on a larger scale."[7] The character and aim of her second open house are neatly summed up in a letter to Auguste Brede: "My efforts at sociability are taking their course. My task is, in my weakened state, to fend off people. They have it good. They can find themselves, firstly. They are being flattered, entertained, cared for, not personally contradicted, attended to, they can come after the theater, find conversation, even when they meet us alone, the newest books, always a ready refreshment."[8] The purpose of the open house had changed: conversation was now but one attraction among several rather disparate ones — entertainment, refreshments, books, even flattery.

Readers may recall that there are several accounts of Rahel's "first salon," the most detailed being the portrait of a representative evening in 1801 by Count von Salm. An anonymous visitor wrote a similar description of an evening in 1830 at the "second salon," detailing its ambiance and visitors. By this time, the Varnhagens had moved into their own home on Mauerstraße. Here Rahel was finally able to set up a home to her liking and taste. It would also be her last. As the anonymous visitor described it, the light blue rooms were large and airy. On one side they looked out on the street and, on the other, onto high trees. The furnishings were simple but elegant. Sofas, Rahel's forte-piano, books, and plants were arranged in a pleasing and harmonious fashion. However, while in the Levin home a portrait of G. E. Lessing symbolically represented the spirit of the Enlightenment, the present living room was graced by the bust of Prince Louis Ferdinand, given to Rahel for safekeeping by Pauline Wiesel,[9] and the bust of Friedrich Schleiermacher. The likeness of Louis Ferdinand, the highest-born person to visit her first open house, was surely meant to remind the visitor not only of the possibilities of a more open society but also of the fact that this project remained unfinished in the 1820s. The meaning of Schleiermacher's bust is more elusive. On the one hand, he was a friend, a frequenter of salons, and an admirer of the Jewish salonnières, as well as a liberal theologian; on the other, he had also on various occasions aroused Rahel's (and her brother Ludwig's) disapproval. Both men lacked the model character of the single-minded, rational, tolerant, and now often conveniently forgotten Lessing. Instead, each in his own particular manner bore within him the contradictions and ambiguities of the age.

Like so many who came before, the anonymous visitor was immediately struck by Rahel's special talent as a hostess as well as by her notion of sociability, evidently still experienced as new and unusual.[10] Rahel's insistence on genuine relations, no matter how brief or transient, must have contrasted in obvious ways with the prevailing form of social interaction, where convention and empty formalities still dictated the tone, manner, and content of conversation.

The visitor describes Rahel's manner of interaction:

A kind as well as lightening-quick grasp of human nature gave her the ease with which she could quickly find the favorable side of every person, which she then promptly brought to light and animated, while the less favorable side automatically remained in the shadow. In this way, she had a personal relation with each individual. . . . Here then was a true coming together, no . . . empty form . . . never did anyone, man or woman, feel like an empty social decoration, a lifeless salon caryatid; whereas, in other circles, I have often seen how, because they have nothing in common with their host, even outstanding persons served as mere room fillers . . .

Quite obviously, the intent behind this manner of treating a conversational partner was consistent with Rahel's original one—to overcome social barriers. By treating each person as an individual, the importance of social status and other limiting categories receded in favor of meritorious human criteria, such as talent, strength of character, kindness, intelligence, and wit.

Also aimed at overcoming class distinctions and thus similarly consistent with her earlier gatherings was Rahel's insistence on a heterogeneous society. In the course of the evening described, the guests included aristocrats, artists, and learned men, including the diplomat Wilhelm von Reden and his family (an acquaintanceship dating from the time in Frankfort and Karlsruhe) and the renowned singer Anna Milder, who later in the evening entertained the guests with lieder by Kreutzer, Schubert, and Beethoven. Ludwig Robert attended with his wife Friederike, admired primarily for her beauty but also recognized for the poems she wrote. Then there was a young American, Albert Brisbane, who was to become important for bringing the teachings of Saint-Simon to Berlin. The young professor of jurisprudence Eduard Gans (1797–1839), a pupil of Hegel and founder of comparative jurisprudence, was also present, as was the explorer and natural scientist Alexander von Humboldt, then at the height of his fame. Quite late in the evening the eccentric Bettine von Arnim appeared. In those years, and especially after her husband's death in 1831, Bettine von Arnim became an increasingly intimate friend, one of the very few women in Berlin whom Rahel considered her intellectual equal and therefore singled out by calling her "my *pair*" (peer).[11]

That the composition of her society was not merely adventitious but the result of considerable effort by the hostess is revealed in Rahel's letters. In 1827 she wrote to Ludwig Robert enumerating a long list of very diverse visitors who took up her time—men, women, families, foreigners, men in politics, as well as men of learning: "All sorts of passers-through, strangers, the Countess Henckel and daughter and sister. The Barnekows, Count Yorck, the Willisens, Hegel, Humboldt, Ranke. Why mention another forty names! Each contradicts the other."[12] The intent behind naming all these guests was to convey to her brother her success in assembling a mixed and cosmopolitan society. The term *contradicts* is indicative of the variety of views and perspectives her guests must have felt free to express. Rahel's care in bringing together people of disparate orientations is also explicit in a letter of 1829 to Varnhagen, to whom she communicated a similar list, adding that she wrote in such detail "on account of the heterogeneity."[13]

Although Rahel still gathered a mixed society at her house, the character of this society had changed. Whereas earlier, free-lance intellectuals or dilettantes constituted a significant part, it was now oriented around professionals and, especially, academics, as the names Gans, Hegel, Alexander von Humboldt, and Ranke indicate. The conversation still ranged freely over a wide variety of topics, but it was also often dominated by these learned men, with Gans, for example, injecting his political observations, or Alexander von Humboldt steering a scientific discussion. According to the visitor's description, there was a lengthy discussion of music as well as one regarding religious belief among various peoples, to which Alexander von Humboldt contributed his extensive knowledge and experiences among both "primitive" and "civilized" cultures. Gans, who was at the time deeply immersed in the revolutionary events of 1830 in France, liked to turn the conversation to politics. His power of argumentation was as effective in a small circle as in the lecture hall, where he attracted hundreds of students, among them the young Felix Mendelssohn-Bartholdy and Karl Marx.

Politics, which had received little attention in Rahel's first salon, now played a prominent role. The momentous events of the past quarter of a century had left a deep impression on her. She had also benefited from Varnhagen's passion for politics and history, so that she now followed such discussions with great interest and considerable insight. That evening she outlined for her guests her understanding of the progressive unfolding of history, set down by the anonymous visitor as follows. Referring to the revolutionary events in France, she was said to have stated: "All Frenchmen . . . have the republic in their bones, and a republic they shall have. Whether it will be to their benefit or their harm. . . . I also consider the success of the constitutions, after which everyone hankers and strives nowadays, not necessarily certain, they may be of the greatest harm, but that does not prevent us from having to go through with them, *there is no other path to the future*. For the French, who are always ahead—my vanguard people, as I call them—the republic is as unavoidable as the constitution is for us."

This forthright endorsement of political progress, traceable also in many of her letters, reveals that the Varnhagen salon, in addition to its cultural importance, also had a political dimension. It served as a refuge for liberals as well as a forum where they could engage in the free exchange of ideas. There they felt safe from spies and censors that infiltrated the public sphere everywhere during the Period of Restoration. The liberal orientation at the Varnhagen's soirees was noted, for example, by the historian Leopold von Ranke. Although he evolved into a very conservative historian, as a young man he enjoyed and benefited from his interaction with various guests at the Varnhagens. In his autobiography, he relates that it was there that he became acquainted with the "communist journal *Globe*," the representative publication of the Saint-Simonians.[14]

In certain respects then, the assemblies of the 1820s required greater courage and more solid convictions than the open house of the previous era of tolerance and cosmopolitanism. The repression was so pervasive that few dared speak openly. Rahel, keen observer of society, was fully aware of the consequences. A diary entry from the year 1825 can be read as her assessment of the onerous influence the repressive period of Restoration exerted at every level: "To have freedom means simply to have what we need in order to be what we really should be; and to have what we really should have. . . . From this consideration follows one about the cause of lying. The primary lack of freedom results from not being permitted to say what we desire and what we lack. We tell it in secret prayers to our God; or he knows it anyhow. . . . From this again follows the thought that only he to whom we can show ourselves completely can be our friend: . . . He . . . doubles our existence. Deepest requirement of all sociability. Aim and purpose of our language."[15]

Lack of progress and political freedom was, in Rahel's view, not restricted to the public realm but affected all human endeavors and all social and personal interaction. The suppression of freedom as well as material deprivation prevented the individual from reaching his or her potential; it led to lying, deception, secrecy, and to the betrayal of trust and friendship. Only in freedom could people recognize each other as fellow human beings; only in freedom could the purpose of language as true, and truthful, communication be achieved. Thus, Rahel stood by her old conviction in seeing the state of sociability as a reflection of the freedom or lack thereof within the larger society.

The Varnhagen salon may have represented an oasis of liberalism that quietly but firmly opposed the prevailing reactionary spirit, but it did not remain entirely immune. The manner in which the repressive climate spilled over into these assemblies constituted another important difference between the first and the second salon (besides the greater ostentation and the professional character of its frequenters). In 1830 the conversation is shown to have been contentious and frequently dominated by others. In other words, the free exchange of opinions within Rahel's heterogeneous society resulted in vehement manifestations of oppositional forces and loyalties that could not always be resolved or dissolved with the former elegance and ease if the hostess wished not to violate her own principle of free sociability. Thus, on the evening described in detail, Gans, Ludwig Robert, and Varnhagen entered together, "all three of them already immersed in an intense quarrel." Another squabble erupted as Anna Milder was about to begin her musical presentation. This time it was Count von Reden who protested "with irate gestures" against an accusation leveled at a Count von Münster, which Ludwig Robert had somewhat incautiously voiced. A third dispute occurred between Dr. Gans and the Spanish diplomat Cordova. It concerned a most touchy subject to be discussed with a Spanish envoy, namely, the question of whether the sovereign was obliged to keep the oaths and promises made to his people. No doubt, it was the academic contingent that contributed substantially to the argumentative spirit.[16] The seriousness of the disputes, however, derived from the social and political problems facing the European nations. It was Rahel's custom to intervene at such moments to appease and reestablish social harmony among her diverse guests. Like Count von Salm and others, the anonymous reporter admired the agility with which she succeeded without detracting from the seriousness of the argument.

Like Count von Salm's report on the first, the anonymous visitor's account has come to be the authoritative source of the second salon. And like the earlier accounts, it raises questions about whether these evenings happened on a regular basis. Rahel's talents as a hostess are described in very similar terms, and the assembled guests are again very distinguished. Rahel's letters reveal that the visitors were often not notable and their numbers much smaller than the twenty-one persons mentioned in the report. More likely, the gatherings at the Varnhagen's must have resembled those earlier ones at the Levin home, which were made up mainly of family members and a few close and not famous friends.[17]

Another constant in Rahel's life, similarly pointing to missed communication and unsuccessful efforts at social relations, was her feelings of being misunderstood, ignored, or unappreciated. Toward the end of her life these feelings took on a more finite and poignant meaning. "That my entire circle does not know me is an old, harsh, and hardened privation of mine. *Every* day, I see it more," she wrote to a young woman friend. Still willing to reveal herself, she invited others "to examine, judge, ask . . . any question." She closed the passage with a wish she had expressed already as a young woman, albeit with a different metaphor. While earlier she had used the image of the cupboard, which, when opened, would show everything arranged neatly on shelves, thus enabling people to know and understand her, she now exclaimed: "If only my breast were a transparent pane."[18]

Rahel and the Younger Generation

Since Rahel was now in her fifties, it may well be asked whether the times were passing her by and the perceived lack of appreciation was to some extent justified, as her younger visitors especially must have been preoccupied with other, newer concerns and tasks. After all, her second salon took place in the third decade of the nineteenth century, whereas she remained firmly committed to eighteenth-century or Enlightenment thinking. The testimony, however, contradicts such an assumption, for the young intellectuals and artists who frequented her soirees were notable precisely because they were forward-looking, and some even radical. Eduard Gans, Heinrich Heine, Ludwig Börne, and Franz Grillparzer were at the forefront of either literary innovation or political thinking or both. Each in his own way felt and expressed admiration for Frau von Varnhagen, who in turn treated each with her customary openness, respect, and even indulgence. More significantly, she showed herself receptive to their ideas and read their writings with great interest and understanding. With some of them she established a working relationship. Gans is reported to have asked for permission to use an argument of hers during a salon conversation for an article he wanted to publish, a request she gladly granted.[19] And Börne printed excerpts of her letters in his journal *Die Wage* (The scale).[20] But even if Rahel had no intellectual difficulty following these young men, she retained a personal reserve and distance that at times took on the severity of a parent toward a rebellious child. This was especially true when it came to the often-disputed Goethe, against whose all-pervasive influence and Olympian stature the young generation of literati struggled, while Rahel's and Varnhagen's admiration remained undiminished and, in the eyes of these younger men, bordered on idolatry.

In contrast to the habitués of the first salon, with whom Rahel often entered into intense epistolary exchanges, a sustained correspondence did not develop with any of these younger friends. In the case of Eduard Gans this was understandable, as he lived in Berlin and was said to be a daily guest at the Varnhagens. Letters were exchanged when they were separated. In 1825 Rahel wrote a detailed and affectionate answer to a missive Gans had sent from Paris, which, to her delight, contained a lively description of people, places, and the political situation.[21] Their common admiration for France, its revolutionary spirit, and its vibrant intellectual life provided the basis for their friendship. Moreover, together with Varnhagen, Gans edited the *Berliner Jahrbücher für wissenschaftliche Kritik* (Berlin yearbooks for scholarly criticism), which required frequent and close collaboration. Gans's name appears often in the letters Varnhagen and Rahel exchanged when they were separated. The tone is almost always one of affection and high regard, conveying an easy relationship. Varnhagen would inquire, for example, whether Gans had provided Rahel with reading material, in particular the *Globe*. In turn, Rahel reported on various visits by Gans, that he was "completely charming," or how he contributed his share to a stimulating conversation.[22]

Franz Grillparzer, Austria's most renowned nineteenth-century poet and dramatist, met Rahel only once, while visiting Berlin in 1826. He made the usual rounds among the city's notables, among them Hegel and Fouqué, the Mendelssohn-Bartholdys, several literary societies, and, quite by chance, the Varnhagen's open house. In his autobiography, written many years later, he remembered the evening and Rahel, who was as yet unknown to him, as follows: "then the aging woman, who had perhaps never been pretty and was now bent over by illness, who resembled a fairy, if not a witch, began to speak and I was enchanted. My tiredness disappeared or rather, gave way to intoxication. She spoke and spoke until almost midnight, and I no longer know whether they chased me away or I left on my own. Never in my life have I heard anyone speak more interestingly or better."[23] Regrettably, Grillparzer fails to relate the contents of Rahel's deliberations. Any number of topics would have been of interest to the shy and withdrawn author of classicist dramas, poems, and novellas, suffering acutely under the repressive as well as capricious censorship laws in force in Vienna. Grillparzer was no friend of intellectual women and perhaps for this reason stressed something others failed to mention: the physical ravages Rahel's illnesses had left on her appearance. The less womanly this unusual woman was, the easier perhaps it was for him to acknowledge her superior intellect. The encounter with Rahel Varnhagen, however, ranked among the memorable experiences of his Berlin visit.

Rahel was made aware of Ludwig Börne in 1819 by her old acquaintance, Friedrich Gentz, who told her that his journal and his drama reviews were easily the most brilliant and witty things to appear since Lessing. Börne belonged to the younger generation in terms of his writings more than his age. Born in the Frankfort Ghetto in 1786 as Judah Löw Baruch, he studied medicine in Berlin and Halle, then political science in Heidelberg and Gießen. In 1811 he returned to Frankfort, where, hoping for a career in government that would permit integration into Gentile society as a Jew, he was appointed to the civil service, specifically to the service of the city police. He was promptly dismissed from this post after the German defeat of the Napoleonic forces in 1814 because of his Jewishness. He converted in 1818, changing his name to Ludwig Börne, so as not to be immediately identifiable as a Jew. He then turned to free-lance journalism, pioneering a field that became uniquely associated with the liberal German Jew. In 1830 he went to live permanently in Paris, from where he wrote his *Letters from Paris* (1832, 1833, 1834), which earned him literary fame. He died in Paris in 1837.

Rahel was deeply impressed by the quality of Börne's writing and in complete agreement with his liberal political views, which, of course, were anathema to Gentz. She promptly wrote to Auguste Brede about her "new friend," urging her to read his highly informative theater and drama reviews: "Doctor Börne . . . is cutting, deep, thoroughly true, courageous, not taken in by faddishness, entirely new, resigned like one of the good old men; and outraged as one should be. And, as sure as I live, a very decent man.

Bold, but thoughtful. In short, a great favorite of mine."[24] Börne's reviews differed greatly from those then current, which related primarily scandals and gossip about actors and singers. He viewed the theater as a serious matter and, in his reviews, he discussed in detail the ideas of a play, their significance for the contemporary audience, the quality and appropriateness of the actors' performances, the scenery, and the direction. Like Rahel in her letters to Auguste Brede and Ludwig Tieck, he demanded that the theater fulfill its role as a public institution by aiding in the formation of a national consciousness and by exposing the public to new political and social ideas.

It is not known how often Börne and the Varnhagens met.[25] Börne lived in the south of Germany and rarely came to Berlin. Moreover, Börne passionately opposed Goethe and felt thoroughly uncomfortable at the Varnhagens, where the poet was incarnate. On the whole, the relationship seems to have remained quite formal, although there is a long letter of Rahel's in 1825 clearly intending to draw him closer to her and her circle. She starts out by encouraging him to come to Berlin, suggesting inns and restaurants along the way and tempting him with the beauties of the route, the weather, the moonshine. She wishes that she could relieve him of all the tedious travel arrangements and then asks how it was that she could so urgently wish his coming to Berlin. Answering her own question, she states that such a visit would be of great advantage to her, to him, and to a great many others. And then she admits: "I miss you, you miss me. You are my *pair* [equal, peer] in the innermost soul, I could also say: I will, I can be like Klärchen in Egmont, carrying the flag that leads all of you. But I am also the drum, the battle music, the army chaplain, the comfort-giving canteen woman, the washerwoman, the nurse, the instigator, the spur, I carry the balsam in the army medical chest."[26]

The list of ways in which she wants to help goes on, changing its venue from the battlefield to Berlin and her society. Significantly, as the allusions to Goethe's *Egmont* and the use of military imagery suggest, Rahel appreciated Börne as a political writer. His polemics served a struggle she fully identified with and was ready to join, encourage, and aid. She saw no break between her Enlightenment principles and the democratic ideals of the nineteenth century; nor did she see a contradiction between her admiration of Goethe and her endorsement of a socially and politically committed literature. Quite the contrary, she considered the younger man's cause as the logical evolution of hers. Since, moreover, she recognized in Börne a capable leader, she was willing to perform the most unglamorous or merely symbolic tasks, as the list of metaphors suggests. Indeed, the battles he fought on the pages of *Die Wage* and other journals, such as Cotta's *Morgenblatt für gebildete Stände* (Morning journal for the educated classes), couched in language aimed at circumventing an ever-vigilant censorship, were entirely consistent with her views. Börne was then espousing the causes of the moderate liberal bourgeois—a constitutional monarchy, civil rights for oppressed groups, such as the Jews, and freedom of the press. Rahel's enthusiastic embrace of Börne was, of course, a compensatory action. Since she was excluded from actively participating in the affairs of the world, she would at least give her full support to those who thought like her. Börne's struggle paralleled her own in so many ways. By coming to Berlin, Rahel's letter implied, he would find like-minded persons not only in her but within the larger oppositional Varnhagen circle.

Like Grillparzer and Heine, as we shall see, Börne suffered under Metternich's harsh censorship policies. With each of these three authors, censorship led not only to rejected or altered manuscripts, but also to self-censorship and reduced literary productivity. Rahel took an interest in Börne's suppressed texts. He responded by sending her one, pleased by her concern and promising to send others, but only if she insisted. He then continued: "I have chosen this essay because it deals with Steffens, about whom we spoke a little yesterday. It was written two years ago, and the Stuttgart censorship didn't approve. Why not—that's what I ask you to consider, as soon as you have time. To me it remains inexplicable. I cannot conceal from you that you have disturbed my peace. I had been living quite contentedly, resigned to my fate, and now you have aroused in me this urgent desire to eat green pea soup with you in Berlin."[27] It must have been this wish of Börne's to be in Berlin and in her company that prompted Rahel's spirited invitation discussed above. In that same letter she sympathized with his publishing difficulties but encouraged him to continue trying to place the "precious manuscript" elsewhere, as the matter was still topical and urgent. She had read the text very thoroughly, marked what pleased her with a +, and what pleased her exceedingly with an x, and also indicated where something seemed unclear. Börne showed his high regard for her not merely by the extremely respectful tone of his letter, but even more so by the fact that he accepted her as one of only three collaborators of note among the occasional contributors to his journal *Die Wage*.[28]

Rahel's relations with Heinrich Heine (1797–1856) were not only more intimate but also a great deal more complex than those with her other young admirers. Heine, who is today recognized as the greatest poet between

Romanticism and Realism, came to Berlin in 1821. He stayed two years, ostensibly to pursue his law studies at Berlin University. He much preferred, however, to attend lectures in philosophy and literature. He eventually received a doctorate of jurisprudence from the University of Göttingen in 1825. In contrast to Rahel, who, as one born and raised in the Prussian capital, had good cause for complaints, the young Heine benefited greatly from his stay in Berlin. Its size and bustle, its cosmopolitanism and active cultural life were all new and exciting to him. Berlin provided his first real introduction to modern European life.[29] He went to the theater and the opera, met some of the leading writers, poets, and scholars, and participated in the famous Berlin social life.

Additionally, the university, although founded only ten years previously, had succeeded in attracting some of the most outstanding and active minds on its faculty. Heine greatly benefited from this stimulating academic environment, attending courses in law, linguistics, classical and Sanskrit literature, and philosophy. Among his teachers were Friedrich Karl von Savigny, Friedrich Wolf, and Georg Wilhelm Friedrich Hegel.

Another formative experience was Heine's association with a group of Jewish intellectuals who, in 1821, founded the Verein für Cultur und Wissenschaft der Juden (Society for the culture and science of the Jews). Its aim was to find, through the study of history and the philosophy of Judaism, some answers to the question, what makes one a Jew. Although the Verein attracted some of the outstanding Jewish minds, including Eduard Gans and Leopold Zunz, it was only moderately successful and dissolved some three years later.[30] Just the same, concern with and discussion of the many conflicting notions of Jewish identity must have helped Heine with his own questions. Although Heine was not initially or inherently preoccupied with being Jewish, his increasingly frequent encounters with anti-Jewish prejudice and attacks forced him to confront his outsider status within a more or less hostile society. Furthermore, it was probably through the Verein that Heine became aware of a tradition of Jewish learning and a Jewish history worthy of study by serious scholars.[31]

Heine was introduced to the Varnhagens soon after arriving in Berlin and quickly became a regular guest at their soirees. Rahel received him warmly, extending a maternal friendship toward him. Understandably, the sensitive, high strung, and rebellious young man caught her interest immediately. Their relationship was not free of tension, but it lasted until her death in 1833, with Heine returning whenever he came to Berlin. Rahel recognized his great talent early on, but she also feared for him, especially when, in the 1820s, he began to achieve a modest literary reputation. She cautioned that his talent "must mature within him, otherwise it becomes devoid of substance, turns into affectation."[32] Her feelings for Heine are summed up in a letter to Gentz: "Like so many, and always too many, Heine came to us several years ago; because he was delicate and singular, I understood him often, and he understood me, where others did not comprehend him, that's how I gained him as a friend; and he made me a patroness."[33]

Heine did indeed regard Rahel with a special kind of awe and romantic reverence. He was deeply grateful for the patience and kindness she showed him. In 1823, as he was about to depart from Berlin, he wrote to her:

Soon I shall be leaving and I beg of you not to throw my image into the lumber room (Rumpelkammer) of oblivion. I truly could not react in kind; and even if I told myself a hundred times a day: "You will forget Frau v. Varnhagen!" it wouldn't work. Don't forget me . . . your spirit has entered into a contract with time; and if perhaps after a few centuries I shall have the pleasure of meeting you again as the most beautiful and marvelous of all flowers, then you shall perhaps again be kind enough to greet me, the poor prickly palm (mich arme Stechpalme) (or shall I be something even worse?), with your friendly glow and lovely touch. . . . Surely you will do it; you have acted similarly toward me already in 1822 and 1823, when you treated me, the sick, bitter, surly, poetic, and insufferable person, with such decency and kindness which certainly I did not earn in this life.[34]

Again and again he conveyed his appreciation for the kindness received. Often he included Varnhagen, writing shortly after his departure from Berlin that he thought of them both almost continuously, as he had so far found very little true goodness and love in his life and "have been treated in a wholly humane fashion only by you and your magnanimous wife."[35] The Varnhagens remained loyal to Heine even when they were critical of his actions and exasperated by the scandals in which he got himself embroiled. The most prominent of these was Heine's attack, in *The Baths of Lucca*, on the poet August von Platen. At such times Varnhagen used his influence in practical ways, mending the impulsive young man's ruptured personal relations, smoothing over ruffled feathers, and writing articles and reviews favorable to him.[36] Varnhagen, moreover, may have helped Heine attain a position as coeditor with the periodical *Neue allgemeine politische Annalen* (New general political annals). Finally, the Varnhagens seemed to have had a hand in Heine's eventual move to Paris.[37]

Heine thus gained in both Rahel and Varnhagen two friends on whom he felt he could always rely for every kind of support and guidance: "you . . .

have cheered, and fortified, and taken the rough off of me, the morose, sick man, you have supported me with word and deed, and refreshed me with macaroni and spiritual food."[38] He promised to be completely candid toward them, to show them "no veiled heart," but one "with all the wounds, indeed, with all the bruises," confident that they, unlike others, would recognize also the "brilliant aspects."[39] Various utterances illustrate how crucial Heine viewed Rahel's influence with regard to both his emotional comfort and intellectual and literary development: "I think of Frau v. Varnhagen—Ergo sum," he wrote to Varnhagen in a very long letter in October 1826.[40] He also admitted that he considered the Varnhagen home his "fatherland."[41] And when he aroused Rahel's anger by dedicating his cycle of poems *Die Heimkehr* (Homecoming) to her without first securing her permission, he apologized to Varnhagen but also gave the following justification: "I believe that she guessed the reasons for my dedication better than I. It seemed to me as if I wanted to express with it that I belong to someone. I run around in the world so impetuously, sometimes people come who would like to make me their property, but they were always the kind that didn't please me much, and as long as this is the case, I shall always have written on my collar: *j'appartiens à* [I belong to] Madame Varnhagen."[42]

Heine, however, revered Rahel not only for her kindness and magnanimity; he was equally taken by her intellect. In fact, Rahel's beneficial effect on both his "mind" and his "heart" is a persistent theme in Heine's statements about her. She was not only a "marvelous woman" but also the "most brilliant woman of the universe." He delighted in the letters she (and Varnhagen) wrote him, claiming that he read "the dear letters three, four, thirty, forty times and my heart became very cheerful and my mind completely clear."[43] Except for a few brief notes, Heine never wrote directly to Rahel. He claimed that there was no need to write to her since she knew everything about him: "Delightful, truly delightful, and almost intoxicating was Frau v. Varnhagen's letter to me. Indeed, I never misjudged her. I know her a little. At the same time, I admit that nobody understands and knows me as thoroughly as *Frau v. Varnhagen*. After reading her letter, I felt as if I had risen in my sleep and put myself in front of the mirror and spoken with myself, and even boasted a little. The best thing is that I don't need to write Frau v. Varnhagen any long letters. As long as she knows that I am alive, she also knows what I am feeling and thinking."[44] This latter assertion appears repeatedly and was more than an expression of youthful arrogance. With it, Heine wanted to stress and set apart the very special relationship between Rahel and himself.

Many years later, in 1840, he returned to this sense of commonalty that required no words. In a letter to Varnhagen he recalled this time not only Rahel but the entire "secret circle, that quiet community" that death had decimated over the past ten years: "We, we understood each other through mere glances, we looked at each other and knew what was happening inside us—this language of the eyes (Augensprache) will soon be lost, and our written testimonials, i.e., Rahel's letters, will become nothing but indecipherable hieroglyphs to those born later."[45]

Rahel, on the other hand, wrote to Heine fairly frequently, usually by including a "more or less fat letter" with one of her husband's. According to Heine, he had at one time in his possession a packet of more than twenty letters, which, to his great regret, fell victim to a fire.[46] But even if the young genius did not feel obliged to answer her directly, he kept up a steady dialogue with his "patroness." He communicated with her through Varnhagen and Ludwig and Friederike Robert. These letters, as well as those exchanged between Rahel and Varnhagen, reveal to some extent the intellectual influence Rahel exerted over her young protégé. Heine himself refers to and cites variously from Rahel's letters in his writings.

Rahel supported Heine in his literary endeavors, made him aware of important authors and works, and helped him acquire some much needed social graces. She encouraged his participation in the salon activities by inviting him, for example, to write a poem of exoneration for an actress who had fallen out of favor with the Berlin public because of a marital scandal, although she was quite innocent.[47] More significant are Heine's own numerous statements about how he profited from Rahel's knowledge of literature and the arts and her insight into human nature and society. To Ludwig Robert he wrote that he was reading Madame de Staël's *Corinne*, a book he would have neither understood nor appreciated at all before his encounter with Rahel.[48]

Even more revealing is a passage at the beginning of his text *Heinrich Heine über Ludwig Börne* (1840, Heinrich Heine on Ludwig Börne), concerning a conversation about the art of writing during which Rahel was to have stated that " 'Börne cannot write, just as I or Jean Paul cannot write.' " Heine explains the meaning of these words, which anyone not familiar with her language could easily misunderstand: "Writing to her meant the calm arrangement, as it were, the editing of one's thoughts, the logical composition of the parts of speech, in short, that particular art of constructing a phrase (Periodenbau) that she admired so enthusiastically in Goethe as well as her husband, and about which we at that time carried on almost daily the most fruitful debates. Today's prose, I'd like to mention parenthetically, was not created without a great deal of experimentation, deliberation, contradiction, and effort."[49]

Heine explicitly credits Rahel with helping him, at a crucial moment, clarify important questions about the direction and function of literature and especially prose. Poetry may have been the genre most suited to his imagination, but prose assumed an increasingly significant role in his work beginning with his *Briefe aus Berlin* (1822, Letters from Berlin) and reaching a first pinnacle with the *Harzreise* (1826, *The Harz Journey*). These works exhibit a complex interweaving of subjective and objective observations, reflections of a general nature as well as specific social and political criticism. For the most part prose, they are also interspersed with poems. The open form of these works permitted Heine to make ample use of his unique satirical, comical, and lyrical gifts. Like Rahel, he saw himself as a keen observer and interpreter of contemporary life, and, like her, he used his personal experiences to arrive at general insights. The older he got the more he felt that prose rather than poetry constituted the appropriate genre of the age.[50]

Heine's remarks were, of course, aimed at Börne. With Rahel's help, he set the scene for a fair evaluation of a writer whose fate and struggle paralleled in many ways his own, only to turn against him in the ensuing pages. By paraphrasing Rahel's literary opinion of Börne and others, Heine identified Rahel as a writer. For he followed the above-quoted words with this observation about her: "Rahel loved Börne perhaps all the more because she too belonged to those authors who, if they are to write well, have to be in a state of passionate stimulation, in a kind of spiritual ecstasy: bacchants of thought who stagger after their god in holy intoxication."[51] Granting Rahel the status of a writer was by then no forgone conclusion. In doing so, Heine went against classicist aesthetics, which had excluded epistolary writing as a legitimate literary genre, as well as against contemporary critics who arrogantly dismissed the "lady authors." Heine's notion of literature was devoid of dogmatism. In his view, the author and artist ought to be free to explore and employ any aesthetic mode, aiming solely for the most appropriate means of representation. It was this encompassing view of literature that enabled Heine to follow an entirely new course in *The Harz Journey* and subsequent works. The extent to which he was influenced by Rahel in this respect as well is difficult to determine.

Another important topic of discussion between the older woman and the young poet concerned the person and writings of Goethe. Rahel urged and pressured Heine to read her favorite author, with whom he and others of his generation went on the warpath. And he seemed to have complied with her request. Not long after his departure from Berlin he wrote to Ludwig Robert, proudly reporting: "And, dear Robert, you can hardly believe how obedient I am toward Frau v. Varnhagen—I have now, except for a trifle, read the entire Göthe! ! ! I am no longer a blind heathen but a seeing one. I like Göthe very well."[52] Actually, it is unclear how thoroughly he had concerned himself at this point with the author. Rahel was of course not the only one who urged Heine to read Goethe. He was often surprised about how many Goethe admirers there were, even among his own generation.

Nonetheless, Rahel's steadfast loyalty and thorough comprehension of the venerable writer's works could not but have impressed the younger poet. Hearing Rahel talk about Goethe must have helped him arrive at a more judicious assessment. He knew Rahel to be a liberal and a rebel, and he admired her for having "fought, suffered, quarreled, and even lied for the truth," yet she saw in Goethe a great humanist and not the servile minister of a tiny principality committed to an outmoded political and social order.[53] It was precisely on this point that the opinions between Rahel and Heine, and the younger generation of liberal intellectuals generally, diverged. They felt oppressed by Goethe's presence and stature as well as his longevity. Literature, the young authors felt, had to become more immediately involved in the affairs of the world. Early on Heine was resolved to take up the pen in the struggle for that which was "good and right. Down with obsolete injustice, with the ruling foolishness and evil! . . . In the end poetry is merely a beautiful trifle."[54]

Above all, the young intellectuals criticized Goethe for his Olympian aloofness and complacency toward the burning issues of the time. They saw him as cold and selfish, unmoved by the atrocious conditions under which the majority of the German people lived. And although most of them acknowledged his poetic genius, they felt that he had failed to use his outstanding talent on behalf of the general good. Thus, Börne wrote in 1830 that "Goethe could have been a Hercules, freeing the fatherland of much ordure; but he merely fetched the golden apples of the Hesperides, which he kept for himself, and then seated himself at Omphale's feet and remained sitting there. How very differently did the great poets and orators of Italy, France, and England live and work!"[55] That same year Heine judged him in very similar terms: "Goethe has become eighty years old, and a minister and prosperous—poor German people! that is your greatest man!"[56] Clearly, Heine was far from being at peace with Goethe, in spite of having listened to Rahel's spirited and intelligent defense and interpretations of his works and in spite of having read and accepted him. More accurately, Goethe became a lifelong preoccupation of major importance, indicated already by the innumerable references to him and his works in Heine's writings.[57]

Returning to the question of whether Rahel was being overtaken by the times as she approached old age, the answer is no. Rahel remained modern and often far ahead of the younger generation. She welcomed and encouraged the direction the young writers and intellectuals took in their writing. Her own work, in both its written and oral form, was partisan almost by definition. But then there was Goethe, whose writings had accompanied her for some forty years. She had admired and defended him when he was still quite unknown and understood him when others were uncomprehending. Again and again she had found her own thoughts and feelings expressed and confirmed by one who could "say everything." Conscious of the encompassing breadth of his work and the revolutionary impact he had had on all genres, she opposed the younger men intent on hastily and impulsively casting overboard the artistic achievements of this epochal figure for the sake of freeing themselves from his long shadow.

Yet, she also knew that Goethe's path was not hers, and surely for this reason she saw fit to pass her legacy on to Heine, an outsider like her, similarly gifted, sensitive, easily outraged, and passionate. This legacy is contained in one of the few extant letters to him, dated 21 September 1830. In summary fashion, she presents the sufferings and dissatisfactions, both personal and general, as well as the palliatives used by various authorities to dissipate and appease. Interestingly, hatred of Jews, suggested by the word *Hep* stands at the outset of all her grievances. This is significant because of Rahel's lack of interest in Jewishness (though not in anti-Jewish hatred). The younger generation viewed Jewishness and Judaism in much more complex terms. For Rahel the optimistic goals of social, political, and cultural assimilation, of which conversion to Christianity was but one aspect, had been real, urgent, and tangible. After 1815 these goals became increasingly elusive, resulting in somewhat different attitudes among the younger generation. On the one hand, a nascent Jewish consciousness began to emerge, as exemplified by the founding of the Society for the culture and science of the Jews. On the other, the repressive climate of the times necessitated accommodations that often went directly against the new Jewish self-affirmation. Rahel, her brothers, and many of her friends, among them Dorothea Mendelssohn-Veit-Schlegel, Henriette Mendelssohn, and Henriette Herz, converted out of a deep inner need and conviction. In contrast, the younger men, Gans, Börne, and Heine, adopted Christianity for opportunistic reasons, in response to renewed legislation aimed at denying Jews civil equality, guaranteed only recently by the 1812 Edict of Emancipation.[58] Of course, Rahel herself had come to see how persistent anti-Jewish attitudes and how tortuous the path toward legal emancipation were. Such considerations must have played a role in her deciding to charge Heine with carrying on her work. She wrote:

Hepp is as little unexpected to me as all other vileness. No great *trumeau* [pier], no "bridal wreath," no elephant crossing stage bridges, no charity list, no hurrah, no condescension, no mixed society, no new hymnal, no award of a bourgeois decoration, nothing, nothing, could ever appease me. The pocks themselves must be extirpated; make-up will not help, even if it is applied with house paint brushes! Only despots can help us, insightful ones, *or*: this said, it shall be done! Unexpectedly I have greeted you with everything I can presently say about the present. You will say all this in wonderful, elegiac, fantastic, incisive, always exceedingly witty, melodic, stimulating, often thrilling ways; say it soon. But the text from my old offended heart will always have to be your own.[59]

Heine's reaction to this message is unknown. The passage was so characteristically Rahel's in style, formulation, and content that it suggests it did not come as a complete revelation to the recipient but built on earlier conversations, during which Rahel opened her innermost soul to him.[60] Consciously or unconsciously, Heine accepted the task by putting his literary talent at the service of progress. Upon receiving notice of Rahel's death, Heine wrote to Varnhagen expressing his condolences and grief. He mentions both Rahel's lifelong struggle on behalf of a more just world and his own. Of her he wrote: "Our friend always fought valiantly and surely earned a laurel wreath." Of himself, he said: "I was very ill. But I remain active. I shall not relinquish the sword, until I fall."[61] Heine thought of Rahel as a person of considerable historical significance. In the prologue to a new edition of the *Buch der Lieder* (*Book of Songs*), he praised Varnhagen for promptly and courageously publishing Rahel's letters: "This book came at the right time, when it could influence, fortify, and console. . . . It is as if Rahel knew her posthumous calling. She, of course, believed that everything would improve and waited; however, when there was no end to waiting, she shook her head impatiently, looked at Varnhagen, and died quickly—in order to arise from the dead all the more quickly. She reminds me of the legend of that other Rahel who climbed out of her grave and stood by the highway and wept as her children went into captivity."[62] Rahel's passing on her legacy to the young Heine is proof that Heine's frequent assertions of a deep bond with the older woman were entirely accurate—the sense of affinity was deep and mutual; each was to the other a comrade in arms.

RAHEL'S LATER LETTERS AND HER APHORISTIC TALENT

Strategies of Writing and Publishing

Rahel's letters now bore all the signs of mature writing in both content and style. Formally, they were still characterized by spontaneity and immediacy—a distinctive mark since the beginning. But this spontaneity was now more than ever a consciously practiced art. Rahel's comments on writing have always shown her to be well acquainted with the rules of literary aesthetics. As she got older such reflections increased in both frequency and incisiveness, indicating greater self-confidence as an author and contrasting sharply with her earlier self-critical and apologetic stance.

Initially, of course, Rahel largely identified with the tradition of eighteenth-century epistolary writing and its explicit demands for "naturalness," "good taste," and "morality." But she quickly pioneered a style of her own that suited not only her needs but also justified her goals. Rahel's statements on writing were almost from the beginning highly individualistic and, in their emphasis on the subjective, fragmentary, nonsystematic, and essayistic, akin to the poetic theories of the early Romantics. With each of her pronouncements, she sought to discover and define her own unique creative process and to distinguish herself from others. Also recalling Romantic aesthetics, her statements combine elements of reflection, critique, and definition. However, equating Rahel's aesthetic concerns with those of the Romantics is not altogether accurate. For, although she felt great affinity with many of the representatives of this movement, sharing their sense of isolation as well as alienation from the increasingly narrow-minded and pragmatic bourgeois world, there were also important differences. As observed earlier, Rahel remained firmly committed to the Enlightenment ideals of tolerance, cosmopolitanism, and perfectibility, and her approach to life was, in spite of being highly emotional, essentially rational. She abhorred the Romantics' turn to irrationality and their glorification of the Middle Ages, not least because it exarcerbated their anti-Jewish prejudice. Moreover, she viewed literature, and therefore also her own writing, as a reflection on and working through of actual life experiences and was therefore averse to texts so fantastic that they lost their connection to social or psychological reality. This becomes clear in her criticism of several highly successful novellas of the time, Fouqué's *Undine* and E. T. A. Hoffmann's *Fräulein von Scuderi*. She maintained that they were replete with "improbabilities and contradictions" and therefore, particularly Hoffmann's tale, in their arbitrariness "hideous, morbid, useless, and actually without any ethical foundation and struggle."[63]

In contrast to the Romantics' aesthetic experimentation, which was often an end in itself, Rahel's aesthetic peculiarities evolved from personal experience. Highly conscious of her marginality as a woman and a Jew, her associative, unsystematic, and subjective approach to writing was for her as necessary as it was intentional. Epistolary writing permitted her to draw on reality in a direct and literal sense. Her domain was everyday life and language, no matter how lofty her imagination or philosophical speculations. Also, since she liked to take the reader on the complex path along which she arrived at her insights, she revealed aspects of herself and others that, in a formally worked-out or finished text, would be neglected or eliminated. In one of his early letters, Gentz suggested that her writing often resembled aromatic strawberries, which, however, still had sand and roots attached to them. Rahel, immediately struck by the appropriateness of this metaphor, remembered and periodically repeated it.[64] "Sand" and "roots" were those aspects that "professional" writers tended to obliterate in an effort to achieve perfection in their work of art.

The frequency of Rahel's reflections on writing was one sign of her growing self-assurance as an author. Another was her willingness to publish selections from her letters and diaries in various journals and collections. These appeared fairly regularly throughout the 1820s and included reviews and essays on music, art, and Goethe, as well as fragments of a more general and philosophical nature.[65] Thus Rahel's personal letters began to make the transition, as literature, into the public sphere. This did not mean, however, that she was ready to give up her anonymity. Whatever she published during her life appeared either anonymously, under the initial G., or under the name Friederike, or submerged in Ludwig Robert's texts. Repeatedly, she implored her editors not to mention her name. But her authorship was in fact a poorly guarded secret. Her editors, Troxler, Börne, Fouqué, Cotta, knew her well, while she herself diligently informed her friends and acquaintances about her publications. Anonymity worked above all because these men were in full agreement with the idea that women should venture into the public realm with their writing only in exceptional cases. Nonetheless, Rahel's tentative steps into the world of printed literature were important because they indicated the extent to which she wanted to be acknowledged as an author whose writings reached beyond her small circle of friends and acquaintances to the public at large.

That writing was a creative process for Rahel is revealed by many of her statements. She could only write if she was seized by a "certain excitement . . . which brings forth and sets in motion spirit, memory, combination, and ideas. . . . [T]here are no finished thought plans within me: rather idea, impulse, thought, expression, all this is one and the same explosion and *a single* flood."[66] Like any writer, however, she was ceaselessly occupied with transforming her thoughts, feelings, and insights into written expression: "As much as the expressions leap from my mind and pen, as decidedly are they distilled beforehand in my mind by all that I experience; by life and property (Gut und Blut); and work, of an incessant kind. . . . Just the same, I cannot write anything, dear Dr. Troxler, that you could use. I can only write letters; and sometimes an aphorism; but absolutely nothing about a subject that is . . . put before me."[67]

Although Rahel's writing was essentially essayistic, her talent, further conditioned by her lack of a formal education, was best suited to the open and infinitely adaptable form of the letter. In contrast, the more rigorous genres, such as the treatise or the formal essay, demanded that a given topic be developed systematically and fully, according to accepted rules. Her special gift for aphoristic combinations, on the other hand, was surely aided by her outsider status, which made her particularly observant of the many contradictions and paradoxes in daily life. Regarding the creative process, Rahel makes clear that her letters contain not the arbitrary thought of the moment but rather the result of a thought process arrived at over time, that often lay dormant within her or her diary. At the moment of writing to a particular person, such insights or thoughts could suddenly become relevant, demanding to be communicated. This explains why passages from diary entries reappear almost verbatim in letters.

Rahel, moreover, remained faithful to the dialogical principle that she had practiced from the start as well: "I never like to write a speech but want to write conversations as they actually occur within the individual."[68] In writing conversations rather than speeches, Rahel took account of the recipient's interest, sensibilities, imaginativeness, and other capabilities and needs. This continuous and demanding creative process rendered her writing lively, relevant, and concrete and helps explain the claim of so many of her correspondents that she understood them perfectly. Additionally, the letter as dialogue was fundamentally democratic and thus permitted Rahel to practice on a continuous basis the principle, most fundamental to her, that "to another—the image of a person—be as it is to us, that *he is* what *we are*."[69]

The "Weather Reports." Also contributing to the immediacy of Rahel's writing and a further illustration of how closely her strategies were related to her personal situation were the weather reports with which Rahel liked to precede her letters. Although she had employed this device for some years, meteorological accounts took on a much more important role as she got older. Originally she confined them to fairly brief statements, such as, "Prag, 10th May 1814. Cold, cloudy, damp, windy, rainy weather to top it all."[70] Later they often became quite lengthy and detailed, at times taking up an entire paragraph. Rahel related the weather conditions almost always to her state of health, which in turn greatly affected her ability to write. For this reason the reports were often quite personal, such as the following opening of a letter addressed to Oelsner:

Berlin, Friday morning 12 o'clock, 13th June 1823. / Hot, bright weather, with decidedly easterly winds. / If this is improbable, it is nevertheless true. I like to put this kind of date before the letters as their weather condition, as the atmosphere in which they grow; and as commentary for the intelligent reader. As a postscript to this date, let me add that today I was very successful with my sulfur bath; I do not feel overheated, not weakened: and am now *precisely* at the point from which this whole letter writes itself; which writing I could not have undertaken without the successful sulfur experiment.[71]

In a letter to Auguste Brede she followed the date and the weather with an even more intimate description of the technique and effects of yet another successful therapeutic treatment, a "spray bath," and a stern warning never to take one without first consulting with her, in spite of the booklet describing the procedure.[72]

Other times the weather report took a poetic and even philosophical turn, as in this missive to Henrik Steffens, natural scientist and philosopher:

Wednesday, 7th March 1827. 11 o'clock in the morning. / Sunshine; yes, but it is melancholy, no matter how bright it renders everything: it raises expectations, memories which it doesn't fulfill: it is nice to see the darkened roofs against the light blue [sky] through the window panes; and the air, the brightness passes through the heart like the lights and airs of spring released; for each time of the year, the month, and the day has its own proportion of light and air. But all this is happening in an unorganized, formless, convulsive weather, where a kind of wind, like a mad, mean dog, has descended and grabbed the world with its snout, shaking it. That is how it has been . . . for some time. . . . For several years there have been only redeemed *moments*, when *one* season rules . . . without . . . being . . . mixed in . . .

and fighting with the others. . . . I am the battlefield, and my entire life's sap is finally used up, destroyed, gone. I have been feeling this already for many years with increased awareness! And now, you wonderful "doctor of body and soul," you'll understand and forgive this long date. . . . I am suffering and struggling with general rheumatism ranting and residing within my very well and finely organized body, where it [the rheumatism] finds the most receptive and harmonizing (all- und anstimmigste) instrument for its fancies. . . . Nothing is therefore as important, as present to me as the weather: yes, I am convinced that this knowledge will be raised to a science . . .[73]

As the above statements illustrate, her ability to write was affected most of all by the state of her health and atmospheric conditions. But other factors—a bad pen, ink that did not flow, poor quality paper, not to mention the incessant interruptions—proved profoundly irritating as well. These were of course the kinds of impediments women authors characteristically had to contend with. But Rahel, owing to her extreme sensitivity and her chronic ailments, was seemingly less able to overcome them through self-discipline. At the same time, suffering was part of life and therefore worthy of observation and description. Rather than consider her body deficient, she conceived of it as a "receptive and well-tuned instrument" from which her writing emanated. Its condition affected everything, "sentence, word, expression, form and sequence of the thoughts" that, accordingly, turned out "bumpy, flowing, gentle, strict, jocular, calm."[74] Rahel's reports on the weather and her health, just like her elaborate descriptions of the associations and events leading to her insights, may be considered as part of the "sand and roots" of Gentz's metaphor.

Gender and Writing. Rahel liked to elaborate on the paradoxical in herself and her writing, especially on the fact that she did not fit the accepted gender categories: "However, I do admit that at first sight my writing does not appear to come from a woman: but if, on second sight, one wants to attribute it to a man, this works even less."[75] As already revealed in her correspondence with David Veit, Rahel recognized herself not only in both male and female characters but also in the thoughts of their [male] creators.

Not surprisingly, her correspondents or acquaintances were either unable or unwilling even to consider Rahel's daring idea that men and women could be intellectually similar. Troxler, the recipient of the above and several other observations on writing, published excerpts from Rahel's letters in his journal *Schweizerisches Museum* in 1816. Well-intentioned, liberal, and enlightened as he was, he commented on the selections with some remarks of his own, thereby granting Rahel her first official recognition as an author, all the same maintaining her anonymity. However, in his preamble he stressed at every step that which appeared to him characteristically feminine and therefore laudable. He wrote: "What a rich profusion of ideas and feelings about the most diverse conditions of life and the world . . . ! These days we have often . . . seen that women too can think and write, however, most of the time, it appeared as an apostasy from their nature rather than a culmination of their destiny." He recommended the selections particularly to the women and daughters of "this free country" [Switzerland] because, in his view, they serve as an admirable example of how a woman could be resigned to her fate and yet remain committed to the idea of freedom: "here, however, is a very different, a deeply intentional recognition of misfortune, a courageous submission to pain, and a firm acceptance of one's destiny without amazonian distortion or frantic convolutions of the mind; finally, [the selections are] the living proof of how closely related the self-educated mind is to enlightenment . . . and to freedom itself."[76] Henrik Steffens, another longtime friend, characterized Rahel in his memoirs as follows: "She was continually occupied with the highest matters and, although an author, thoroughly woman."[77] These men were no exceptions. Similar views were voiced by other notables of the age. The writer, economist, and political scientist Adam Müller (1779–1829) distinguished between male and female styles of writing by contrasting the "iron pen" with the "winged pen." Jacob Grimm determined that women were best at writing letters, and for this reason everything written by women should be treated like letters and published with as much caution.[78]

Although Rahel the author seemed to be at the mercy of a great many constraints and impediments, her writing strategies cannot be viewed merely as reactions to unfavorable conditions. Rather, they were deliberate and creative innovations that gave her certain advantages over women who wrote within the traditional, male-determined genres. This becomes especially clear when considering Rahel's statements on female authorship. Not only did she oppose separate standards for women authors, but she directed her harshest criticism at what she perceived to be women's lack of intellectual independence. Thus, she condemned as misdirected and therefore "reprehensible" flattery if a woman who writes and publishes and therefore surely has something to say continues to behave in a servile manner to men, even in her work, as if she considered herself nothing but a charming usurper, who may be tolerated after all because, in her weakness, she is entirely harmless.

Not her fearful curtsies, the subject matter will put her in her womanly place. Mostly, it will not be one requiring university or other studies (Universität und Studium). If, however, a woman were to have the fortune, discounting whatever else she is deprived of, to be nourished and nurtured by these [university studies] and possessed the mind and talents through which alone a formal education would bear fruit; and she finally did succeed on the market of scholarship (Markt der Wissenschaften); what purpose would the long insipid excuses serve . . . and old-fashioned coquetry? Or should a woman remain stupid? Under any circumstances? Therefore I agree with Friedrich Schlegel . . . "As long as men remain brutes . . . women must be coquettish."[79]

Although Rahel herself was a reluctant author, she could envision a time when men and women would treat each other as intellectual equals. At the same time, she failed to consider some harsh realities—the pressures exerted on women who published in the established genres, where they had to conform to the expectations of male editors or patrons, be they husbands, brothers, or friends. Since Rahel had chosen for herself a medium that freed her from such patronage, she showed little patience toward women who ventured into the public sphere and yet failed to achieve intellectual emancipation. In the semipublic sphere of epistolary writing, she felt sheltered as well as free to express herself without ever having to compromise her authenticity.

Reading Germaine de Staël's works prompted a similarly categorical reaction. Observing that de Staël also could not free herself of the fear that a talented woman might be considered unfeminine or that her works might be judged not on a par with those written by men, she wrote: "Poor fear! A book must be good, even if it is written by a mouse and will not become any better if the author wears angel wings on his shoulders. . . . If Mrs. Fichte had written Fichte's works, would they be worse? Or is it proven that a woman cannot think and express her thoughts? Even if this were so, it would still remain our duty . . . to make the attempt over and over."[80]

Rahel was equally emphatic in refuting the related argument, debated in all the papers since "the time of J. J. Rousseau and long afterwards," that women who write fail to fulfill their womanly destiny. "Granted," said Rahel, "however, since so many women fail to fulfill their destiny, we can count among these also some who fail because of their writing."[81]

A particularly interesting aspect of Rahel's comments on writing concerned language. We saw earlier that she considered her own language deficient and inelegant; but she gradually came to recognize its merits.

In 1816, as she was again reflecting on the backward state of the German lands, she recognized that deep social divisions and the lack of public discourse adversely affected not only social progress but also the evolution of language. Unlike the French, Germans lacked a common language in which to communicate across class lines: "We Germans have as yet no language, driven through all the social conduits like the French; where one can be understood by the lowliest in Faubourg. But there is one prepared within ours; we only have to get it ready, select the words for it—I too am capable of this because daily life is the subject matter of my art as it is for the French—In our land, there existed no opportunity for public speaking, except from the pulpit. All other ideas are obliged to move, devoid of tone or gesture, impersonally, unearthly, from intellect to intellect. . . . Speech must become wholly plain and clear and distinct."[82] Rahel perceptively argued that progressive ideas required a forum for their dissemination and realization. In Germany, such institutions were still lacking, with the result that the most lofty ideas developed in a vacuum. She even included her revered philosopher Fichte among those whose thought tended toward abstract speculation.

In terms of content, Rahel's writing during her later years marks a clear advance in thought and a deepening of it. What in her youth appeared as a wealth of witty aperçus and startlingly original insights evolved more and more into a carefully considered and principled way of looking at and interpreting the affairs of the world. Viewed as a whole, Rahel's epistolary oeuvre shows a clear evolution but no ruptures or radical departures. In her youth as in maturity, she pursued the same goal—the promotion of harmonious and egalitarian human relations. Another constant was her deep commitment to truth and truthfulness: "certain things I like to say, and especially with the pen: then, I think, they can be seen by everyone and need never again be repeated nor contested, because they are so downright true."[83]

Since Rahel's network of correspondences remained as extensive as ever, a discussion of the major themes in her writing is again called for. Moreover, in her later years her diaries assumed greater importance, for they figure substantially in the third volume of the *Buch des Andenkens* (which covers the years 1820–33). Included in such notations are not only personal reflections and observations, often in the form of aphorisms, but also detailed discussions of books and articles she read. Before turning to the major themes in the letters and diaries, however, we shall pause and consider briefly that other genre Rahel excelled in—aphoristic writing.

Rahel's Aphorisms

Aphorisms, like proverbs and jokes, are so closely bound up with the structure and logic of a particular language and culture that they do not lend themselves to translation easily. Nevertheless, since Rahel herself admitted to having a certain talent for this genre, the following selection, consisting of aphorisms as well as lengthier statements, is intended to introduce the reader to Rahel's aphoristic writings. These examples also illustrate how generally aphoristic Rahel's style is, for they do not appreciably differ from the many previously quoted passages. Like aphorisms generally, Rahel's formulations are both striking and surprising. They express in concise terms her insights into complex matters arrived at over a lifetime of careful observation and reflection. Many of them, again in accordance with the aphoristic genre, question or invert established opinions and assumptions. As observed earlier, Rahel's outsider status seems to have predisposed her to look at things and events in novel or original ways. Her statements claim general validity, but they are not necessarily immediately convincing. Because they are open-ended and express her subjective point of view, they demand the reader's active intellectual engagement. The following examples indicate a wide range of concerns and insights—historical, political, social, psychological, moral, and ethical—as well as Rahel's unusual sensitivity to language.

Frankfort, 30 December 1815

It is quite immaterial how someone is, as soon as he cannot be the way he wishes to be.[84]

[Personal] qualities are not talents; however, we must make them into talents, otherwise we are not at all educated.[85]

2 November 1822

I would like to ban the phrase "spirit of the times" (Geist der Zeit); it is terribly confusing. "General conviction," I would rather call [it]. . . . When they burnt the alleged witches, it was the spirit of the times: the general conviction, however, caused this stupid cruelty to be stopped. — These two very different conditions often still rule side by side, but the general conviction must always oust the spirit of the times.[86]

17 January 1824

We hate in a character everything we don't understand; the immoral is really incomprehensible as well. It is incomprehensible why a person would want to cause another disagreeable sensations: since he must surely desire agreeable ones for himself. But it is completely understandable that we want to do good to another: we desire for the other person that which we want for ourselves. Malice, which isn't revenge—the latter derives from a sense of justice—is completely incomprehensible.[87]

September 1827
It is only through love that we know of our existence, otherwise we would merely know of things and thoughts.[88]

To Gentz, 7 February 1831.
I am convinced that it is part of this earthly existence that every individual is hurt by that which is to him the most painful, the most unbearable: the way he comes to terms with this, that is the essential.[89]

To Prince Pückler-Muskau, 6 February 1832
(Regarding the ideas of the utopian socialist, Saint-Simon): I consider it depravity and not lack of reason, if man refuses to take in new and irksome ideas: [it is] stupidity if these ideas appear before him, and he does not notice that they are new; [and it is] the highest infamy if he recognizes them and yet denies them.[90]

The Letters and Diaries

The themes that preoccupied Rahel during the last fifteen years of her life are continuous with those of her earlier years. Literature, the arts, the lot of women, the state of society, history, the endless variety of human interaction, continued to preoccupy and fascinate her. On the whole, her tone was less outraged and more philosophical, although the old "rebel" was still not subdued. Her approach to life remained fresh and unconventional, indicating how very much she was still engaged in the affairs of men and the world.

The Life of the Mind. In youth and in old age, Rahel spent much time reading books on history, political theory, philosophy, the natural sciences as well as literary works and collections of letters. Among the authors whose works Rahel considered at some length in the diaries or letters of the last fifteen years were many contemporaries—the writers Ludwig Börne, Germaine de Staël, Madame de Genlis, Lady Morgan, the very young Victor Hugo, and, of course, Goethe, the philosophers Herder and Hegel, and Heinrich Pestalozzi, the Swiss educational reformer. Increasingly, her custom was to excerpt passages from a work that intrigued her, to which she then joined her own commentaries. Besides the names of the above-mentioned luminaries, a great many other names appear in her writing, showing that she was familiar with the legacy of the great minds of the Western world—from Plato to Cervantes and Shakespeare. Among the great British authors she knew the writings of Thomas Hobbes, John Milton, and Henry Fielding. In her own German literature she read and reread Lessing, Schiller, Jean Paul, the aphorist Georg Christoph Lichtenberg, the Romantics, with Goethe being her constant literary companion. The French authors included Blaise Pascal, Racine, Molière, Rousseau, Mirabeau, Lafontaine, Lamartine, besides the already mentioned Victor Hugo. Among the Italians she appreciated especially Alessandro Manzoni, the author of the famous novel *I promessi sposi* (1825–27, *The Betrothed*). Of further note are several lengthy letters devoted to music. In one she discusses musical developments from Bach to Mozart and Gluck to Karl Maria von Weber; in another she elaborates on the differences between Handel and Bach; while a third is concerned with the then popular contemporary Italian composer Gasparo Spontini. Some of these appeared within reviews published in Ludwig Robert's name. She delighted in the youngest composers, Felix Mendelssohn and Nicolò Paganini. She was also knowledgeable about painting, as indicated by a published review of a portrait of a woman (her beautiful sister-in-law Friederike Robert) in the journal *Morgenblatt für gebildete Stände* (Morning journal for the educated classes). Her writings furthermore show her continued lively interest in the performance arts, music, acting, and dance. Thus, in spite of her poor health and advancing age, Rahel's mind remained ever active, curious, and involved.

Rahel's attitude toward philosophy was highly personal and, one is tempted to say, pragmatic. Like literature, philosophy was in her view neither esoteric nor abstract but concerned with aiding man in mastering life's dilemmas. She maintained that the greatest philosopher could provide no better answers than the common intelligent person. What mattered in philosophy, however, was to pose or formulate the questions properly, to clear and pave the way, so that we would not attempt to answer the wrong queries. It was the business of philosophy to ask questions, straightforwardly and dispassionately, down to the last unanswerable ones.[91]

Since Fichte was the philosopher she revered above all, Rahel came to the philosophy of Hegel late in life, but then immersed herself in its study with diligence by excerpting and commenting. Quoted passages are followed by remarks of approval or questions, or they serve as a point of departure for her own reflections, as the following example illustrates. Like so many others, she found Hegel's style arduous; but she was also able to appreciate his occasional aphoristic conciseness. Thus, she wrote in 1827: "Language is the center and apex of all that is marvelous. Hegel says: 'If you want to live, you must serve; if you want to be free, you must die.' I love such sayings which constitute a wellspring: which contain whole thought families."[92] Elaborating the idea further, she reflected that in order to arrive at such an insight, Hegel had to have considered and experienced a great deal. And, speculating further, she observed that "he to whom such true power of thinking and reflection was given, would have to arrive at a single word which would contain all knowledge. . . . This is surely 'the word' from the Bible, about which so much is being said! — In any case . . . we only speak a great deal if we are unable to say what we would like to say."[93]

She understood Hegel's notoriously difficult philosophical writings well enough to recognize his roots in Fichte's thought. To Ludwig Robert she wrote about Hegel's *Encyclopedia*: "Excellent. Almost every line [is] an irrefutable definition. I underline and write on the side. I find Fichte. What else? He who traced the outline of the human spirit . . . must find it again in each new depiction. All thinking and investigating is a rediscovery of a method."[94] In her diary she remarked that the meaning of Hegel's "investigating the instrument" was the same as Fichte's knowing (erkennen). And therefore, there remained only one thing to do — to start with Fichte; that is, "with the question: How do I come upon my self?" (Wie find' ich mein Ich vor?)[95] It is interesting and symptomatic of Rahel's lack of self-assurance that, even as a mature woman, she did not tell the philosopher, who visited the Varnhagen home quite often, how deeply she was immersed in his *Encyclopedia*. Only to Ludwig Robert did she admit that she was "one of the students who loves and understands it best: or rather understands and loves it."[96]

Another philosopher, writer, and critic who shaped Rahel's world view in significant ways was Johann Gottfried Herder (1744–1803). Herder stood poised between the Enlightenment and what came to be known as the Storm and Stress period in German literature. He is well known for his seminal influence on the young Goethe, particularly in regard to his ideas about aesthetics and history. He introduced Goethe [to the writings of Shakespeare and Oliver Goldsmith, to Homer and Pindar, and to folk poetry.] His advocacy of intuition over a strict rationality also had an immediate impact on the young poet and, moreover, formed the basis of German Romanticism. Rahel had been acquainted with his work since the 1790s. In 1815 she related to Varnhagen about how impressed she was with Herder's *Ideen zur Philosophie der Geschichte der Menschheit* (*Outline of a Philosophy of the History of Man*), a massive work in four volumes that appeared between 1784 and 1791, for which Herder is still known and remembered today. It laid the foundation for a new philosophy of history in Germany. Herder began with a discussion of man's place in nature and the links that connect him to other forms of organic life; he went on to a consideration of the primitive or prehistoric phases of human society and ended with an examination of recorded history up to the beginning of the sixteenth century. The thought underlying the work as a whole was that there was an analogy between a biological organism and human society. Herder maintained that every known society had grown and developed in a distinctive manner and in response to a particular time and place. It is not difficult to see correspondences between Herder's conception of history as an organic process of evolution and his stress on the uniqueness of each historical age and Rahel's own, although the extent to which his ideas helped shape hers is difficult to determine. No doubt, however, Herder, along with Lessing, Fichte, and Goethe, was important in reinforcing Rahel's progressive view of history, even as the political clocks were turning back during the Restoration, the Romantics looking back to the Middle Ages for a solution to their alienation, and the Hep Hep riots appearing to be an actual refutation of historical progress.

In 1821 Goethe published *Wilhelm Meisters Wanderjahre oder die Entsagenden, Teil 1* (*Wilhelm Meister's Journeymanship, or the Renunciants, Part One*), the sequel to his earlier epoch-making *Bildungsroman, Wilhelm Meister's Years of Apprenticeship*. No part 2 ever appeared. Instead, after this early version met with a rather negative reception, Goethe revised and expanded until, in 1829, he republished it in its final, more rounded and highly symbolic form. Even the earlier edition, however, the one Rahel read, was both formally and thematically so revolutionary that it foreshadowed the development of the novel far into the twentieth century.[97] The work had a long evolutionary history, its conception dating back to the time of *Wilhelm Meister's Years of Apprenticeship*. In his study, *Goethe and the Novel*, Eric Blackall beautifully and cogently summed up the encompassing scope of the initial version of the *Wanderjahre*:

> In the process it became a novel about the fullness of life, a novel with perspectives that reach almost into infinity, a novel of serene irony as well as of passionate anguish. It has a testamentary quality about it, something of the nature of a summing-up by one who has lived long, experienced widely and reflected deeply. The central ethical thread running through it is the necessity of renunciation, of *Entsagung* . . . but this attitude is presented as a positive quality, as achievement rather than deprivation. It is an "encyclopaedia" of the inner and outer life of man such as the German Romantics wished for from the novel as a genre, even though its content and ethical position

are in no wise Romantic. But as a structure it not only absorbs into itself and fuses into one whole every kind of experience and every form of communication—letters, conversations, poems, stories, diaries and reflections—but seems also to be Goethe's final resolution of the tensions of epic and drama, novel and romance, prose sobriety and poetic boldness, characters and sentiment, deeds and events, realism and the marvelous—a novel concerned but also content with the fact of being a novel.[98]

The open, even fragmentary structure of this work, the incorporation of multiple genres, the intermingling of realistic and fantastic or utopian elements, as well as the fact that there was no all-knowing narrator but rather an author-narrator who turned to the reader, asking him to fill in the gaps for himself and thus contribute toward the realization of the work, understandably caused consternation among its readers. Rahel was one of the few who was ready for Goethe's innovative work, both in terms of its content and its form. Although *Wilhelm Meister's Years of Apprenticeship* remained her favorite Goethe novel, she immediately grasped the meaning of the sequel as well as the relationship between the earlier and the later work. She recognized it as the summation of all his previous works, which were

nothing less than so many intellectual viewpoints about our earthly existence, the consideration of the human spirit included. We have to keep all his works, even the smallest, in mind if we want to understand each one better and more thoroughly and abundantly; one illuminates the other . . . and it is with these works as with the world itself [which also] consists of innumerable creative manifestations. However, the more we come to know of it, the richer and more perfect the concert becomes and, in its newness, again quite simple. An artistically talented intellect is the Creator's imitator (der Nachschöpfer des Urschöpfers). A great poet takes the world itself with all its occurrences as the subject matter for his works. . . . He is free to choose; but in all that he chooses he remains true because he only selects that which is true, showing that which is already false and pathological in nature as such, without arbitrarily setting up such abominations as a model as so many newer [writers] like to do out of weakness. . . . I see in him a mighty historian; what he describes must happen for he only describes that which happens. . . . At every step in life, at every new hurdle we have just overcome within our soul, something else of Goethe's becomes remarkable and clear.[99]

Again and again, Rahel refers to the striking confluence between Goethe's art and life or reality itself.

Rahel's ease of comprehension and sure judgment surely derived from her encompassing knowledge of literature. But there was also from the beginning this special affinity between her and Goethe. The more she read, the more she became convinced of his greatness. And although, she loved and appreciated a great many other poets, her thoughts and feelings resonated with no other as deeply as with Goethe. In 1827, for example, even though she read some letters and poems of Schiller that left her with a great admiration for his language, his soul, and his mind, she could not help comparing him to Goethe, as she writes to Varnhagen:

I loved him [Schiller] completely: I was full of joy to find him so charming and noble. But then there is Goethe with his power, his lines, his perfection and imagination, his thinking, maturity, perfection and power of expression, his battle-fought wisdom, his contemplative comprehensive melancholy, his wise, struggled-for serenity, with his *vue d'oiseau* [bird's eye view], with his celestial glance, as we would say in German—looking down from a star—, with his divine breast, upon which one not only rests but also finds peace—and all other poets lack something—great. No wonder that we still have to explicate him daily.[100]

Goethe's sweeping view of historical developments—including scientific and technical innovations, his awareness of the painful tensions between society and the individual, his explorations of human predicaments and potential, as well as his affirmation of life corresponded to Rahel's own.

It is perhaps in connection with the far-reaching perspectives contained in Goethe's novel that Rahel began to think of literature and art in terms of their utopian potential. The thought that the task of art was "to portray with talent that which could be according to our better judgment" appeared in various formulations throughout the 1820s.[101] She compared the role of art to that of play for children—as a deeply serious endeavor—as the most gifted individuals' attempt to work out problems, to find a way out of misery and limitation:

Art strives to fulfill all the conditions required to satisfy spiritual human nature; particularly, by presenting a better state than the one which we find ourselves in. . . . This may be accomplished through images—of any kind—or through speech—of any kind—through images which may refer to our physical existence or to that produced by our thoughts. Art is nothing but the children's play of grown-ups. They endeavor to present an existence which they cannot attain, over which they have no control. This great drive, this inevitable striving, this search for a surrogate, this creativity—is already highly venerable in children, no jest at all, but deeply serious.[102]

The Woman Question. Among Rahel's most interesting and forward-looking ideas are those concerning the conditions of girls and women and the need for improving their position in society. It is the topic that appears most frequently throughout her writing, undoubtedly because it was closest to her heart. As a young woman she railed against the constraints imposed on girls, demanding self-determination, freedom of movement, and the possibility to study and take up a profession. Her love relations failed to some extent because she was too much of a "rebel," unable and unwilling to subordinate herself to the will of another. She had identified for some time with the feminine ideal set forth by Goethe and the Romantics. However, through personally experienced deep disappointments she came to understand the inequity and injustice underlying this kind of thinking. She married eventually, but her husband proved to be an exceptional man for his time, granting her not only her much needed personal freedom but also genuine intellectual respect.

She nevertheless remained opposed to the institution of marriage. A lengthy passage at the very end of her life reveals just how radical her views on the subject were. Understandably, she confided her remarks to her diary. As in her younger days, she set pleasure, even sexual pleasure, above a narrow kind of moralism, but now she also went considerably further. She questioned outright the superiority and morality of legally sanctioned marriage and family life by juxtaposing it with friendship, which existed successfully without legalization: "Can liking exist without attraction? Is there a legal outer guarantee for established and known friendships? Is a *household* alone holy? Is the raising of children or their treatment? Do they have any guarantee? Cannot parents especially torture them unto death, physically and morally? Is intimate living together, without magic and delight, not more indecent than ecstasy of any other kind?"[103]

Earlier, in a letter to her sister, Rahel had put forth the equally modern argument that marriage and family could not fulfill a woman's life, and, given that she had no other occupation, she should at least have the right to diversion in order to periodically escape her confined state. Nonetheless, she was extremely fond of children and held the mother-child relationship in the highest regard. In fact, it was this lifelong concern that led her to consider the problem of illegitimacy, which was for her as well a result of women's low social status:

Natural children is the name given to those who are not children of the state, like natural law and state [constitutional] law. Children should have mothers only and bear their names; and the mother [should have] the wealth and power of the families: this is how nature ordained it. [Nature] must only be made more ethical; to act against it will never solve the problem completely. Nature is terrible only in that a woman can be abused and forced to produce a human being against her pleasure and will. This great wrong must be made right again through human efforts and institutions and shows how much the child belongs to the woman.[104]

How little regard Rahel had for moralistic thinking is shown by the fact that she never disapproved of women who bore children out of wedlock but remained friends and rejoiced with them in the rewards of motherhood. In 1811 Rahel herself seriously but unsuccessfully attempted to adopt such a child.[105] The mother-child relationship seemed to her unique and self-contained, almost unaffected by the presence or absence of a father. Her greatest disappointment was that she had no child of her own and was forced to look on as parents failed their children or treated them indifferently. Her letters contain long passages about the pleasures of having her nieces and later her grandniece on extended visits and the sense of loss when they returned to their parents.

In principle Rahel demanded full equality between women and men, although she knew only too well how remote were the chances of this. Full equality, of course, went against all contemporary theories on women. In philosophy, Fichte, Hegel, Humboldt, and others wrote extensively on the differences between men and women, insisting that it was women's fate to be and even want to be subjugated to man. Marriage and motherhood were the true destiny of woman and, although they welcomed women who could inspire and respond to them intellectually, such intellectuality and creativity were not supposed to become sovereign but remain subordinate to male endeavors. Interestingly, Rahel never took issue with such statements, not even in her diaries. She simply wrote down the ideas that her own experience and insight taught her. She was in many respects far ahead of the active feminists of the second half of the nineteenth century. Among the pioneers who wrote on behalf of women were Hedwig Dohm, Louise Otto, and Fanny Lewald. In contrast to Rahel they quite agreed with the notion that marriage and motherhood were the natural profession of women. They advocated women's work outside the home but intended it primarily for those remaining single. Thus, employment was a means to respectable economic survival and independence rather than self-fulfillment, as Rahel proposed. The early feminists also disavowed sensual pleasure, concerned as they were with what was then perceived as the rampant spread of prostitution. They directed their efforts toward improving the moral climate and thus, although they also attacked men's double standard and hypocrisy, it was women's freedom that was sacrificed for the sake of morality. Rahel's affirmation of sensuality, in part rooted in the pleasure-seeking courtly eighteenth century, contrasted starkly with the newer bourgeois moralism of the early feminists.

Whether young or old, single, in love, or married, Rahel never stopped protesting the restrictions imposed on women. Toward the end of the 1820s, her old friend Gentz began writing again. In the course of the next few years, Rahel exchanged a number of letters with the famous statesman and bon vivant, now aged and afraid of death. As always, he requested reassurance and cheering up from his brilliant, wise, and, most of all, kind friend. In 1831 his melancholy reached crisis proportions, primarily a result, as he wrote, of the disorder created by the revolutionary events of 1830 and the Polish uprising. These were the first signs that the Restoration, instituted by the major powers following the Napoleonic wars, was doomed. Looking back on his life, Gentz began to have doubts about the cause he had devoted his career to, vaguely feeling that the fruits of his forty years' labor in the service of a reactionary political order had come to naught. Rahel at first responded with empathy, but then spoke at length plainly.

In answer to his query, she exclaimed: "I should tell you about politics?" She reminded him how much of what happened and had been in his sphere of influence, she—"a mere woman!"—had foreseen; he, however, had paid no attention to her. She urged him to pull himself together and to see not just the chaos of the moment but to look forward and, based on his forty years of labor, search for solutions. She then contrasted his privileged and influential position in the world with her own life of privation, telling him of her vexations, suffering, and disappointments that she neither liked nor accepted: "No! No! No! And eternally No! But I have honestly worked through them." She had received no personal satisfaction but compensated for this deprivation by extending her empathy and interest to others and by devoting herself to "meditation, reason, ardor, joyfulness, kindness, innocence. . . . I despaired *often,* raged, *considered* myself already mad: because I also did not have peace and quiet. And you speak of forty years of labor. It was *pleasure*: and what did it bring you! All the joys of life and wealth, personal satisfaction: honor, respect, wealth, social enjoyment; travels, garden, horses, stimulation, life of any sort. (I should tell you!!) How humbly I peek out and up from my corner! How thoughtfully and happily. . . . *Me voilà.* I am consoling you and me."[106]

There is a companion to this letter, written almost forty years earlier, at the beginning of Rahel's "invented career" as epistolary writer and salonnière. In her very first missive to David Veit, dated April 1793, she had launched into a similarly vehement protest against the curtailments of girls and women. Then it was the young medical student's detailed and well-intentioned account of meeting the literary luminaries of the age that brought her face to face with the disadvantages of being female. In 1831 it was the statesman Friedrich Gentz, who, plagued by sudden self-doubt and self-pity, impressed upon her once more the extent to which she, as a woman, had been prevented from applying and realizing her considerable talents. As she looked back over her own life, she was not troubled by regrets or remorse, however. Lack of opportunity, what she called the inability to move, also effectively precluded making the kinds of mistakes a person in power was apt to make. Her account to Gentz reveals the extent to which she had invested her energy, creativity, and resourcefulness into merely maintaining her self-respect and sense of self. Although she achieved a certain prominence, she had no illusions about her accomplishments but saw them for what they were, compensatory efforts for want of real opportunities. Her letter to Gentz also sheds light on her testimonial letter to Heine, written in the same year. There, too, she included the "mixed society"—in other words, her life's work—among the palliatives that would never satisfy her because she recognized that such gatherings, no matter how free and tolerant, were too esoteric and limited. A much more radical cure was required to change a fundamentally divided society.

The two letters, with their impassioned outcry against and keen analysis of women's restricted existence, act like a frame to Rahel's written oeuvre. As such, they provide further proof of how profoundly this inequality affected her. So much of what was unsatisfactory in her life originated and was shaped by what had been denied her as a woman. Her Jewish origins and the accompanying lack of social status also affected her deeply, but in her eyes their effect was not as devastating because there seemed to be a way out of the Jewish ghetto, whereas the female ghetto remained as tightly locked as ever.

Jewish Matters. Although writing about Jews never again took on the urgency it did during the Hep Hep riots of 1819, Rahel remained conscious of their precarious position in society. She was watchful of any sign pointing to renewed outbreaks of violence and related these mainly to Ludwig Robert, whose thinking on these matters was most like hers. At the same time, she noted with satisfaction how, in times of emergency, Jews tended to be among the most generous donors and supporters of charity. Moreover, she never had any illusions about her own marginality.

Having had little contact with traditional Jewish life and no religious education, Rahel never attributed much value to Judaism, except as a historical phenomenon. Since her youth, she firmly believed that Judaism, once the most advanced form of religious thinking, was now surpassed by Christianity. Thus, assimilation entailed more than social integration and acceptance. Escape from Jewishness was seen as a necessity and obligation—a matter of keeping pace with the course of history. In the 1820s her long-held views must have received further confirmation through the philosophy of Hegel as well as her friend, Eduard Gans, Hegel's gifted and devoted disciple. To join the large class of enlightened humanity had been Rahel's wish almost from the beginning. "You know that I can't stand classes and don't like to be restricted to one, except to that of human beings," she had written to David Veit in 1795.[107] Some twenty years later, she gave the following advice to her longtime friend Ernestine Goldstücker, who was about to adopt Christianity. The passage contains the most detailed statement about how Rahel viewed conversion and its consequences. Beginning with the name change and ending with a warning, she wrote:

I consider this changing of names important. You thereby become to some extent outwardly a different person; and this is especially necessary. . . . You will have the children baptized as well. They have already received a Christian education and may, possibly, come to know of that crazy history (von jenem Verrückthistorischen) nothing more than about history generally!—You, however, have no reason to want to remain in the appearance of your birth faith. You must also outwardly . . . commit yourself to the large class with whose customs, opinion, education, conviction you are one. You will thereby not join in the one bad thing which this avowal might lead to, the new hatred against Jews; and continue to stand by the unhappy remnants of a great and gifted nation, far ahead in the knowledge of God (weit in Gotterkenntniß vorgeschrittenen Nation). . . . You will not be ashamed of your Jewish descent and abandon the nation whose misfortune *and* deficiencies you know only too well, in order that one may not say, there is still something Jewish about her! Find the courage to ignore such reproaches in the newly acquired religious tenets![108]

There is no explicit statement about her own conversion, and the very absence of one or other reflections surrounding this step suggests that for Rahel baptism raised no questions regarding her identity. She who analyzed and reflected on just about every aspect of her life seems to have taken this step as a matter of course. Was she so thoroughly imbued with the ideals of Enlightenment and the Romantic notion of self-realization that Jewishness constituted a minor and mostly negative part of her identity? Did becoming a Christian imply no change in allegiance because she had never felt part of traditional and, especially religious, Jewish life? If this is so, she differed markedly from her brother Ludwig Robert, who was plagued by doubts when, in 1819, he resolved to convert in order to marry Friederike Braun, a Gentile. At that time, he confessed to his sister: "Since you know me well, you will also know that I am taking this step [conversion] as earnestly as I have earlier refused it. We cannot escape our individuality . . . rest assured that I shall not permit a *foreign* one to be forced . . . on me. . . . I try not to lie to myself. . . . It is true that this step and my love have produced a great change in me; it is equally true that this change has not come about without struggle—after all, the individual *too* has his historical epochs."[109] Ernestine Goldstücker, judging from Rahel's answer, appears to have voiced in her letter similar reservations regarding her loyalty toward the Jewish community.

Nonetheless, although Rahel seemed to pursue assimilation, including conversion, quite single-mindedly, this did not mean that she had no interest or concern for her fellow Jews. She was intensely loyal to those Jews whose intellectual goals were similar to hers and for whom assimilation was a matter of personal and human growth, whether they remained Jewish or not. In time she also became able to appreciate Jews who pursued paths other than her own. It may be recalled that, as a young woman, she came to regard her uncle and aunt in Breslau, who remained committed to traditional, if enlightened, Jewish life, in the highest esteem. Much later she expressed genuine admiration for the ways and person of Bernhard Freiherr von Eskeles, von Arnstein's business partner in Vienna, remarking that "he has remained entirely Jewish, with spiritual gifts, and a rich life . . . which he has cultivated entirely according to his own manner, from which he derives completely original insights, with the ease of the most experienced person in good Jewish fashion."[110] Moreover, as her letter to Ernestine Goldstücker indicates, she was unforgiving toward those who succumbed to anti-Jewish sentiment, especially if they were Jews who had recently converted to Christianity. Jewishness was important in one other respect: it constituted the foundation upon which her life developed—in its tragic as well as its enriching aspects.

This is not to deny that Rahel's religious outlook, however, was deeply and sincerely Christian without being tied to any confession or religious institution. "The human soul is by nature Christian," she wrote in her diary in 1817, by which she meant that humans were by nature kind, charitable, and tolerant.[111] She found solace and inspiration in the writings of those Christian mystics whose religiosity affirmed both life and the world as well as independence of thought. The ideas of original sin and life after death, however, remained foreign to her. And she was insistent that God was not removed from and indifferent to humanity and the world but manifested himself through and within his creation. This notion of an immanent divine presence as well as her rationality are as akin to Jewish as to certain kinds of Christian religious thought. Rahel developed a highly personal form of religion not tied to any doctrine. In 1811 she replied to Fouqué's queries about his daughter's religious upbringing by posing further questions: "can one person teach another—without revelation—a feeling of religion, belief, or opinion? Is this not the ultimate intimate act between created man and that which I don't want to name? . . . Only for God's sake! Let her [Fouqué's daughter] find for herself the Great, Divine, Infinite. How outrageously sinful! not to let a person ask all the questions, make all the discoveries himself!"[112] This and other statements could easily be seen as combining aspects of both faiths. In this respect, too, she was essentially in agreement with Hegel and Gans, for whom Judaism did not simply disappear but was contained within the later stage of Christianity.

It was Hannah Arendt who proposed that Rahel came to terms with her Jewishness at the end of her life. Seizing upon the words Rahel had uttered to Varnhagen, Arendt concluded that Rahel finally, after so many years as a parvenu, acknowledged what she had denied throughout her life—her "schlemihldom" or "pariahdom." Varnhagen relates having written down Rahel's words precisely and immediately after hearing them. Rahel was reported to have said: "What a history! . . . A fugitive from Egypt and Palestine, and here I find your help, love, and care! . . . With sublime rapture I think back upon these, my origins and this whole web of destiny, by which the oldest memories of the human race are connected with the latest circumstances, and the greatest distances of time and space are bridged. The thing which for the most part of my life was my greatest shame, my bitterest suffering and misfortune—to have been born a Jewess—I would not now miss at any price."[113] But Arendt did not quote the entire passage, for Rahel continued: "Dear August, my heart is refreshed in its inmost depths. I have thought of Jesus and cried over his passion; I have felt—for the first time so felt it—that he is my brother. And Mary, how did *she* suffer! She saw her beloved son suffer but did not succumb; *she stood* at the cross! *That* I could not have done; I would not have been that strong. May God forgive me, I confess how weak I am."[114]

This is one of the few explicit statements about her Christian beliefs—explicit because it refers to Christ and Mary rather than to God, this quite personal God of hers whom she invoked so often in her letters and diaries. Perhaps prompted by physical suffering and a premonition of death, she seems to have sought solace and strength among those symbolic figures of Christianity whose sufferings were still on a human scale.

The affirmation of her Jewish roots, however, cannot be seen as a return to Jewishness, something she was never allowed to deny in the first place. Rather, the entire passage represents another of her sweeping historical analyses. Looking back upon the course of her life as an outsider and member of a despised minority, she now found herself loved and cared for by Christians—her husband and her faithful servant Dore as well as Bettine von Arnim, who had become a close and devoted friend.[115] Her life must have appeared to her as a small token of historical progress. Although deeply dissatisfied with the general state of the world, she could at least look with satisfaction upon her own case.

The Perfectibility of the World. Very late in life, Rahel came across the writings of the utopian socialist Claude-Henri Comte de Saint-Simon (1760–1825). With Armand Bazard and Barthélemy-Prosper Enfantin, among other followers, Saint-Simon proposed the complete reordering of society, envisioning in his last work, *The New Christianity* (1825), a form of state socialism based on the Christian principle of brotherly love and cooperation.[116] A few years after his death, his devotees, a group of brilliant if troubled young men, began to organize and propagate Saint-Simon's ideas. In 1828–29, they held a series of lectures, which they subsequently published as *The Doctrine of Saint-Simon*, a distillation of what they conceived to be the salient features of Saint-Simon's theory. To this they added their own ideas about free love, the emancipation of women, and a critique of the bourgeois family and morality. In 1830, in the wake of the July revolution, they acquired the journal *Le Globe*, in which they published the programs and writings of the Saint-Simonians. The journal had previously served as an organ for the popularization of Goethe in France, especially his *Wilhelm Meister* novel. Because of the egalitarian relationships depicted in the work and the search for more adequate forms of social organization, it was considered by many, including, for example, Varnhagen and George Sand, to contain socialist ideas as well.[117]

Saint-Simon and his followers were important in that they moved away from the rather mechanistic eighteenth-century view of man as primarily a rational being. Rather, they recognized three cardinal capacities present in all men—utilitarian, religious, and activist. These capacities, moreover, were not limited but would, in a good society, be nurtured and developed infinitely and in all directions. Man could at one and the same time progress in power over nature, in expansive feeling, and in the endless accumulation of knowledge. The Christian duality of the spiritual and the corporeal, the contempt for the body and its desires, and the repression of feeling were refuted. Instead of the limited rationalistic "progress of the human mind," the Saint-Simonians proposed "progress toward the emancipation of humanity."

Although the Saint-Simonian social movement evolved within a short time into a religious one, Saint-Simon himself had paid close attention to the social and economic ills of the age. He was alarmed by the glaring differences between the leisure and the laboring classes. He also observed the rapid pace of industrialization in France and England and the role of science in making these developments possible. He was thus among the first to recognize that a new social order would fundamentally have to reorganize production and the distribution of wealth. In both their philosophical and historical import, Saint-Simon's ideas contained the seeds of the later scientific socialism of Marx and Engels.

Saint-Simonism reached Berlin through the *Globe*, to which Varnhagen had been subscribing for years, and Albert Brisbane, a young American who had come to Berlin in 1829 for the purpose of acquainting himself with German philosophical thought. While there, he was also introduced to the famous Berlin intellectual circles. He was delighted with German hospitality, much preferring it to "the stiff reserve of the English or the calculated exclusiveness of the French." He frequented the homes of the Mendelssohns, the Beers, the Varnhagens, being particularly impressed by two women, Rahel and Bettine von Arnim.[118] In 1831 after a further sojourn in Paris Brisbane returned to Berlin full of enthusiasm for the teachings of Saint-Simon and the Saint-Simonians, whose association he had joined. He found a most receptive audience at the Varnhagens, and especially in Rahel. Her immanent religiosity and her lifelong interest in human progress, both social and spiritual, predisposed her in an ideal way to this kind of thinking. Throughout the winter of 1831–32, she immersed herself in the writings of Saint-Simon, her "nourishment, entertainment, occupation," as she wrote to Heine. She declared Saint-Simonism "the new, grandly conceived instrument which finally touches the great old wound, men's history on this earth. It operates and sows; and has brought to light irrefutable truths. It put in order the true questions: answered many important ones. . . . To beautify the earth. My old topic. Freedom for men to develop."[119]

Saint-Simonism became a frequent and much debated topic at the Varnhagen gatherings. In fact, at a time when Saint-Simonism caught the fancy of progressive minds throughout Europe, the Varnhagen salon became a center for the dissemination of these ideas in Berlin. To further spread the good news, Brisbane and Varnhagen also regularly placed the *Globe* in one of the major coffeehouses in Berlin. After three months the police discovered the dangerous character of the publication and suppressed it.

To Brisbane's regret, Rahel was not very impressed by Saint-Simonian proposals for industrial reform and the dignification of labor. She was much more taken with his philosophical arguments and historical analyses. Brisbane relates in his autobiography how, when reading about the "subversion of society: a world invertedly organized, in which all the principles of normal organization were violated," Rahel was said to have exclaimed: " 'I have said this a thousand times. . . . I know that this world is in a false state, and that society is upside down.' "[120] Her lack of interest in the passages dealing with labor reform is to some extent understandable. A privileged woman from a country where industrialization was only just beginning, she had very little idea of the turbulent changes taking place in the industrially and technically more advanced nations. Moreover, coming from a community of bankers and schooled on Fichte's *Der geschlossene Handelsstaat* (1800, The closed commercial state), she viewed money, rather than labor, as the foundation of a nation's economy. She was well aware of the poverty all around her, observing in 1823 that the "laboring class is larger than we think."[121] But she saw no solution to the problem other than alleviating the suffering through generous charitable gifts. Saint-Simonism was to her a continuation of Enlightenment thinking, an educational project, a project of *Bildung*, bringing light and knowledge not only to a few but to all men: "This old earth must be made brighter and future men must be better and happier."[122] Another passage from a letter to the young writer Karl Schall similarly articulates her indebtedness to Enlightenment thinking: "I am the most deeply convinced Saint-Simonist. Namely: I believe completely in the progression, the perfectibility, the continued improvement of the universe, toward ever greater understanding and wealth in the highest sense; happiness and the giving of happiness. . . ."[123] Progress and perfectibility, those two seminal eighteenth-century concepts, retained their urgency for Rahel throughout her life, that is, until well into the nineteenth century.

In one crucial respect, however, Rahel was more realistic than Brisbane, Heine, and her other visitors. For, although she wrote of Saint-Simonism in a reverent, almost religious tone, she insisted that it was a secular theory and not a religion. A religion, she maintained, cannot be deduced; it must be either revealed through commandments or proven through miracles. Everything else is a theory produced by reason. "The beauty of our present state is that whatever is good and beneficial can be proven—and thus must be proven—and that which we recognize as right and proper *leads us to the height of perfection within us*; we honor it like the most unexpected revelation, handed down to us from the clouds by a chorus of angels! This irrefutable recognition of what is right and proper and appropriate and our holy reverence for it, is now religious, but no longer religion. Now our knowledge is the holy countenance of God which we recognize: it is evidence which can be resisted by nothing, which gradually excludes all visions."[124] Rahel adamantly refused to relegate the Saint-Simonian insights to the realm of religion. She recognized their potential for changing the world and therefore wanted them to be in the world in order that they may be realized and put into practice. The protosocialist ideas contained in Saint-Simonism completely captivated Rahel. They held the solution to the grave and pressing problems of humankind and thus represented the logical next stage in the evolution of men and society. After a lifelong search, she finally found what she considered to be real answers to the essential questions facing humanity. Her spirits lifted and her zest for life revived. She regretted being "so old already," as she wished "to still partake of the feast [of life]"[125] One of her favorite thoughts was by Saint-Martin: " 'Our future happiness will consist of our coming to know something new every moment.' " To this she added: "Then only shall we be free and take part in the creation."[126]

She had only another year to live, however. All around her, her contemporaries were dying: Hegel died in 1831, Goethe and Gentz in 1832. Ludwig Robert and his wife succumbed to the cholera epidemic that same year. Rahel said little about the loss of these people. The more she loved them, the less she tended to express her grief. About Goethe she wrote simply: "Children's kisses are milder than May showers. The fragrance of roses, the sound of nightingales, the whirl of larches—Goethe no longer hears it. A great witness is no more."[127] Ludwig Robert, her favorite brother, she remembered this way: "Words are too pale. Silence the only form of speech. My soul mate. We shared every conviction. We experienced together all matters of the intellect and life. I raised, nurtured him; in all aspects. A good part of my youth lies buried in the earth of Baden."[128] Rahel did not succumb to the epidemic, but her own health steadily deteriorated so that she could not leave the house or bed for long periods at a time. She was often unable to write and had to resort to dictation. But her letters were to the end missives of encouragement and empathy, expressions of gratitude, love, and friendship. She died on 17 March 1833, after prolonged suffering. Varnhagen, her loyal maid Dore, Bettine von Arnim, her brother Moritz and his wife, Ernestine, whose beautiful singing voice cheered her often, were among those who stood by her during the last months.

Fittingly, in 1831, she wrote her own epitaph. Prompted by yet another attack on Jews, this time in Königsberg, she confided to Ludwig Robert her concern over the deteriorating conditions in Prussia at all levels, the political disorder and repression, and the deep dissatisfaction communicated to her by "all classes." She concluded her historical analysis with the following words, probably the last of her many self-appraisals: "When I must die, do think: she knew everything: because everything was familiar to her; she was never anything, aimed for nothing, and filtered everything through her mind and brought it into a general context; she grasped Fichte; loved green things, children; understood the arts, humanity's helpmate. She wanted to help God in his creatures. Always; uninterruptedly; and thanked him for this her disposition. 'This was the old dragon's good side.'"[129] These words accurately sum up what she accomplished in life. Her extensive writings, however, tell a much more complex story—the life story of a woman with grand ambitions, hopes, and dreams, not just for herself but for all, and how they were thwarted.

Barely four months after her death, Varnhagen published *Rahel: Ein Buch des Andenkens für ihre Freunde*, the work by which she is still known today. Both he and Rahel had spent the last several years preparing her letters and diary entries for publication. With this and subsequent publications as well as the establishment of the Varnhagen Collection, the couple made certain that the voice of an outstanding and penetrating witness and critic of her time would be preserved for posterity.

NOTES

ABBREVIATIONS

GW *Rahel-Bibliothek, Rahel Varnhagen: Gesammelte Werke*, ed. Konrad Feilchenfeldt, Uwe Schweikert, and Rachel E. Steiner (Munich: Matthes & Seitz, 1983), vols.1-10

Kemp *Rahel Varnhagen: Briefwechsel*, ed. Friedhelm Kemp (Munich: Winkler, 1983), vols.1-4

Varnhagen/Wiesel *Rahel Varnhagen: Briefwechsel mit Pauline Wiesel*, ed. Barbara Hahn, with the cooperation of Birgit Bosold (Munich: C. H. Beck, 1997)

SV Sammlung Varnhagen (Varnhagen Collection), Biblioteka Jagiellonska, Cracow, Poland

INTRODUCTION

1. Thomas Carlyle, *Critical and Miscellaneous Essays*, vol.4 (London, 1899), 115.

2. Cited in Carlyle, *Essays*, 110.

3. Heinrich von Treitschke, *Deutsche Geschichte im Neunzehnten Jahrhundert*, Viertes Buch: *Das Eindringen des französischen Liberalismus 1830–1840* (Leipzig: S. Hirzel, 1897–1904), 434. Ludwig Börne and Heinrich Heine were Jewish writers; Eduard Gans, a student of Hegel's, was a highly successful professor of jurisprudence at Berlin University. All were a generation younger than Rahel but knew and admired her. Heine and Börne are often counted among the Young Germans, a progressive literary movement (1830–50) advocating a politically committed literature. Its major representatives, Heinrich Laube, Theodor Mundt, Karl Gutzkow, and Georg Büchner, were not Jewish.

4. Fanny Lewald, *Meine Lebensgeschichte*, Zweiter Band: *Leidensjahre*, ed. Ulrike Helmer (Frankfort on the Main: Ulrike Helmer Verlag, 1989), 156. Abbreviated English version: Fanny Lewald, *The Education of Fanny Lewald: An Autobiography*, ed., trans. Hanna Ballin Lewis (Albany: State U of New York P, 1992), 185.

5. Lily Braun, "The Female Mind," *Selected Writings on Feminism and Socialism*, ed., trans. Alfred G. Meyer (Bloomington: Indiana UP, 1987), 184.

6. Terry H. Pickett, *The Unseasonable Democrat: K. A. Varnhagen von Ense, 1785–1858* (Bonn: Bouvier, 1985).

7. The most notorious "treatise" is that of Kurt Fervers, *Berliner Salons: Die Geschichte einer großen Verschwörung* (Munich: Deutscher Volksverlag, 1940).

8. The autobiographical connections to this early work are explored by Dagmar Barnouw in her study *Visible Spaces: Hannah Arendt and the German-Jewish Experience* (Baltimore: Johns Hopkins UP, 1990), especially chapter 2.

9. Hannah Arendt, *Rahel Varnhagen: The Life of a Jewess*, ed. Liliane Weissberg, trans. Richard and Clara Winston (Baltimore: Johns Hopkins UP, 1997), 81.

10. Although scholarship on Rahel and Karl August Varnhagen has been prolific since the rediscovery of the Varnhagen Archive in the late 1970s, both in its wealth of new historical information and interpretive approaches, Barnouw does not draw on these new insights. She thereby simply takes over and perpetuates Arendt's negative portrait of Varnhagen, falling short in her attempt to analyze Arendt's perspective on this unusual couple. Ursula Wiedenmann's dissertation, *Karl August Varnhagen von Ense: Ein Unbequemer in der Biedermeierzeit* (Stuttgart: Metzler, 1994), provides an excellent analysis of Varnhagen's maligned reputation as well as a fair assessment of his accomplishments as a journalist and man of letters. Although Wiedenmann is critical of Arendt's book, it too remains her primary source of information on Rahel.

11. Lotte Kohler and Hans Saner, eds., *Hannah Arendt/Karl Jaspers Correspondence, 1926–1969*, trans. Robert Kimber and Rita Kimber (New York: Harcourt Brace Jovanovich, 1992), no.134.

12. Elisabeth Young-Bruehl, *Hannah Arendt: For Love of the World* (New Haven: Yale UP, 1982), 109.

13. Kohler and Saner, *Arendt/Jaspers Correspondence*, no.135. Arendt herself admits: "[The book] was written from a Zionist critique of assimilation, which I had adopted as my own and which I still consider basically justified today. But that critique was as politically naive as what it was criticizing."

14. Arendt, *Rahel Varnhagen*, 3–5.

15. Kemp, 4 vols.

16. GW, 10 vols.

17. For the adventurous story of the Prussian State Library's manuscript collection, see Deborah Herz, "The Varnhagen Collection Is in Krakow," *The American Archivist* 44/3 (1981): 223–28; Dieter Henrich, "Beethoven, Hegel und Mozart auf der Reise nach Krakau," *Neue Rundschau* 2 (1977): 165–99; Peter Whitehead, "The Lost Berlin Manuscripts," *Notes: The Quarterly Music Journal of the Music Library Association* 33 (1976): 165–99.

18. Barbara Hahn, *"Antworten Sie mir!" Rahel Levin Varnhagens Briefwechsel* (Basel: Stroemfeld/Roter Stern, 1990), 12–13; Ursula Isselstein, *"Der Text aus meinem belei-*

digten Herzen": Studien zu Rahel Levin Varnhagen (Turin: Tirrenia Stampatori, 1993), 25–26.

19. Isselstein, *Studien zu Rahel Levin Varnhagen*, 25–119; Ursula Isselstein, "Rahel Levins Einbrüche in die eingerichtete Welt," *Von einer Welt in die andere: Jüdinnen im 19. und 20. Jahrhundert*, ed. Jutta Dick and Barbara Hahn (Vienna: Christian Brandstätter, 1993), 93–108; Heidi Thomann Tewarson, "Jüdinnen um 1800: Bemerkungen zum Selbstverständnis der ersten Generation assimilierter Berliner Jüdinnen," *Von einer Welt in die andere*, 47–70. Heidi Thomann Tewarson, "German-Jewish Identity in the Correspondence between Rahel Levin Varnhagen and Her Brother, Ludwig Robert: Hopes and Realities of Emancipation, 1780–1830," *Leo Baeck Institute Yearbook* 39 (1994): 3–29; Barbara Hahn, "'Lernen Sie europäisch!' Die Rolle Frankreichs bei der Akkulturation deutscher Juden," *Athenäum: Jahrbuch für Romantik* 4 (1995): 319–40.

20. Uwe Schweikert, "'Am jüngsten Tag' hab ich recht': Rahel Varnhagen als Briefschreiberin," GW 10:17–42; Marianne Schuller, "'Unsere Sprache ist unser gelebtes Leben': Randbemerkungen zur Schreibweise Rahel Varnhagens," GW 10:43–59; Barbara Hahn, "Rahel Levin Varnhagen und Bettine von Arnim: Briefe, Bücher, Biographien," *Frauen, Literatur, Politik*, ed. Annegret Pelz et al. (Hamburg: Argument Verlag, 1988), 115–31; Barbara Hahn, "'Weiber verstehen alles à la lettre . . .' Briefkultur um 1800," *Deutsche Literatur von Frauen*, ed. Gisela Brinkler Gabler (Munich: C. H. Beck, 1988); Barbara Hahn, *Antworten Sie mir!*; Heidi Thomann Tewarson, "Lebensprojekte deutscher Jüdinnen während der Emanzipationszeit: Rahel Levin Varnhagen und Fanny Lewald," *Lektüren und Brüche: Jüdische Frauen in Kultur, Politik und Wissenschaft*, ed. Mechtild M. Jansen and Ingeborg Nordmann (Wiesbaden: Hessische Landeszentrale für politische Bildung, 1993), 22–47; Barbara Hahn, "Goethe lesen—über Goethe schreiben: Briefe und Aufzeichnungen deutscher Jüdinnen um 1800," *Lektüren und Brüche*, 48–71; Barbara Hahn, "Schriftstellerin zwischen allen Grenzen: Rahel Levin Varnhagen (1771–1833)," *Frankreichfreunde: Mittler des französisch-deutschen Kulturtransfers (1750–1850)*, ed. Michel Espagen and Werner Greiling (Leipzig: Universitätsverlag, 1997), 243–60.

21. Of these, the first has appeared (see Varnhagen/Wiesel in Abbreviations). This excellently conceived and painstakingly researched volume appeared too late to be considered in any detail in this study. All quotes from this correspondence, however, refer to this edition.

22. The most important publications based on archival research are listed below. Barbara Hahn and Ursula Isselstein, eds., *Rahel Levin Varnhagen: Die Wiederentdeckung einer Schriftstellerin* (Göttingen: Vandenhoeck & Ruprecht, 1987). See the essays by Barbara Hahn, Ursula Isselstein, Consolina Vigliero, and Renata Buzzo Màrgari. Several contributions address questions of a future edition of unpublished

material: Günter de Bruyn, ed., *Rahels erste Liebe: Rahel Levin und Karl Graf von Finckenstein in ihren Briefen* (Berlin: Der Morgen, 1985); Heidi Thomann Tewarson, *Rahel Levin Varnhagen mit Selbstzeugnissen und Bilddokumenten* (Reinbek: Rowohlt, 1988); Deborah Hertz, ed., *Briefe an eine Freundin: Rahel Varnhagen an Rebecca Friedländer* (Cologne: Kiepenheuer & Witsch, 1988); Barbara Hahn, *Antworten Sie mir!*; Barbara Hahn, ed., *"Im Schlaf bin ich wacher:" Die Träume der Rahel Levin Varnhagen* (Frankfort on the Main: Luchterhand, 1990); Isselstein, *Studien zu Rahel Levin Varnhagen*; Heidi Thomann Tewarson, "Jüdisches und Weibliches: Rahel Levin Varnhagens Reisen als Überschreitungen," *German Quarterly* 66 (1993): 145–59; Tewarson, "German-Jewish Identity"; Hahn, *Rahel Levin Varnhagen: Briefwechsel mit Pauline Wiesel*. Others will be cited in the course of this study.

23. Information of this kind had not been available to Hannah Arendt, who knew little about Jewish history. Belonging to the very assimilated German Jews, she had, by her own admission, been not at all interested in the "so-called Jewish question" until forced to concern herself with it in the early 1930s. See Kohler and Saner, *Arendt/Jaspers Correspondence*, no.135.

24. The most detailed analysis on this subject can be found in Ursula Isselstein, "Costruzione e ricostruzione di un'identità: Rahel Levin Varnhagen e i suoi diari," *Ricerche di identità*, ed. Cesare Cases (Turin: La Rosa 33, 1985), 135–55.

25. Isselstein, *Studien zu Rahel Levin Varnhagen*, 199–200.

26. *Letters of Alexander von Humboldt Written Between the Years 1827 and 1858 to Varnhagen von Ense: Together With Extracts from Varnhagen's Diaries, and Letters of Varnhagen and Others to Humboldt*, authorized translation from the German, with explanatory notes and a full index of names, preface Ludmilla Assing (London, 1860).

27. Rudolf Haym [rev.], "Varnhagen von Ense: Tagebücher von K. A. Varnhagen von Ense, 6 Bde. Leipzig 1861 u. 1862, Zweite Aufl. 1863," *Preußische Jahrbücher* 11 (1863): 445–515.

28. Heinrich von Treitschke, *Deutsche Geschichte im Neunzehnten Jahrhundert*, Zweites Buch: *Bis zu den Karlsbader Beschlüssen* (Leipzig: Hirzel, 1897–1904), 370–73.

29. Among those viewing Varnhagen positively were Heinrich König, "Erinnerungen an Varnhagen von Ense," *Deutsches Museum* (1859), nos.27 and 28; Ludwig Geiger, *Das Junge Deutschland und die preußische Zensur: Nach ungedruckten archivalischen Quellen* (Berlin, 1900); Heinrich Hubert Houben, *Gutzkow-Funde: Beiträge zur Litteratur- und Kulturgeschichte des neunzehnten Jahrhunderts* (Berlin, 1901); Otto Berdrow, *Rahel Varnhagen: Ein Lebens- und Zeitbild* (Stuttgart: Greiner & Pfeiffer, 1900).

30. Arendt, *Rahel Varnhagen*, 80–81.

31. See Varnhagen's instructions regarding future publications: Isselstein, *Studien zu Rahel Levin Varnhagen*, 199–205.

32. GW 4/1:xii–xiii.

33. Arendt, *Rahel Varnhagen*, 196.

34. Varnhagen's rehabilitation began in the 1970s, when a more objective assessment acknowledged his commitment to a liberal-progressive interpretation of history. See Konrad Feilchenfeldt, ed., *Varnhagen als Historiker* (Amsterdam, 1970); Werner Greiling, ed., *K. A. Varnhagen von Ense, Kommentare zum Zeitgeschehen: Publizistik, Briefe, Dokumente 1813–1858* (Leipzig: Reclam Universal-Bibliothek, 1984); Pickett, *The Unseasonable Democrat*; Werner Greiling, *Varnhagen von Ense—Lebenswege eines Liberalen: Politisches Wirken zwischen Diplomatie und Revolution* (Cologne: Böhlau, 1993). Increasingly, studies are drawing on the collection, disclosing Varnhagen's many-sided achievements. See Cornelia Fuhrmann, *Varnhagen von Enses Denkwürdigkeiten als "Dichtung und Wahrheit"* (Frankfort on the Main: Peter Lang, 1992); Wiedenmann, *Karl August Varnhagen von Ense*.

35. Kemp 4:222.

36. How much Rahel is still read and cherished in the twentieth century is shown by the following moving story. I have recently come into possession of documents owned and written by a German Jewish family. When going through the wife's pocket calendars (from the years 1933–45), I found in one of them, tucked into the covers, a piece of paper with a quote by Rahel about the power of love. Rahel's words thus accompanied this brave woman from Berlin, where she married a blinded war hero, to the concentration camp Theresienstadt, where she gave birth to a son whom she miraculously kept alive, then back to Berlin and finally to New York.

I. BEGINNINGS

1. Kemp 4:365.

2. The number of resident "protected" Jews had been fixed at 120 families and 250 domestic and public servants by the edict of 1737. As a result, 584 persons were expelled. In 1743, there were 333 resident Jewish families, the total Jewish population amounting to 1,945, and no fresh expulsions. See Alexander Altmann, *Moses Mendelssohn: A Biographical Study* (Tuscaloosa: U of Alabama P, 1973), 16. Two good historical studies in English are Jacob Katz, *Out of the Ghetto: The Social Background of Jewish Emancipation, 1770–1870* (Cambridge: Harvard UP, 1973) and Steven M. Lowenstein, *The Berlin Jewish Community: Enlightenment, Family, and Crisis, 1770–1830* (New York: Oxford UP, 1993).

3. Bildarchiv Preußischer Kulturbesitz, *Juden in Preußen: Ein Kapitel deutscher Geschichte* (Dortmund: Harenberg, 1981), 76–84.

4. Stefi Jersch-Wenzel, *Juden und "Franzosen" in der Wirtschaft des Raumes Berlin/ Brandenburg zur Zeit des Merkantilismus* (Berlin: Colloquium Verlag, 1978); Anna-

Ruth Löwenbrück, *Judenfeindschaft im Zeitalter der Aufklärung: Eine Studie zur Vorgeschichte des modernen Antisemitismus am Beispiel des Göttinger Theologen und Orientalisten Johann David Michaelis (1717–1791)* (Frankfort on the Main: Peter Lang, 1995) 21–60.

5. Mirabeau, *De la Monarchic Prussienne sous Frédéric le Grand* (Paris, 1788), cited in *Juden in Preußen*, 130.

6. On the extent of Jewish poverty in the eighteenth century, see Löwenbrück, *Judenfeindschaft im Zeitalter der Aufklärung*, 42–51, and Steven M. Lowenstein, "Two Silent Minorities: Orthodox Jews and Poor Jews in Berlin, 1770–1823," *Leo Baeck Institute Yearbook* 36 (1991): 3–25.

7. Dolf Michaelis, "The Ephraim Family," *Leo Baeck Institute Yearbook* 21 (1976): 208–9.

8. Ursula Isselstein, *"Der Text aus meinem beleidigten Herzen": Studien zu Rahel Levin Varnhagen* (Turin: Tirrenia Stampatori, 1993), 30.

9. Rainer Schmitz, ed., *Henriette Herz in Erinnerungen, Briefen und Zeugnissen* (Frankfort on the Main: Insel, 1984), 40, 42.

10. GW 1:51.

11. GW 5/3:311.

12. GW 1:324–25.

13. The two gates were the Hallisches and the Prenzlauer Tor. Gatekeepers, which the Jewish community had to provide, issued passes and removed those whose presence was illegal, for the elders of the community were charged with keeping the number of Jews at the required level. Altmann, *Moses Mendelssohn*, 16.

14. *Henriette Herz*, 64.

15. The ballets referred to earlier, which the children performed on Saturday mornings, were in actuality an attempt at religious instruction or, rather, a compensation for the lack of it, since "no one had any idea how this was to be done" (Rahel to Markus, 17 Jan. 1817, in Isselstein, *Studien zu Rahel Levin Varnhagen*, 30).

16. GW 3:376.

17. The following discussion is based on an essay by Julius Carlebach, "Deutsche Juden und der Säkularisierungsprozeß in der Erziehung: Kritische Bemerkungen zu einem Problemkreis der jüdischen Emanzipation," *Das Judentum in der deutschen Umwelt, 1800–1850: Studien zur Frühgeschichte der Emanzipation*, ed. Hans Liebeschütz and Arnold Paucker (Tübingen: Mohr, 1977), 55–94.

18. *The Life of Glückel of Hameln, 1646–1724: Written by Herself*, trans. from orig. Yiddish and ed. Beth-Zion Abrahams (New York: Thomas Yoseloff, 1963).

19. As outlined by Carlebach, "Deutsche Juden und der Säkularisierungsprozess," 91.

20. SV, Box 202.

21. See, for example, the passages on Klopstock and Lavater in Goethe's autobiography, *Poetry and Truth*, Books XIII and XIV.

22. GW 7/1:201–2.

23. Peter Berglar, *Wilhelm von Humboldt in Selbstzeugnissen und Bilddokumenten* (Reinbek: Rowohlt, 1970), 83–97.

24. GW 1:325.

25. Jeffrey L. Sammons, "The Mystery of the Missing *Bildungsroman*, or: What Happened to Wilhelm Meister's Legacy?" *Imagination and History: Selected Papers on Nineteenth-Century German Literature*, ed. Jeffrey L. Sammons (New York: Peter Lang, 1988), 7–31.

26. GW 1:435.

27. GW 1:62–63.

28. "Rahel Levin und ihre Gesellschaft: Gegen Ende des Jahres 1801 (Aus den Papieren des Grafen S*** [Salm])," *Ausgewählte Schriften*, vol.19, ed. Ludmilla Assing, publ. K. A. Varnhagen (Leipzig: 1876), 158–82.

29. Ulrich Im Hof, *Das gesellige Jahrhundert: Gesellschaft und Gesellschaften im Zeitalter der Aufklärung* (Munich: C. H. Beck, 1982).

30. Clemens Brentano to Sophie Mereau, Berlin, 24 Nov. 1804. In Isselstein, *Studien zu Rahel Levin Varnhagen*, 114.

31. Wilhelm von Humboldt, *Briefe an eine Freundin*, sel. and ed. Albert Leitzman (Leipzig: Insel, n.d.), 288–89.

32. Gustav von Brinckmann, "Rahel: Brief an Varnhagen von Ense," Karl August Varnhagen von Ense, *Denkwürdigkeiten und Vermischte Schriften*, vol.8 (Leipzig, 1859), 653.

33. GW 9:321.

34. Deborah Hertz, *Jewish High Society in Old Regime Berlin* (New Haven: Yale UP, 1988).

35. See Wilhelm von Humboldt to Henriette Herz in 1786–87: "Oh, and how many, many thanks do I owe you, dearest friend, for all the kindness, the friendship you have shown me, for the pleasures which I enjoyed in your company." Henriette Herz, *Berliner Salons: Erinnerungen und Portraits*, ed. Ulrich Janetzki (Frankfort on the Main: Ullstein, 1984), 135–36. In 1799 the philosopher Johann Gottlieb Fichte wrote about Dorothea Mendelssohn-Veit: "Praise of a Jewess may sound strange coming from me. But this woman has robbed me of my belief that nothing good will come of this Nation. She is unusually intelligent and knowledgeable; with little or actually no outward glamour, complete lack of pretension, and much kindheartedness. One grows gradually fond of her, but then from the bottom of the heart." Quoted in Josef Körner, "Mendelssohns Töchter," *Preußische Jahrbücher* 214 (1928): 170–71.

36. GW 2:69.

37. Barbara Hahn, "Der Mythos vom Salon: 'Rahels Dachstube' als historische Fiktion," and Ursula Isselstein, "Die Titel der Dinge sind das Fürchterlichste! Rahel Levins 'Erster Salon.'" *Salons der Romantik: Beiträge eines Wiepersdorfer Kolloquiums zu Theorie und Geschichte des Salons*, ed. Hartwig Schultz (Berlin: de Gruyter, 1997), 171–212, 213–34. Hahn goes so far as to attribute the authorship of this as well as a similar report about the so-called second salon to Karl August Varnhagen. Isselstein states that Varnhagen was more likely to have suggested and edited the pieces. In this study, the term "salon" is used for convenience's sake.

38. Joan B. Landes, *Women and the Public Sphere in the Age of the French Revolution* (Ithaca: Cornell UP, 1988), 22–28.

39. Friedrich Schleiermacher, *Werke*, vol.2 (Leipzig: F. Meiner, 1913), 1–31.

40. GW 1:16.

41. GW 2:616.

42. Kemp 4:265.

43. GW 3:540.

44. Kemp 1:340.

45. Peter Seibert, *Der literarische Salon: Literatur und Geselligkeit zwischen Aufklärung und Vormärz* (Stuttgart: Metzler, 1993), 347–77.

46. Edmund Dörffel, *Briefwechsel Lessing und Eva König* (Stuttgart: Verlag der J. G. Cotta'schen Buchhandlung, n.d.), 1:26.

47. Franz von Taxis instituted the first postal service between Vienna and Brussels in 1500. It was expanded and eventually became the official imperial post. Although the north German territories instituted their own postal service, the Taxis system remained dominant in southern and western Germany, as well as in Thuringia, throughout the eighteenth century and survived until 1866. Johann Wolfgang Goethe, *From My Life: Poetry and Truth*, parts 1–3, trans. Robert R. Heitner, intro. and notes Thomas P. Saine, ed. Thomas P. Saine and Jeffrey L. Sammons (New York: Suhrkamp, 1987), 512, n.82.

48. Goethe, *From My Life*, 411.

49. GW 3:396.

50. "Bruchstücke aus Briefen und Denkblättern: Mitgetheilt von Karl August Varnhagen von Ense," *Schweizerisches Museum* 1 (1816): 212–42, 329–75.

51. GW 2:406.

52. GW 3:397–98.

53. GW 3:396.

54. GW 7/2:135.

55. GW 4/1:79, 92.

56. GW 7/1:15.

57. Kemp 3:121.

58. Kemp 3:126.

59. GW 7/1:86.

60. GW 7/2:130, 149.

61. GW 7/2:177.

62. GW 7/2:261.

63. Kemp 1:337.

2. THE EARLY LETTERS

1. GW 7/2:175.

2. GW 7/1:68.

3. GW 7/1:12–13.

4. GW 7/2:32–33.

5. GW 7/2:204.

6. GW 7/1:13.

7. See Michael A. Meyer, "The Orthodox and the Enlightened," *Leo Baeck Institute Yearbook* 25 (1980): 101–10.

8. For example, Rahel broke the Sabbath law by accompanying the singer Maria Marchetti, whom she greatly admired, to a rehearsal (GW 7/1:76). And after the birth of her brother's child, she expressed her satisfaction that it was a girl because it meant that "religious neutrality can be preserved for a while longer" (GW 7/1:24).

9. GW 7/1:263.

10. GW 7/1:114–17.

11. K. G. Lessing, ed., *Gotthold Ephraim Lessings Leben, nebst seinem noch übrigen litterarischen Nachlasse*, 2 vols. (Berlin: Voss'sche Buchhandlung, 1793).

12. GW 7/1:52.

13. GW 7/1:80.

14. GW 7/1:88.

15. Mendelssohn published *Letters on the Sentiments* in 1755; between 1759 and 1763 he contributed to Lessing's *Letters Concerning the Newest Literature. Jerusalem* and *Morning Hours* appeared in 1783 and 1785, respectively. (I am using the English titles in Altmann's *Moses Mendelssohn*.)

16. GW 7/1:121.

17. GW 7/1:140.

18. GW 7/1:270.

19. GW 7/2:15.

20. GW 7/2:79–80. Translation in Hannah Arendt, *Rahel Varnhagen: The Life of a Jewess*, ed. Liliane Weissberg, trans. Richard and Clara Winston (Baltimore: Johns Hopkins UP, 1997), 88.

21. GW 7/2:99.

22. Moses Mendelssohn, jointly with F. Bamberger, H. Borodianski, S. Rawid-owicz, B. Strauss, L. Strauss, *Gesammelte Schriften: Jubiläumsausgabe*, ed. Elbogen et al. (Berlin, 1929–1938), cont. by A. Altmann, vol.12/2 (Leipzig, 1971ff), 200.

23. GW 7/2:99.

24. GW 7/2:80–81.

25. Theodor Zondek, "Dr. med. David Veit (1771–1814): Eine Gestalt aus der Emanzipationszeit," *Bulletin des Leo Baeck Instituts* 52, n.f. (1976): 49–77.

26. GW 7/1:56.

27. "Eduard Gans: Dritter Bericht im Verein für Cultur und Wissenschaft der Juden, abgestattet am 4ten May 1823, Hamburg 1823." Quoted in H. G. Reissner, "Begegnung im Zeichen der Romantik," *Judentum in der Deutschen Umwelt, 1800–1850: Studien zur Frühgeschichte der Emanzipation*, ed. Hans Liebeschütz and Arnold Paucker (Tübingen: Mohr, 1977), 336.

28. GW 7/1:82–83.

29. GW 7/1:71–74.

30. See chapter 1.

31. Käthe Hamburger, "Rahel und Goethe," GW 10:183. This essay, first presented as a lecture in 1963, assesses in detail Goethe's significance for Rahel. Hamburger observes that Rahel's understanding of Goethe represents not only an important chapter in German intellectual history but also in the history of German Jews.

32. GW 7/2:223.

33. GW 7/2:234.

34. GW 7/2:234.

35. GW 7/2:119.

36. For examples of how Goethe incorporated fragments of reality into his writings, see Katherine R. Goodman, "The Sign Speaks: Charlotte von Stein's Matinees," *In the Shadow of Olympus: German Women Writers around 1800*, ed. Katharine R. Goodman and Edith Waldstein (Albany: State U of New York P, 1992), 71–93.

37. GW 7/2:133–34.

38. GW 7/2:233.

39. The work appeared anonymously in the journal *Die Horen*, ed. Friedrich Schiller (1795–97). It is modeled after Boccaccio's cycle of novellas, a work that Rahel disliked as well. In Goethe's work, the émigrés are a German family fleeing from the French revolutionary troops who have occupied the left bank of the Rhine. It starts out with a discussion of the pros and cons of the Revolution. But a deep rift causes the group to abandon the topic and turn instead to telling exemplary stories that deal with the idea of a falsely understood freedom and renunciation. From

Rahel's remarks it is not clear whether she disliked the work because of its political conservatism. In contrast to Goethe, she appreciated the French Revolution and she vehemently disliked the French émigrés, whom she considered social parasites.

40. GW 7/2:238.

41. GW 7/2:1–20. All subsequent quotes are from this letter, written over a period of three days (15 to 17 Nov. 1794).

42. Little attention has been given to Wilhelm von Humboldt's literary criticism. Richey A. Novak, in his *Wilhelm von Humboldt as a Literary Critic* (Berne: Herbert Lang, 1972), writes that Humboldt was important not so much for the positions he developed or the specific doctrines he articulated, but rather for the kinds of probing psychological questions he asked, the kinds of answers he gave, and the unusual dimensions he added to critical thinking in literary matters (134). In many respects, Humboldt's ideas were comparable to Rahel's and similarly unsystematic.

43. Rahel could not know how right she was with regard to the choice of the work. Humboldt was a friend of Jacobi's and knew how touchy he was about criticism. He therefore formulated his review so as not to offend the author, although he considered it a "failed imitation of Goethe." See Albert Leitzmann, ed., *Wilhelm von Humboldts Werke*, vol. 1 (Berlin: B. Behr, 1903), 435.

44. GW 7/2:22.

45. GW 7/2:235.

46. GW 1:74.

47. GW 1:61.

48. GW 1:128.

49. GW 1:63.

50. GW 1:170.

51. GW 1:76–77.

52. GW 1:79.

53. GW 1:180–81.

54. GW 1:185.

55. GW 1:259.

56. Kemp 3:122.

57. Rahel asked Finckenstein to return her letters. Henriette Mendelssohn, however, wrote in 1801 that Finckenstein was reluctant to part with them, promising that someday he would return them to her personally. While Henriette recognized Finckenstein's vapidness, she nevertheless intervened on his behalf, reassuring Rahel that she didn't think he would misuse the epistles since he felt such boundless respect for Rahel. Henriette thought that he would lose a part of himself if he had to return them. See Günter de Bruyn, ed., *Rahels erste Liebe: Rahel Levin und Karl Graf von Finckenstein in ihren Briefen* (Berlin: Buchverlag Der Morgen, 1985), 306.

58. De Bruyn, *Rahels erste Liebe*, 69–81. These pages contain excerpts from letters about Madlitz and the Finckenstein family by John Quincy Adams, Wilhelm von Burgsdorff, Friedrich Schleiermacher, Clemens Brentano, Ludwig Tieck, and others.

59. De Bruyn, *Rahels erste Liebe*, 121, 124.

60. De Bruyn, *Rahels erste Liebe*, 126, 147, 170.

61. De Bruyn, *Rahels erste Liebe*, 269.

62. De Bruyn, *Rahels erste Liebe*, 203.

63. De Bruyn, *Rahels erste Liebe*, 183.

64. De Bruyn, *Rahels erste Liebe*, 281–82.

65. De Bruyn, *Rahels erste Liebe*, 298–99. Even now she was solicitous about him without, however, avoiding the truth: "Don't be frightened about this letter . . . you yourself have composed it."

66. De Bruyn, *Rahels erste Liebe*, 199.

67. GW 1:207–8.

68. GW 1:212.

69. Kemp 1:353.

70. Kemp 1:354.

71. Kemp 1:352.

72. GW 4/1:11, 33.

73. GW 4/1:33.

74. "Aus Dorothea's Tagebuch," *Dorothea von Schlegel und deren Söhne Johannes und Philip Veit*, vol.1, ed. J. M. Raich (Mainz, 1881), 448.

75. GW 4/1:109.

76. Of the approximately six thousand preserved letters, some sixteen hundred are written to and by women (six hundred by Rahel and over a thousand to her). Of these only 233 by Rahel are printed and a mere 64 by her friends. Varnhagen provided descriptions of and commentaries about many of these women. (Information from Barbara Hahn.)

77. Although Dorothea Schlegel destroyed the greater part of her correspondence because she did not want to have it published, a few of her letters can be found in Ernst Behler et al., eds., *Kritische Friedrich-Schlegel-Ausgabe* (Paderborn: Schöningh; Zurich: Thomas, 1980–85), sec.3, vols.23, 24, 30. Caroline von Humboldt's correspondence has been published in its entirety. Sophie von Grotthuß corresponded with Goethe, but only seven of her letters have been printed in excerpts while all of his twenty-six letters to her are published. Esther Gad's letters to Jean Paul have been published by Barbara Hahn, " 'Geliebtester Schriftsteller': Esther Gads Korrespondenz mit Jean Paul," *Jahrbuch der Jean-Paul-Gesellschaft* 25 (1990): 7–42.

78. Behler, *Kritische Friedrich-Schlegel Ausgabe*, 23:62–65.

79. GW 1:216–19.

80. GW 1:216–19.

81. Isselstein, Ursula, *"Der Text aus meinem beleidigten Herzen": Studien zu Rahel Levin Varnhagen* (Turin: Tirrenia Stampatori, 1993), 51–58. This and all subsequent quotes are from this transcription, unless otherwise noted. Isselstein's is the exact transcription of this letter, of which Varnhagen published about a third in combination with another one under the same date. See GW 1:81–83.

82. GW 1:86, 90, 93.

83. GW 1:96.

84. GW 1:85–86.

85. Isselstein, *Studien zu Rahel Levin Varnhagen*, 41–51.

86. SV, Box 209. Moritz to Rahel, 14 Jan. 1802.

87. The foregoing quotes are in Consolina Vigliero, "'Mein lieber Schwester-Freund': Rahel und Ludwig Robert in ihren Briefen," *Rahel Levin Varnhagen: Die Wiederentdeckung einer Schriftstellerin,* ed. Barbara Hahn and Ursula Isselstein (Göttingen: Vandenhoeck & Ruprecht, 1987), 47–55.

88. SV, Box 216. Printed in Heidi Thomann Tewarson, "German-Jewish Identity in the Correspondence Between Rahel Levin Varnhagen and Her Brother, Ludwig Robert: Hopes and Realities of Emancipation, 1780–1830," *Leo Baeck Institute Yearbook* 39 (1994): 3–29.

3. HOPES BETRAYED

1. GW 1:328–29.

2. GW 4/1:236.

3. GW 4/1:236.

4. GW 1:311.

5. GW 3:313.

6. Barbara Hahn, *"Antworten Sie mir!" Rahel Levin Varnhagens Briefwechsel* (Basel: Stroemfeld/Roter Stern, 1990), 62–64. The letter is printed here in its entirety for the first time.

7. See Hahn, *Antworten Sie mir!* 62.

8. Henri Campan, French civil servant during the occupation in Berlin and a friend of Rahel's with whom she corresponded for some time. He was the son of Madame Campan (1752–1822), author of memoirs and pedagogical texts and lady in waiting to Queen Marie Antoinette. Rahel explains that she was not Campan's lover, that she trusted him because he loved and respected her. Love and respect were precisely what she claimed her brothers had withdrawn from her (GW 4/1:308–9).

9. GW 1:436.

10. GW 1:444.

11. GW 1:585.

12. GW 3:55.

13. GW 1:441.

14. GW 1:287.

15. Reinhold P. Kuhnert, *Urbanität auf dern Lande: Badereisen nach Pyrmont im 18. Jahrhundert* (Göttingen: Vandenhoeck & Ruprecht, 1984), 35.

16. GW 1:337.

17. In another to Brinckmann, Rahel relates how desperate she had been during the winter and anxious about having to spend another "walled-in summer in Berlin, where I would go evenings at 11 a little through the *streets* with the servant" (GW 1:333–34).

18. GW 1:317–18.

19. GW 1:288–89.

20. GW 9:29.

21. GW 9:31.

22. GW 1:480–83.

23. SV, Box 219. Moritz to Rahel 13 Feb. 1810.

24. They were published within a collection, *Briefe des Prinzen Louis Ferdinand an Pauline Wiesel: Nebst Briefen von A. von Humboldt, Rahel, Varnhagen, Gentz und Marie von Meris*, ed. Alexander Büchner (Leipzig, 1865). Two years later, Ludmilla Assing published those letters Varnhagen had copied, once again in combination with many other prominent personalities, under the title, *Briefe von Chamisso, Gneisenau, Haugwitz, W. von Humboldt, Prinz Louis Ferdinand, Rahel, Rückert, L. Tieck u.a. Nebst Briefen, Anmerkungen und Notizen von Varnhagen von Ense*, 2 vols. (Leipzig, 1867). Significantly, Pauline Wiesel's name does not appear in the title. Hannah Arendt recognized the importance of this friendship and considered this collection the most important source material for Rahel's life after her marriage. See *Rahel Varnhagen: The Life of a Jewess*, ed. Liliane Weissberg, trans. Richard and Clara Winston (Baltimore: Johns Hopkins UP, 1997), 79–80. Barbara Hahn states that Varnhagen had spent a great deal of time collecting, organizing, and copying this correspondence, without success (Varnhagen/Wiesel 710–14).

25. GW 6/1:31.

26. Varnhagen/Wiesel 91–93.

27. GW 9:518–19; Varnhagen/Wiesel 216.

28. Varnhagen/Wiesel 20.

29. Varnhagen/Wiesel 95.

30. Varnhagen/Wiesel 114–15.

31. Christel Eigensatz, an actress and friend of Rahel's from the time of her first salon and a lover of Friedrich Gentz in 1802; she later married an innkeeper named Pedrillo and moved to Venice with him.

32. Varnhagen/Wiesel 87–88.

33. Varnhagen/Wiesel 120–21.

34. Varnhagen/Wiesel 94.

35. Varnhagen/Wiesel 24.

36. Varnhagen/Wiesel 161.

37. GW 2:407; Varnhagen/Wiesel 157.

38. GW 9:65; Varnhagen/Wiesel 99–100.

39. Varnhagen/Wiesel 220.

40. Pauline too was an avid reader. On 22 July 1822 she wrote that she read more than she ought to in her solitude: Goethe, Schiller, and Voltaire, whose entire works she had at her disposal (Varnhagen/Wiesel 340).

41. Varnhagen/Wiesel 160.

42. Varnhagen/Wiesel 362.

43. Varnhagen/Wiesel 123.

44. Varnhagen/Wiesel 388–90.

45. Kemp 1:17.

46. Kemp 1:64.

47. GW 1:551.

48. GW 4/2:27.

49. See Marwitz's letter of 11 July 1811 (Kemp 1:67–69). In his *Hausbuch*, a kind of memoir covering the years 1809–27, Ludwig Marwitz wrote of Alexander: "He lived in close connection with people I avoided and believed that a better age should be brought about through a general revolution" (Kemp 1:407).

50. Arendt, *Rahel Varnhagen*, 209.

51. Kemp 1:38–40.

52. Kemp 1:32.

53. Kemp 1:24.

54. GW 1:534–35. Translation for the most part as in Arendt, *Rahel Varnhagen*, 202.

55. Kemp 1:95. Translation for the most part as in Arendt, *Rahel Varnhagen*, 212–13.

56. Kemp 1:123. Translation in Arendt, *Rahel Varnhagen*, 215.

57. Kemp 1:126. Translation in Arendt, *Rahel Varnhagen*, 216.

58. Kemp 1:138–39. Translation for the most part as in Arendt, *Rahel Varnhagen*, 217.

59. Arendt, *Rahel Varnhagen*, 216–18.

60. "Now I want to write down my *five dreams*, in the sequence in which I dreamed them." This is how Rahel started her "dream book." Other shorter dreams or dream fragments are contained within letters. All the dreams and dream sequences are now

accessible in Barbara Hahn, ed., *"Im Schlaf bin ich wacher: Die Träume der Rahel Levin Varnhagen* (Frankfort on the Main: Luchterhand, 1990), 11–38.

61. Translation in Arendt, *Rahel Varnhagen*, 186–88.

62. In the manuscript the name is not abbreviated but spelled out. See Hahn, *Im Schlaf bin ich wacher*, 37, n.10.

63. Translation in Arendt, *Rahel Varnhagen*, 189–90.

64. Hahn, *Im Schlaf bin ich wacher*, 22–25.

65. Translation in Arendt, *Rahel Varnhagen*, 192.

66. Karl August Varnhagen, *Denkwürdigkeiten des eigenen Lebens*, vols.1 and 2, ed. Konrad Feilchenfeldt (Frankfort on the Main: Deutscher Klassiker Verlag, 1987). A good English introduction is Terry H. Pickett, *The Unseasonable Democrat: K. A. Varnhagen von Ense (1785–1858)* (Bonn: Bouvier, 1985).

67. Kemp 3:360.

68. GW 2:395.

69. GW 4/1:297.

70. GW 5/3:373.

71. GW 4/1:125–26, 175, 259.

72. GW 4/2:101–2.

73. GW 4/1:259; GW 4/2:99.

74. GW 4/2:258.

75. SV, Box 78. Rahel to Sara Grotthuß, 14 Nov. 1811.

76. GW 4/1:25.

77. GW 4/2:93.

78. GW 4/2:108.

79. GW 1:529.

80. GW 4/2:148.

81. GW 5/3:159.

82. GW 5/3:173–74. See other letters and diary entries written between April 1813 and February 1814 in GW 2 and 5.

83. GW 5/3:174.

84. GW 5/3:170.

85. GW 1:380.

86. GW 1:580–81.

87. GW 5/3:189.

88. GW 1:339.

89. GW 2:190–91.

90. GW 1:400–401.

91. GW 2:189.

92. GW 7/2:79–80.

93. GW 1:212, 329–30.

94. GW 1:383.

95. GW 1:383–84.

96. GW 1:316 and 2:190.

97. Ursula Isselstein, *"Der Text aus meinem beleidigten Herzen": Studien zu Rahel Levin Varnhagen* (Turin: Tirrenia Stampatori, 1993), 76–119.

98. GW 7/2:260.

99. Hahn, *Im Schlaf bin ieh wacher*, 16–19.

100. GW 2:572.

101. For a more detailed analysis of this dream, see Heidi Thomann Tewarson, "Der 'zweite' Traum—Entwurf einer ästhetischen Selbstbestimmung," Hahn, *Im Schlaf bin ich wacher*, 39–58.

4. MADAME VARNHAGEN VON ENSE

1. In 1795 she wrote to David Veit: "Write me: to Mlle Robert." GW 7/2:154.

2. GW 3:158.

3. For both the technicalities of the baptism and marriage and the newly gained respect see GW 5/4:46–71.

4. Conversion, although quite common at the time, was still disapproved of by many. Jews taking this step therefore were discreet or even secretive about it to lessen offending opponents.

5. GW 5/4:54.

6. Terry Pickett, *The Unseasonable Democrat: K. A. Varnhagen von Ense (1785–1858)* (Bonn: Bouvier, 1985), 41–42.

7. Hilde Spiel, *Fanny von Arnstein oder Die Emanzipation: Ein Frauenleben an der Zeitenwende, 1758–1818* (Frankfort on the Main: Fischer, 1978), 423–29.

8. GW 2:284, 255.

9. GW 2:272.

10. GW 5/4:258, 269, 284.

11. GW 5/4:268.

12. GW 5/4:325–28.

13. GW 5/4:296–97.

14. Pickett, *The Unseasonable Democrat*, 39–45.

15. Stephanie Beauharnais, Grand Duchess of Baden, an adopted daughter of Napoleon for whom he arranged the marriage to Karl Duke of Baden in order to tie Baden permanently to France.

16. GW 6/5:109.

17. GW 6/5:173.

18. GW 2:409–10.

19. GW 9:458–59; Varnhagen/Wiesel 189.

20. Line Brack, the first one, was now in the employ of Moritz's family.

21. Konrad Feilchenfeldt, "Die Beziehungen der Familie Carel und Rose Asser-Levin zu ihren Berliner Verwandten, *Studia Rosenthaliana* 4 (1970): 181–211.

22. GW 6/5:112–16.

23. Varnhagen/Wiesel 144.

24. GW 2:375.

25. GW 2:446. See also her letter to Varnhagen, where she informs him that there were twenty-nine people waiting for letters from her, not counting the ones she may have forgotten (GW 6/5:176).

26. GW 6/5:142.

27. GW 6/5:139, 171–72.

28. Peter Berglar, *Wilhelm von Humboldt in Selbstzeugnissen und Bilddokumenten* (Reinbek: Rowohlt, 1970), 119–27.

29. Karl August Varnhagen von Ense, ed., *Galerie von Bildnissen aus Rahel's Umgang und Briefwechsel*, vol.2 (Leipzig, 1836), 144.

30. GW 6/5:137.

31. GW 2:417 and to Pauline (Varnhagen/Wiesel 166–67).

32. See the tender and affectionate letters of Delphine de Custine in Custine, Astolphe, Marquis de, *Lettres à Varnhagen d'Ense* (Paris: Slatkine Reprints, 1979; originally published in Brussels, 1870), 21–25, 64, 69–73, 109–13, 124, 125–28, 188–89, 242–44, 308–10.

33. GW 6/5:133. Varnhagen replied that if he had been in Rothschild's place, he would have simply thrown the count out of the house over the insult. GW 6/5:143.

34. GW 5/3:175.

35. GW 6/5:145.

36. Anna von Sydow, ed., *Wilhelm und Caroline von Humboldt in ihren Briefen*, vol.6 (Osnabrück: Otto Zeller, repr. 1968), 59–60.

37. GW 6/5:157.

38. Albert Leitzmann, ed., *Briefwechsel zwischen Karoline von Humboldt, Rahel und Varnhagen* (Weimar, 1896), 94.

39. Sydow, *Wilhelm und Caroline*, 4:80.

40. Sydow, *Wilhelm und Caroline*, 4:395.

41. Sydow, *Wilhelm und Caroline*, 5:112.

42. Sydow, *Wilhelm und Caroline*, 5:122.

43. Sydow, *Wilhelm und Caroline*, 5:219.

44. Jonathan Katz, *Emancipation and Assimilation: Studies in Modern Jewish History* (Westmead, England: Gregg International Publishers, 1972), 265–73.

45. Jonathan Katz, *From Prejudice to Destruction: Anti-Semitism 1700–1933* (Cambridge: Harvard UP, 1980), 96.

46. Sydow, *Wilhelm und Caroline*, 5:236.

47. Barbara Hahn, "Der Mythos vom Salon: 'Rahels Dachstube' als historische Fiktion," *Salons der Romantik: Beiträge eines Wiepersdorfer Kolloquiums zu Theorie und Geschichte des Salons*, ed. Hartwig Schuetz (Berlin: de Gruyter, 1997), 230–32.

48. *Letters of Ludwig Tieck: Hitherto Unpublished 1792–1853*, col. and ed. Edwin H. Zeydel, Percy Matenko, and Robert Herndon Fife (New York: Modern Language Association of America, 1937), 430.

49. GW 10:419.

50. Sander Gilman, *Jewish Self-Hatred: Anti-Semitism and the Hidden Language of the Jews* (Baltimore: Johns Hopkins UP, 1986), 156–62.

51. Varnhagen, *Ausgewählte Schriften*, vol.18, ed. Ludmilla Assing (Leipzig: 1876), 112–18. Contemporary opinions were very much divided, many siding with Itzig. Reinhold Steig, in his *Heinrich von Kleist's Berliner Kämpfe* (Berlin, 1901; repr. Bern: Herbert Lang, 1971), provides a blatantly anti-Semitic version. See especially the sections: "Angriffe auf Achim von Arnim," "Überfall auf Achim von Arnim," and "Die Macht der Verhältnisse," 630–43.

52. Ludwig Robert to Rahel, 27 Jan. 1816. Quoted in Heidi Thomann Tewarson, "German-Jewish Identity in the Correspondence Between Rahel Levin Varnhagen and Her Brother, Ludwig Robert: Hopes and Realities of Emancipation, 1780–1830," *Leo Baeck Institute Year Book* 39 (1994): 3–29. The following discussion and all the quotations are based on this article. See also: Consolina Vigliero, "'Mein lieber Schwester-Freund': Rahel und Ludwig Robert in ihren Briefen," *Rahel Levin Varnhagen: Die Wiederentdeckung einer Schriftstellerin*, ed. Barbara Hahn and Ursula Isselstein (Göttingen: Vandenhoeck & Ruprecht, 1987), 47–55.

53. Ludwig Robert was not the only one to suspect Arnim of cowardice. The precise reasons why Arnim was apparently not permitted to join, although he volunteered, remain unclear. See Jürgen Knaack, *Achim von Arnim—Nicht nur Poet* (Darmstadt: Thesen Verlag, 1976), 95, n.250.

54. Ludwig Robert, *Kassius und Phantasus oder der Paradiesvogel: Eine erzromantische Komödie mit Musik, Tanz, Schicksal und Verwandlungen; in drei großen und drei kleinen Aufzügen* (Berlin: Vereinsbuchhandlung, 1825), 136.

55. Robert, *Kassius und Phantasus*, 137. "Das Fatum ist die Bestimmung des Menschen, und des Menschen Bestimmung ist—über Bestimmung nichts Bestimmtes zu wissen." The word *play* cannot be rendered in translation.

56. *Riches* (Hebr.): antipathy toward the Jews.

57. Ludwig Robert converted in Frankfort in March 1819 prior to marrying

Friederike Braun. The conflicting feelings with which Robert undertook this step are revealed in his letters to Rahel. See Tewarson, "German-Jewish Identity," 22–23.

58. The expression "Hep" was believed to have originated from the Latin— H(ierusalema) E(est) P(erdita). The brothers Grimm had a different explanation. According to them, it derived from the call "hep hep," used by Franconian shepherds.

59. Katz, *From Prejudice to Destruction*, 74–91.

60. Katz, *Fram Prejudice to Destruction*, 92–97.

61. Monica Richarz, ed., *Jüdisches Leben in Deutschland: Selbstzeugnisse zur Sozialgeschichte 1780–1871* (Stuttgart, 1976, Veröffentlichung des Leo Baeck Instituts) contains only two passing references to the riots, see 187 and 453.

62. See Horst Fischer, *Judentum, Staat und Heer in Preußen im frühen 19. Jahrhundert: Zur Geschichte der staatlichen Judenpolitik* (Tübingen: Mohr, 1968), 54–56. The prospect of a civil service job had prompted many young men, including Jews, to enlist in the army in 1813. Fischer relates the case of the rifleman Moritz Seligmann, who in April 1815 was slated to become an excise man but was subsequently refused the position by the ministry of finance because of his Jewish religion. By 1816 all Jewish civil servants in the Prussian monarchy, even those who had occupied their posts for years, were forced to give them up.

63. GW 9:579–82.

64. GW 9:582–85.

65. Eleanor O. Sterling, in her study, "Anti-Jewish Riots in Germany in 1819: A Displacement of Social Protest," *Historia Judaica* 12 (1950): 105–42, comes to similar conclusions, without the benefit of Rahel's analysis. Jonathan Katz, *From Prejudice to Destruction*, 97, knew Rahel Varnhagen's letter. He nevertheless refutes Sterling's thesis about displaced social protest, arguing that those in German society who attacked the Jews were not identical with those who opposed the government. Katz seems to have misunderstood Sterling's notion of "displaced" protest, which Rahel also described so succinctly.

66. GW 9:585.

67. GW 2:383–84.

68. Tewarson, "German-Jewish Identity," 19.

69. Tewarson, "German-Jewish Identity," 25.

70. Kemp 4:118.

71. Kemp 4:443.

72. GW 6/5:130–31.

73. GW 2:367.

74. Varnhagen/Wiesel 175–76.

75. Kemp 4:157; similarly to Pauline (Varnhagen/Wiesel 166).

76. GW 2:355–56.

77. GW 2:564–65. The next two quotes are from the same letter.

78. GW 2:524.

79. GW 2:414–15.

80. GW 9:435.

81. Kemp 4:115–16.

82. For a portrait of the man and the significance of his writings, see George F. Kennan, *Marquis de Custine and His "Russia in 1839"* (Princeton: Princeton UP, 1971).

83. The book has been periodically republished, the most recent edition being Astolphe, Marquis de Custine, *Empire of the Czar: A Journey through Eternal Russia*, foreword Daniel J. Boorstin, intro. George F. Kennan (New York: Anchor, Doubleday, 1989). Chapters 1–3 contain autobiographical information.

84. Custine signed his very first letter with Astolphe, and Rahel closed her reply with the words: "If you write Astolphe, then I call myself Rahel." Custine, *Lettres à Varnhagen d'Ense*, 28, 30.

85. GW 3:412.

86. In his portrait of Custine, Varnhagen gives a discreet but fairly detailed account of his contradictory and volatile character, his several attempts at marriage, his close friendship with men, the sensational attack on him, and the rumors it generated in French high society. But it is unclear whether the reader of that time would have drawn conclusions in the same way we would today. See Custine, *Lettres à Varnhagen d'Ense*, vii–xii.

87. Kemp 4:139–43.

88. GW 9:489–90.

89. GW 9:527–29.

90. See GW 8:second part.

91. GW 2:436–43.

92. Kemp 4:89–91.

93. See Kemp 4:437–38.

94. GW 2:548–49. Here also the next two quotes.

95. GW 2:542.

96. Custine, *Lettres à Varnhagen d'Ense*, 311–14.

97. GW 9:777–79.

98. See Introduction.

99. In all, the Varnhagen Collection contains 46 letters and 3 notes by Rahel and 82 by August Brede. Information from Barbara Hahn.

100. GW 2:561.

101. GW 9:695–96.

102. GW 2:576.

103. Barbara Hahn, *"Antworten Sie mir!" Rahel Levins Briefwechsel* (Basel: Stroem-

feld/Roter Stern, 1990), 177. Since this study contains the most detailed discussion of the correspondence so far, including quotations from unpublished letters, this presentation draws on Hahn's.

104. Hahn, *Antworten Sie mir!* 177.

105. GW 2:574–75.

106. Hahn, *Antworten Sie mir!* 178.

107. Hahn, *Antworten Sie mir!* 176.

108. GW 3:121–22. The trend originated with August Wilhelm Iffland, playwright, actor, and director of the National Theater in Berlin. He had exerted an immense influence on the German stage. Rahel, who had observed these developments in Berlin over the course of many years, always viewed them critically.

109. Hahn, *Antworten Sie mir!* 170.

110. Hahn, *Antworten Sie mir!* 170, n.2.

111. GW 2:215.

112. Pickett, *The Unseasonable Democrat*, 48.

113. GW 6/6:29, 31.

5. RETURN TO BERLIN

1. Varnhagen/Wiesel 211–12.

2. GW 2:603–5.

3. SV, Box 11. Rahel to Rose, 20 June 1820.

4. GW 2:609–10.

5. Terry Pickett, *The Unseasonable Democrat: K. A. Varnhagen von Ense (1785–1858)* (Bonn: Bouvier, 1985), 51.

6. GW 9:777. See also GW 6/2:66, 266.

7. GW 3:390.

8. GW 3:47.

9. Wiesel/Varnhagen 28.

10. N.n., "Der Salon der Frau von Varnhagen," in Karl August Varnhagen von Ense, *Denkwürdigkeiten und Vermischte Schriften*, vol.8 (Leipzig, 1859), 595–630.

11. GW 9:776.

12. GW 3:281. Gustav von Barnekow served as officer and later as major of the First Regiment of the Guards; Count Yorck, son of the field marshall Yorck von Warteburg; Wilhelm von Willisen, his companion; Leopold von Ranke (1795–1886), historian and professor of history at the University of Berlin.

13. GW 6/6:228.

14. Leopold von Ranke, *Zur eigenen Lebensgeschichte* (Leipzig: Duncker und Humblot, 1900).

15. GW 3:209.

16. See Peter Seibert, *Der literarische Salon: Literatur und Geselligkeit zwischen Aufklärung und Vormärz* (Stuttgart: Metzler, 1993), 344–45. However, Seibert's contention that Rahel's role and influence were diminished is not borne out by the report.

17. Barbara Hahn, "Der Mythos vom Salon: 'Rahels Dachstube' als historische Fiktion," und Ursula Isselstein, "Die Titel der Dinge sind das Fürchterlichste! Rahel Levins 'Erster Salon,'" *Salons der Romantik: Beiträge eines Wiepersdorfer Kolloquiums zu Theorie und Geschichte des Salons*, ed. Hartwig Schultz (Berlin: de Gruyter, 1997), 181 and 227. A historically more accurate assessment of the salon will have to await the publication of the correspondence with the family and the friends.

18. GW 3:528.

19. "Der Salon der Frau von Varnhagen," 615–17.

20. (Rahel Varnhagen). "Briefe," *Die Wage*, 2 May 1821, 1–28.

21. GW 3:210–14.

22. GW 6/6:196, 305; GW 3:373.

23. Franz Grillparzer, "Selbstbiographie," *Sämtliche Werke* (Munich: Carl Hanser, 1965), 4:137.

24. GW 2:577.

25. Rahel may have met the sixteen-year-old Börne when, between 1800 and 1803, he was a student and border at the home of Marcus Herz. In any case, she was familiar with and admired the passionate love letters young Börne subsequently wrote to the middle-aged Henriette Herz.

26. GW 9:679–82.

27. GW 9:678–79.

28. Helmut Bock, *Ludwig Börne: Vom Gettojuden zum Nationalschriftsteller* (Berlin: Rütten und Loening, 1962), 116. Börne wrote most of the contributions himself.

29. Jeffrey L. Sammons, *Heinrich Heine: A Modern Biography* (Princeton: Princeton UP, 1979), 75.

30. Michael A. Meyer, *The Origins of the Modern Jew: Jewish Identity and European Culture in Germany, 1749–1824* (Detroit: Wayne State UP, 1967), 163–82.

31. Sammons, *Heinrich Heine: A Modern Biography*, 93.

32. GW 6/6:356–57.

33. GW 3:452.

34. Heinrich Heine, *Säkularausgabe*, vol.20 (Berlin: Akademie-Verlag; Paris: Editions du CNRS, 1970), 77.

35. Heine, *Säkularausgabe*, 20:94.

36. Heine, *Säkularausgabe*, 20:387–90.

37. Heine, *Säkularausgabe*, 20:270.

38. Heine, *Säkularausgabe*, 20:94.

39. Heine, *Säkularausgabe*, 20:421.

40. Heine, *Säkularausgabe*, 20:273.

41. Heine, *Säkularausgabe*, 20:307.

42. Heine, *Säkularausgabe*, 20:254.

43. Heine, *Säkulareusgabe*, 20:270.

44. Heine, *Säkularausgabe*, 20:254.

45. Heine, *Säkularausgabe*, 21:345.

46. Heine, *Säkularausgabe*, 21:272.

47. Elke Fredericksen, "Heinrich Heine und Rahel Levin Varnhagen; Zur Beziehung und Differenz zweier Autoren im frühen 19. Jahrhundert; Mit einem unbekannten Manuskript von Heine," *Heine Jahrbuch* 29 (1990): 9–38.

48. Heine, *Säkularausgabe*, 20:125.

49. Heinrich Heine, *Sämtliche Werke*, vol. 4, ed. Klaus Briegleb (Munich: Carl Hanser, 1968–75), 11.

50. Heine, *Säkularausgabe*, 21:338: "I no longer put much faith in my poetry. My age and perhaps our time generally is not propitiate for verses and is asking for prose."

51. Heine, *Sämtliche Werke,* 4:11.

52. Heine, *Säkularausgabe*, 20:125. Goethe's world view was pantheistic rather than narrowly Christian, and he was therefore often accused of being a heathen.

53. Heine, *Säkularausgabe*, 20:390.

54. Heine, *Säkularausgabe*, 20:62.

55. Ludwig Börne, *Sämtliche Werke*, vol.2, comp., ed. Inge and Peter Rippmann (Düsseldorf: Joseph Melzer Verlag, 1964), 819.

56. Quoted in Sammons, *Heinrich Heine: A Modern Biography*, 101.

57. George F. Peters, *"Der große Heide Nr. 2": Heinrich Heine and the Levels of His Goethe Reception* (New York: Peter Lang, 1989).

58. In 1822 Jews were excluded from the higher ranks in the army and explicitly denied public academic posts. Meyer, *Origins of the Modern Jew*, 178.

59. GW 9:813.

60. In 1838 Heine wrote to Varnhagen: "It is strange that the time has not yet come and surely will not come very soon, when I would be able to say candidly, what Rahel told me from the depth of her soul, in agitated (bewegten) hours" (*Säkularausgabe*, 21:272).

61. Heine, *Säkularausgabe*, 21:51.

62. Heine, *Sämtliche Werke*, 1:10. By the other Rahel, Heine meant the biblical Rachel, of whom it is said in Jer. 31:15, "A voice was heard in Ramah, lamentation,

and bitter weeping: Rachel weeping for her children refused to be comforted for her children, because they were not."

63. GW 3:13–15, 224.

64. GW 3:456.

65. Her publications included (titles translated here into English) "Fragments from Letters and Diaries" in Troxler's *Schweizerisches Museum* (1816); "Letters" in Börne's *Die Wage* (1821); "About 'Wilhelm Meister's Wanderjahre'" in *Der Gesellschafter* (1821); "From Letters: Goethe in the Testimony of His Contemporaries": A supplement to accompany all editions (1823); "Berlin, 19 September" in Cotta's *Morgenblatt für gebildete Stände* (1825); "News about Spontini" in *Morgenblatt für gebildete Stände* (1825); "From the Papers of a Contemporary Woman" in *Eos* (1826); Ludwig Robert, "Remarks Less for the Germans than for the French about Goethe's *Tasso* and that by the Frenchman Alexis Duval" in *Morgenblatt für gebildete Stände* (1826); "About a Portrait of a Woman" in *Morgenblatt für gebildete Stände* (1827); "Berlin, in March" in *Morgenblatt für gebildete Stände* (1827); "From the Diaries of a Berlin Woman" in *Berlinische Blätter für Deutsche Frauen* (1829).

66. GW 3:177–78. This recalls Heine's characterization in his Börne text.

67. GW 2:369–70.

68. GW 3:456–57.

69. GW 2:616.

70. GW 2:211.

71. GW 3:102.

72. GW 3:499.

73. GW 3:268–69.

74. GW 3:178.

75. GW 2:435.

76. GW 10:421–22.

77. GW 10:418.

78. Quoted in Herta Schwarz, "'Brieftheorie' in der Romantik": *Brieftheorie des 18. Jahrhunderts: Texte, Kommentare, Essays*, ed. Angelika Ebrecht et al. (Stuttgart: Metzler, 1990), 232.

79. GW 3:116.

80. GW 3:10.

81. GW 3:221–22.

82. GW 2:410–11.

83. GW 2:350.

84. GW 2:368.

85. GW 2:368.

86. GW 3:72.

87. GW 3:133.

88. GW 3:309.

89. Kemp 3:192.

90. GW 3:554.

91. GW 3:309–10.

92. GW 3:258–59.

93. GW 3:259. In 1824 she expressed this same thought as an aphorism: "We only speak so much because we cannot express ourselves; if we could, we would say one thing only" (GW 3:160).

94. GW 3:282–83.

95. GW 3:275.

96. GW 3:283.

97. There is no satisfactory English version of this unusual work, except for Thomas Carlyle's translation of the first edition (reissued by Camden House, Camden, N.C., 1991).

98. (Ithaca: Cornell UP, 1976), 226.

99. GW 9:606–10.

100. GW 3:299–300.

101. GW 3:113. See also GW 3:77–80, 121.

102. GW 3:356.

103. GW 3:559. Regarding the marriage of one of her nieces, she stated to Moritz that she would never give permission to marry to anyone, in spite of her own happy marriage. GW 2:445.

104. GW 3:19.

105. GW 2:56–58. Marwitz, the supposed father, was to provide for the child financially, while Rahel would be the legal mother.

106. Kemp 3:191–92.

107. GW 7/2:204.

108. GW 2:536–37.

109. Quoted in Tewarson, "German-Jewish Identity," 22.

110. GW 2:258–59. In the printed version "ancestral" (altväterisch) replaced "Jewish."

111. GW 2:447.

112. GW 1:584–85.

113. See (in a somewhat different translation) Hannah Arendt, *Rahel Varnhagen*, 85.

114. GW 1:43–44.

115. Opinions are divided regarding Bettine's anti-Jewish hatred. In her letters and diaries, Rahel speaks often of this delightful and intelligent friend. On two

occasions, however, she also refers to anti-Jewish behavior. In 1810 she wrote in her diary about a long conversation with Bettine: "She also spoke about Christianity, succumbing suddenly to her Frankfort hatred of Jews, which offended me deeply, that is, it tarnished the image I had of her. Such a noble and pure soul should have no room for such confusion" (GW 9:60; see also 4/2:216–17).

116. For a helpful historical survey of this movement, see Frank E. Manuel, *The Prophets of Paris: Turbot, Condorcet, Saint-Simon, Fourier, and Conte* (New York: Harper and Row, 1962), 103–93.

117. Werner Vordtriede, "Der Berliner Saint-Simonismus," *Heine-Jahrbuch*, 14 (1975): 93–110.

118. Albert Brisbane, *A Mental Biography: With a Character Study by His Wife, Redelia Brisbane* (New York: Burt Franklin, repr. 1969), 76–97. In his discussion Brisbane confuses Saint-Simonism with the teachings of Charles Fourier, which he embraced only after he had left Berlin and the Saint-Simonists had disbanded. See Terry H. Pickett and Françoise de Rocher, *Letters of the American Socialist Albert Brisbane to K. A. Varnhagen von Ense* (Heidelberg: Carl Winter Universitätsverlag, 1986), 23–44.

119. GW 9:894. See also GW 3:560, 568, 569.

120. Albert Brisbane, *A Mental Biography*, 172–73.

121. GW 3:129.

122. GW 3:557.

123. GW 3:570.

124. GW 3:556.

125. GW 3:561.

126. GW 3:581.

127. GW 3:573.

128. GW 3:583. Baden was the town in southern Germany where Ludwig and Friederike had settled and where they died.

129. GW 3:509.

INDEX